THE ROYAL OBSERVER CORPS UNDERGROUND MONITORING POSTS

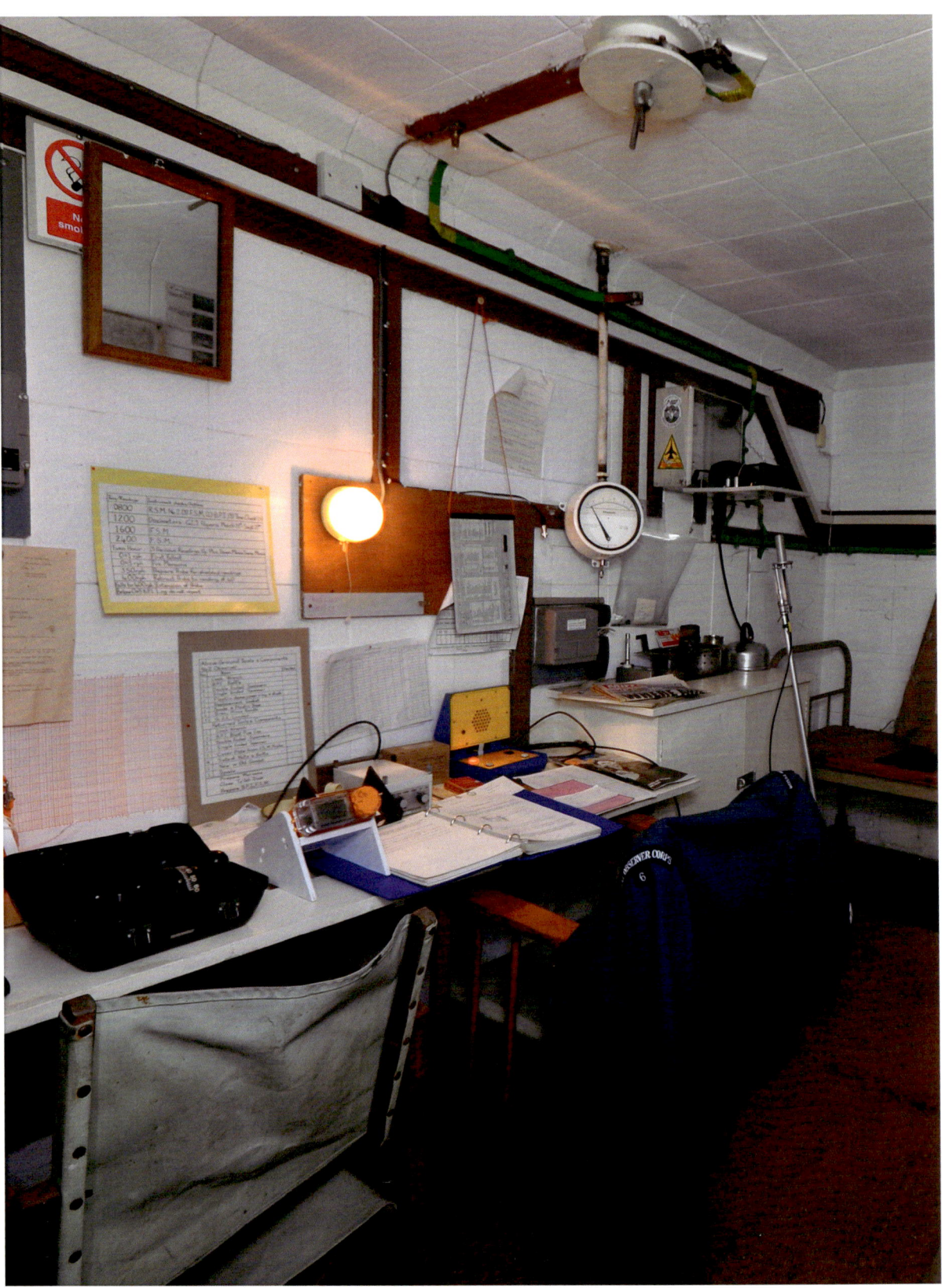

THE ROYAL OBSERVER CORPS UNDERGROUND MONITORING POSTS

Mark Dalton

FOLLY BOOKS

Folly Books 2017, 2023

© Mark Dalton 2011, 2017, 2023

All rights reserved. No part of this publication may be produced or stored in a retrieval system or transmitted, in any form or by any means, electronic, mechanical, photocopying, recording or otherwise, without prior permission in writing from the publisher.

A catalogue record for this book is available from the British Library.

ISBN 978-1-9161789-6-0

Published by Folly Books Ltd
Monkton Farleigh
BA15 2QP
www.follybooks.co.uk

Designed and typeset by Vicky

Printed and bound in the UK by Corsham Print.

ACKNOWLEDGEMENTS

I would like to thank all the contributors who have made this book possible and all those who offered to help or directed me to someone who could.

In particular I would like to thank David Ross, Peter Broom and Steve Scanlon for help with proof reading and technical questions plus David for his recollections of No.25 Group and Peter for capturing the last days of No.16 Group and letting me use his photographs for the book; Ernie Guy for the record of the ROC in the 1960s; Neville Cullingford for his patience and enthusiasm plus the many unique photographs and equipment he dug out for me; Terry Tracey for his series of 1980s and 1990s ROC photographs plus Don Brereton for his recollections of 'Hornbeam', and Elaine Norris who put me in touch with both of them; Roger Thomas of English Heritage whose help with original drawings was invaluable; Lawrence Holmes for photographs and articles; Dave Peace and Pete Owen for the great story about intercepting the Russian 'Bears'; Terry Bottrill and Martin Cooke for all their help with photographs and equipment; all the post restorers, many who also provided additional information and photographs, including John Jenkinson, Jack Hanlon, Mark Russell, Ed Combes, Andy Ramek, John Smiles, Nick Garside, Dave Arnold and Frank Alexander. I would also like to thank Alistair McCann – the Northern Ireland section could not have been attempted without his considerable help; Craig Smith for arranging access to the Severn Trent reservoirs; Simon Craine, John Shere, Chas Parker, Jamie Cross and Nick Catford for photographs; Rod Seibert at Hack Green and Mike Smith at the Newark Aviation Museum; Nick and Vicky at Folly Books who took on this book and put it all together; and, finally, last but by no means least, Hazel.

Mark Dalton
June 2011

LIST OF CONTRIBUTORS

I would like to thank the following for contributing photographs and other illustrations for this book:

10 Group ROCA Newsletter *29 top; 168 bottom left, bottom right; 210 top, bottom; 211 top, bottom left, bottom right*
Frank Alexander *96 bottom; 201 top left*
Adrian Angove *76 bottom; 77 top; 80 top left, bottom*
Ayrshire Post *96 middle*
Terry Bottrill *205 bottom*
Don Brereton *72 bottom left, bottom right; 73 top, bottom*
Peter Broom *70 bottom; 79 top, bottom left bottom right; 80 top right; 93 bottom; 96 top*
Des Brown (Chop Gate ROC Post) *71 top; 172 bottom*
Nick Catford *13 bottom right; 165 bottom left; 167 bottom; 170; 205 top left*
Martin Cooke *202 top, bottom; 203 top, bottom right, bottom left; 204 top, bottom*
Ed Combes *180 bottom left; 188 top, bottom; 189 top, bottom left, bottom right*
Jamie Cross *Frontispiece; 142 bottom; 174 top*
Crown Copyright *8 top; 9 top; 16 top, bottom; 17 bottom left; 25 bottom left, bottom right; 37 top; 50 bottom; 60 top, middle, bottom; 65 top, bottom middle; 87 top left, top right, bottom left, bottom right; 95 bottom; 144 top; 146 top right; 167 top*
English Heritage *17 bottom; 18 bottom; 19 top, bottom; 20 top, bottom; 21; 28 top, bottom; 29 bottom left*
Ed Gamble *173 top*
Ernie Guy *26 bottom left, bottom right; 27 top left, bottom; 76 top left, top right; 77 bottom; 78 bottom*
Jack Hanlon (Chop Gate ROC Post) *11 top right; 173 bottom left, bottom right*
Lawrence Holmes *78 top*
John Jenkinson *171 series of six photographs; 172 top, middle*
George Jones / The Royal Observer Corps Museum *12 top, bottom; 44 top; 82 bottom left, bottom right; 86 top left, top right, bottom left, bottom right*

Brian Marston *99 bottom; 100 top, bottom; 101 top left, top right, bottom left, bottom right*
Steve May *10 top*
Geoff McAuley *26 top left, top right*
Nick McCamley *11 bottom*
Alistair McCann *27 top right; 190; 191 top, bottom; 192 top, bottom; 193 top; 194 top, bottom; 195 top, bottom; 213*
Pete Owen *74 top, bottom left, bottom right; 75 top, bottom*
Chas Parker *62 top*
Andrew Ramek *181 bottom; 182 top, bottom; 183 top left, top right, bottom; 184 top left, top right, bottom; 185*
ROCA National Archive *24; 25 top; 66 bottom; 85 top, bottom*
The Royal Observer Corps Museum *22 top, middle, bottom; 23 top, top middle, bottom middle, bottom; 65 bottom left, bottom right; 84 bottom;*
David Ross *13 top left, top right, bottom left; 81; 83 top, bottom; 84 top left, top right; 134 top*
Mark Russell *117 top, bottom; 169 bottom; 171 top; 178 bottom; 179 middle right, bottom left; 180 top left*
John Smiles *186 bottom left, bottom right; 187 top, bottom left, bottom right*
Mike Smith (Newark Air Museum) *119 bottom*
South Yorkshire ROC Collection *128 top*
Ron Swain *70 top; 108 top*
Ricky Thomas *186 top*
Terry Tracey *67 bottom; 94 top, bottom left, bottom right; 143 top, bottom; 148 top, bottom; 149 top, bottom; 151 bottom left; 152 top*
J. H. Walter *163 bottom right*
Colin Woods *195 middle*

While every effort has been taken to ensure the original copyright owner is attributed there may be instances where this has not been possible due to the archive nature of the material and the difficulties in tracing ownership.

CONTENTS

		Page
1	ORIGINS OF THE ROYAL OBSERVER CORPS	1
2	UKWMO AND THE ROC NUCLEAR ROLE	6
3	THE UNDERGROUND MONITORING POSTS	16
4	POST EQUIPMENT	31
5	LIFE IN THE ROYAL OBSERVER CORPS	66
6	MANNING THE POSTS	81
7	ABANDONED POSTS	97
8	RESTORED POSTS	170
9	THE ROYAL OBSERVER CORPS LEGACY	212
	BIBLIOGRAPHY	216

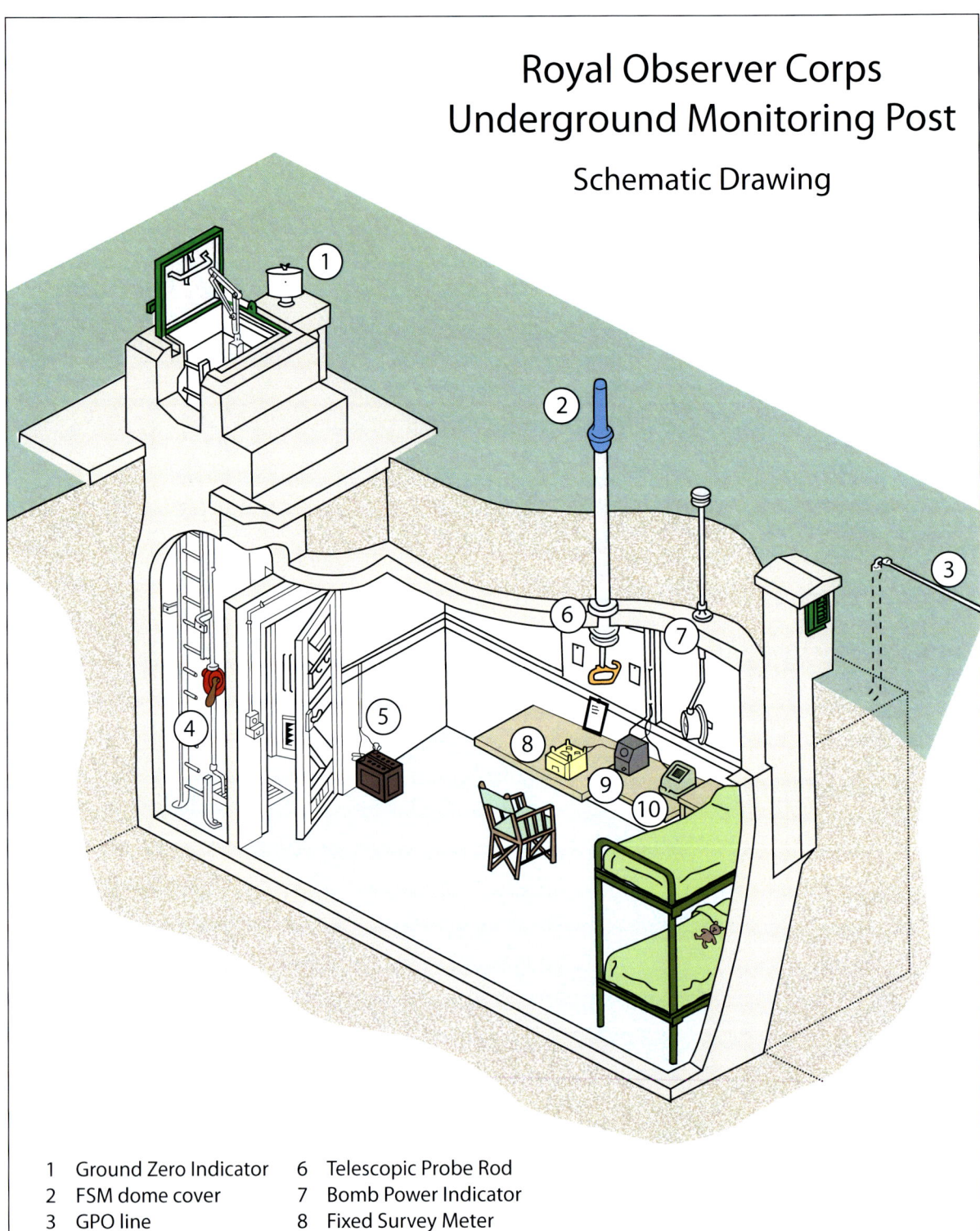

Chapter 1

ORIGINS OF THE ROYAL OBSERVER CORPS

The origins of the Royal Observer Corps (ROC) can be traced back to the deployment by Imperial Germany of airships and subsequently of aeroplanes, as offensive weapons against the British Isles during the Great War. These initial incursions into British skies were countered by army and naval artillery. Defensive measures included rings of anti-aircraft guns and searchlights and introduced the notion of 'observer' volunteers who were recruited as Special Constables.

Zeppelins were the real fear during the early stages of the war and there was little consideration that the aeroplane could also be a menace. The large and relatively slow-moving airships would be spotted by observer volunteers and by the regular police who would telephone a central control room with location, direction and other information to enable countermeasures to be taken. In reality this was an ineffective system and with the focus being on the Channel ports and London it should not have come as a surprise when a raid on the Norfolk coast went unopposed in the early part of 1915. The authorities responded to the outcry that followed by issuing a warning poster showing representations of the key British and German machines. It was requested that if a German machine was spotted, the time of appearance and direction of flight should be telephoned immediately to the authorities.

Further raids and more fatalities were to follow, still with no effective defence. The number of official observers was increased by using coastguard stations and shipping, along with gun and searchlight crews, to report aircraft movements. In addition, the movements of home aircraft were reported by their flying stations so that the whereabouts of friendly aircraft could be understood. This information was passed back to a central office for assessment. If enemy activity was identified then appropriate actions were communicated to the gun and searchlight crews and to the fighter stations. However, this was in practise a very slow process and undefended airship attacks continued. Success against the Zeppelins finally came towards the end of 1915 with improved Royal Flying Corps tactics and equipment, especially the introduction of incendiary ammunition which allowed a small biplane fighter to bring down the huge hydrogen-filled Zeppelins.

Any relief was short lived as the Germans then switched to the twin-engine Gotha bomber, with immediate and devastating effect. Hundreds of people were killed and injured when large formations of these aeroplanes flew and bombed unopposed over London. This was highly audacious and for a while the Gothas bombed with impunity, often in broad daylight. In response the London Air Defence Area (LADA) was created. Under this scheme the gun rings were set further from the capital to disperse enemy formations and radio-equipped aircraft could track the intruders and report back from the air. This met with some success but it was recognised that the only way to effectively direct guns and fighters was to have a better observation and reporting system that could provide accurate and up-to-date information as to where the enemy was and where he was heading.

The man for the job was Major General Ashmore. He had commanded artillery in the field in France and the work he did from the Great War until the end of the 1920s established the reporting systems that became the mainstay of Great Britain's air defences in the Second World War and beyond. The LADA concept originally instigated by Ashmore became known as the Metropolitan Observation Service and had expanded by the end of the Great War beyond the original boundaries to include more rural areas and hence allow earlier warning on the approaches to the city. This expanded system also included the concept of 'posts' where observers were situated at fixed locations, usually in a farmer's field, and linked by telephone to one of twenty-five sub-controls. The posts had a basic instrument that could give bearing and angle to target with the height being estimated. Information from several posts could then be used to triangulate the position of the aircraft over the ground. This was the start of the system that became familiar during the Second World War. Information fed from the field would be filtered and plotted before being used to direct the defences and warn the public.

After the Great War

Following the end of hostilities the theories of air defence were held to be of value, but the observer organisation soon fell away and it was not until the mid-1920s and the establishment of the Air Raid Precautions committee that the idea of the observer was again considered. The ARP committee took the view that any new observer network would have both military and civilian responsibilities and this concept continued during the subsequent iterations of what became the Observer Corps and later the Royal Observer Corps.

Fortunately, the original champion of the observer network, General Ashmore, was still much involved with home defence matters and he took the opportunity to develop his ideas further with a small trial using Special Constables in Kent. This proved that fast and accurate information could be obtained from a volunteer field force using rudimentary instruments and communications if organised properly. Ashmore expanded the scheme to Suffolk for the next trial and, based upon its successful outcome, the Observer Corps was officially inaugurated in October 1925, with a further two counties being added in 1926. There followed a period of consolidation and improvement with the existing groups (which roughly aligned to the counties) exercising during the annual Air Force manoeuvres. During this period it was realised that observer numbers would have to be increased within the existing groups to allow shift relief at both posts and controls.

Ashmore retired in 1929 and in that year the Corps was transferred from the War Office to the Air Ministry, a reflection on the fact that the RAF was the main beneficiary of the Observer Corps system. During this period the famous Corps crest of an Elizabethan beacon lighter and the motto 'Forewarned is forearmed' was introduced. Qualified observers were allowed to purchase and wear an Observer Corps lapel badge. The equipment used by the posts was also improved with better height estimation methods and the introduction of the Mark IIa post instrument. This instrument in modified Mark IIb form, along with the Micklethwaite Height Corrector, continued in service until the 1950s.

Expansion

Following Hitler's rise to power in 1933 it was soon apparent to the British government that an urgent expansion of its offensive and defensive capability was required. These expansion plans rapidly pushed the Observer Corps out from its traditional south-eastern heartland and into the wider nation. Key to the rate of expansion was the ability of the General Post Office (GPO) to establish the necessary communication lines, and the ability to staff the expanding Corps. These changes also resulted in the Corps moving its headquarters staff to RAF Bentley Priory near Stanmore in Middlesex, where they remained for the rest of the life of the Corps.

By 1936 tension in Europe was high and the Spanish Civil War gave the pilots and crews of the German Condor Legion the opportunity to develop and hone their skills while the world looked on. At home, the country started to move to a war footing and combined forces exercises in Britain included the Corps (and also the new radio-location system, later to become RADAR) and tested the nation's defences. It also placed the Observer Corps firmly in the public eye as the country's early warning system. By 1939 a much expanded Observer Corps was in place, although its members were still classed as 'Police Specials' and were only paid on call-out. Even at this point the observers were only to report and plot aircraft and no official role was given to the actual recognition of the types themselves. One final tweak to the system meant that the radar sites would hand over responsibility to the Observer Corps once incoming aircraft had reached the coast, thus allowing a continuous picture to be maintained.

The question of aircraft recognition was not addressed in the armed forces as a whole until February 1940 when formal courses started at Anti-Aircraft Command. Observer Corps members had been running an unofficial recognition club since 1939 and this finally became official in 1941, well after the Battle of Britain. The RAF finally got in on the act rather late when it established a Recognition Training Wing which ran its first course in February 1941 having taken much advice from the Army.

The Royal Observer Corps

A defining moment occurred in April 1941 when the Corps was granted the status of 'Royal' to become 'The Royal Observer Corps'. This was largely an acknowledgement of the role the organisation had played in the Battle of Britain but it also brought the Corps more into the traditional establishment of the day. This change in status introduced a new rank structure, new uniforms and more alignment with the radar reporting system. Women were also now free to join the Corps. The same year also saw the famous incident when Scottish posts tracked the flight of the then Deputy Führer, Rudolph Hess on his mission to betray Hitler. The eventual crash of the Messerschmitt Me 110 transporting Hess resulted in his capture and a propaganda victory for the country.

The Corps were still primarily focused on reporting and plotting aircraft but it also took on the duty of localised warning. The idea was that general alerts lost war production and so more localised warnings would mean less time wasted in shelters. Initially this was a fairly ad hoc arrangement with air raid spotters, provided by factory management, perched on rooftops looking for enemy formations. A more formalised arrangement meant that the local ROC control could be linked to a factories control for early warning, with the raid spotters in place as a last line of defence. Aircraft recognition was now a mandatory part of observer training and the growth of aircraft spotting, and the usefulness of aircraft recognition reached new heights of official awareness.

With the war turning in the Allies' favour the next role for the ROC was an unusual but critical one, although it would only affect a small proportion of the organisation. The invasion of Europe was imminent and with the volume of shipping planned to cross the Channel on D-Day, plus the sheer scale of the Allied air forces overhead the beaches, there was great concern that many Allied aircraft would be lost to friendly fire. It was felt that the Navy had trained Gunnery Officers who would have some knowledge of aircraft recognition but that armed merchant vessels were a potential liability. Consequently a call was made to the ROC for assistance, and 796 members were subsequently selected. Those serving with the fleet

ORIGINS OF THE ROC

Above: Observers manning a post. The equipment includes the post instrument which was used to determine the position of an aircraft on a map grid on the post plotting table. The position, height and numbers of aircraft were reported to Centre using the head and breast set which the observer with binoculars is wearing.

Below: An observer centre during the early part of the Second World War. The central map table is surrounded by plotters who were in direct contact with clusters of posts. The information received was plotted on the map and viewed from the raised area by tellers who would pass this on to fighter groups, sectors and other centres. Uniforms had not been issued at this time – the black and white armband seen here denoted an Observer Corps member. Standardised group headquarters started to be built in 1942 and these had a two-level operations room with a balcony looking down onto the main map table. A long-range board was introduced soon after.

operated in teams of two per ship and, as volunteers in the ROC, had to be inducted into the Navy as Petty Officers under the 'Seaborne' scheme. Members who served were entitled to wear a Seaborne badge on their uniforms and some of these members proudly served into the 1980s with the Corps in the nuclear role.

Just after D-Day the ROC was back in action on dry land when the first V-1 flying bomb attacks began. Forewarned of the new weapon, procedures to prioritise the flying bomb attacks were already in place and the typical characteristics of these attacks were quickly determined, if never really countered effectively. While the use of anti-aircraft fire and fighters 'tipping' the V-1s reduced the number that got through, there was no defence against the next German technological step, the V-2 rocket. The existing systems could not detect this unseen threat and the Corps were reduced to confirming impact rather than tracking the weapon itself – a prelude to the later nuclear role.

Germany capitulated on 7 May 1945 and within a week, on 12 May, the ROC was stood down. The wider world entered the atomic age on 6 August 1945 with the dropping of the atomic bomb, 'Little Boy', on Hiroshima. This development would result in a wholesale change in role for the Corps within a decade.

The importance of the Corps to the defence of UK airspace and its efforts during the war were not forgotten and, with increasing tension over Russian ambitions, the Corps was reformed in January 1947.

Although only a relatively short time period had elapsed since stand-down, much of the wartime infrastructure had badly deteriorated and it took some years to get back to an acceptable level, with many observers operating old equipment in exposed, unprotected locations.

By the end of 1947 it was apparent that the Soviet Union had made significant advances in their jet fighter force and, more worryingly, were developing a long-range bomber force. UK air defence exercises at this time highlighted the poor performance of the radar system but showed that the ROC network functioned well. Later trials with jet aircraft indicated that the increased speed of these aircraft needed a correspondingly speedy response from the Corps, which was difficult to achieve with the existing system. The upgrading of Britain's air defence network took on a new impetus with the perceived increase in Soviet belligerence. Their recent atomic bomb test and the emergence of new advanced aircraft types woke the Western Allies from the traditional view of the Soviet Union as an agricultural nation who copied Western designs.

The 1950s – Terriers, Rats and Orlits

The early 1950s saw the increase in aircraft speeds outstripping the Corps' attempts to plot them using existing Second World War methods and equipment. The post instrument was too cumbersome and 'finger-plotting' was used to speed up the process – the post instrument being removed completely. 'Very' pistols were also provided to signal to fighters *(Terriers)* that low-flying intruders *(Rats)* were in the area.

Further posts opened in Scotland and the north of England as it was realised that earlier warning of inbound aircraft was needed. Shelter and accommodation for post crews was also improved with the introduction of the *Orlit* post. These were simple prefabricated concrete structures that could be assembled on site. A doorway opened into a small storeroom on the left-hand side of the structure. A sliding door then led off the storeroom to the main observation area which contained the plotting table which was open to the elements. A removable corrugated iron roof was fitted when the post was not in use. Approximately 400 of these structures were installed in two basic types; the *Orlit A*, which was erected at ground level, and the *Orlit B*, which was identical but raised on concrete stilt legs to provide better visibility.

During the early and mid-1950s there was a massive programme of bunker building as new RAF radar facilities (the *ROTOR* plan) were provided with hardened underground accommodation. This resulted in a new RAF sector distribution and the ROC took the opportunity to realign to this new set-up. Almost as soon as they were completed many of these *ROTOR* plan sites became redundant. A major advance in radar technology, the Type-80 set, meant that only a small number of sites were now necessary as the new equipment could provide extended range and coverage far out over the approaches to the country. This new technology together with the new jet interceptors being developed meant that any threat could be detected and dealt with well out to sea. The use of the ROC as an aircraft plotting and reporting organisation was beginning to look superfluous.

By 1953 a new role was being envisaged for the ROC and this had evolved by 1955 into an official, albeit secondary, role of reporting radioactive fallout. 'Shadowgraph' units were also being considered. These later becoming known as ground zero indicators (GZI) and could be used to determine the position of a strike. By 1960, with a new building programme well underway, the nuclear role officially became the primary function of the Corps and aircraft reporting was reduced to a few hundred posts around the V-bomber bases on the east coast. This latter task was finally abandoned in 1965, and although the Corps' interest in aircraft recognition never diminished, its official role from then on was solely nuclear.

Chapter 2

UKWMO AND THE ROC NUCLEAR ROLE

In 1955 the United Kingdom Warning and Monitoring Organisation (UKWMO) was created by the Home Office. This positioned the Corps as the field force in a larger organisation that provided nationwide warning of attack, confirmed nuclear strikes and tracked and warned of fallout. Additionally, the UKWMO could provide an emergency weather service and would disseminate information on nuclear bursts and fallout to a number of government and armed forces headquarters as well as NATO partners. In order to achieve this goal a decision was made that the Corps would require protected accommodation both for post crews and headquarters staff.

Originally a total of thirty-one groups was thought to be needed to provide nationwide coverage but this was reduced to twenty-nine before any building started. Several groups used existing structures but most required new buildings. The Bristol and Belfast group headquarters reused redundant anti-aircraft operations rooms. These monolithic concrete structures were built in the early 1950s and were modified for ROC use. Preston and Inverness were also built into modified structures – this time RAF Sector Operations bunkers. These were much larger structures and the headquarters at Preston was subsequently modified to become a Sector Control and ultimately the standby war headquarters of the UKWMO.

This still left twenty-five groups without protected accommodation and a new building programme started in 1959. The buildings were constructed to two designs; either semi-sunken with the lower levels being protected by an earth mound, or as surface blockhouses. The interior arrangement of the rooms was different depending on the type, but they served an identical purpose. They were large reinforced concrete structures with the hub of activity being a two-level operations room where information would be collated, interpreted and actioned. Typically, around forty to fifty people would be required to man the headquarters and three crews would operate on a shift pattern to keep it fully operational during exercises or in a real emergency.

Right: Leaflets outlining the role of the UKWMO. The smaller leaflet is from 1976 and the cover shows the golf ball radomes of the Ballistic Missile Early Warning System (BMEWS) at Fylingdales in Yorkshire. The leaflet at the rear is from 1987. The substantial upgrades made to the system in the early 1980s are obvious when comparing the contents of the two leaflets.

Six of these group headquarters were also designated as Sector Controls and had additional responsibilities and larger staffs. Modifications were made to these headquarters with the addition of a new sector operations room – either by boarding over the two-level control room or, in the case of Horsham, building an extension. Existing external office accommodation was available on some sites while new facilities were built at many others. This allowed training and administration to take place away from the bunker in a more comfortable environment.

Following further reorganisations in 1968 and 1973 the final network at stand-down consisted of twenty-five group headquarters and five Sector Controls.

Below: This mock-up at the Hack Green Secret Nuclear Bunker museum in Cheshire shows the principal equipment in the WB1400 Wire Broadcast System used to warn of air and nuclear attack and subsequent fallout. The blue-cased unit on the desk nearest the camera would have been situated at the United Kingdom Regional Air Operations Centre (UKRAOC) at High Wycombe, where a threat assessment would have been made based on information coming in from a range of systems including BMEWS, North American Aerospace Defense Command (NORAD) and ground and airborne radars. If there was a genuine threat then a key would be turned in this unit and a spoken warning message would be transmitted to the 250 Carrier Control Points located at major police stations throughout the United Kingdom. The Carrier Control Points are the two large units in the picture with red and black telephone handsets. Two were provided at each designated police station – one as a primary unit and one as a back-up. These could be used to operate powered sirens to warn the public and to alert warning points in their area, including ROC posts, via the installed carrier receiver.

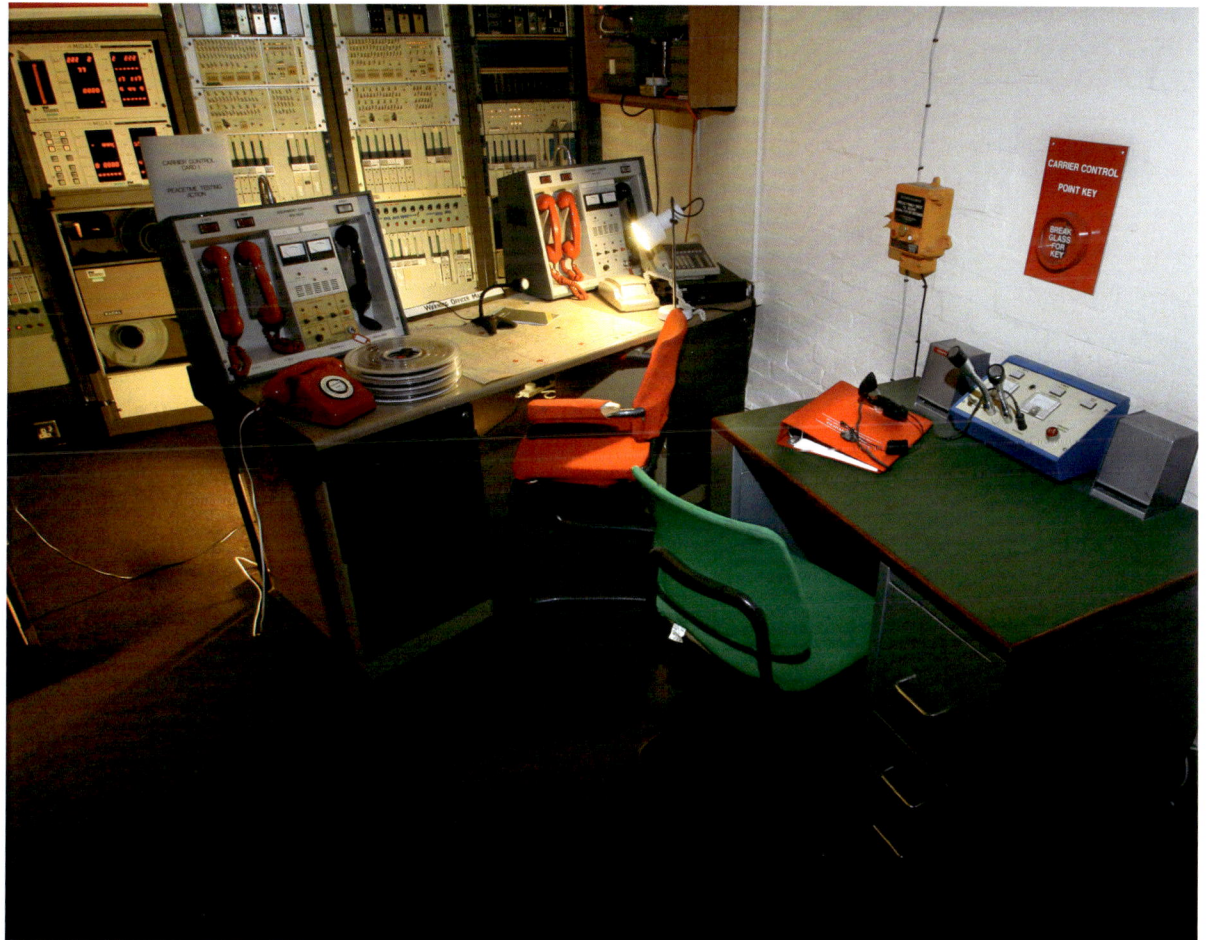

Right: This drawing, which appeared in the appendix of the 1976 edition of the UKWMO leaflet shows the layout of the organisation and the various interdependencies.

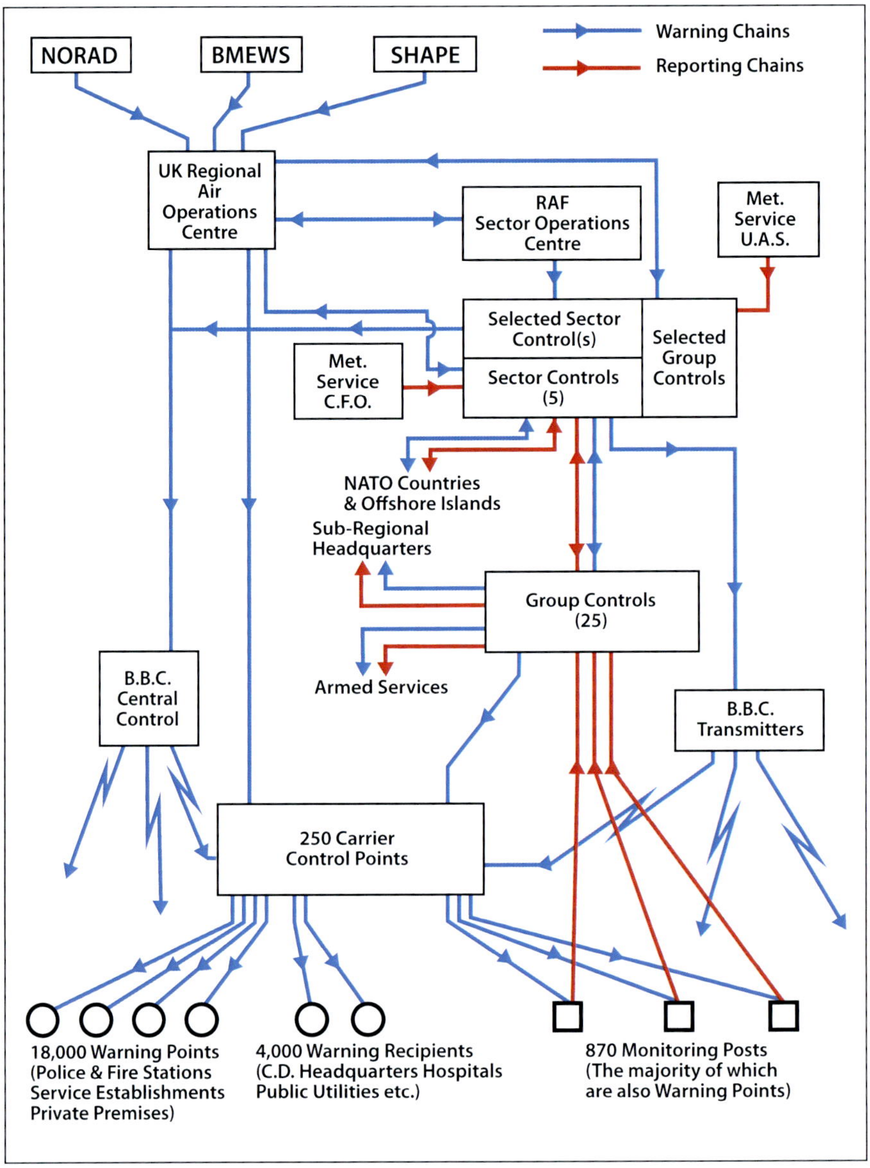

Below left and right: Including the ROC posts, there were around 11,000 warning points throughout the country, and a further 7,000 power operated sirens. These warning points were usually issued with a carrier receiver and a siren to warn the public. Maroons and a Radiac Survey Meter (RSM) would also be issued during an emergency. Locations for warning points included pubs, hospitals, government buildings and even private dwellings. This system was the reality that would provide the public with the famous four-minute warning.

KENT COUNTY CONSTABULARY

INSTRUCTIONS

TO

WARNING POINT OPERATORS

AT A TIME

OF INTERNATIONAL TENSION

WHICH MAY LEAD TO WAR

Warning and Monitoring Office
Maidstone (0622) 65432 Ext. 252

November, 1984

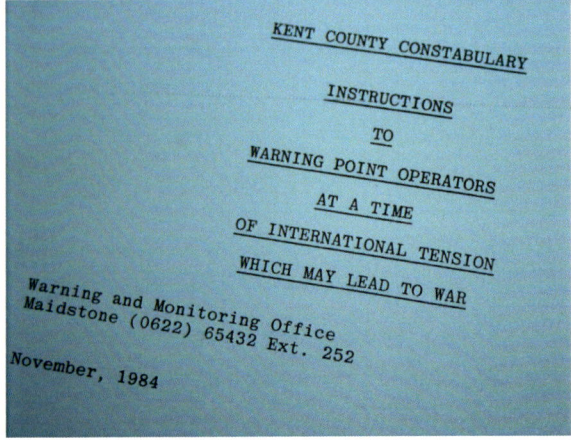

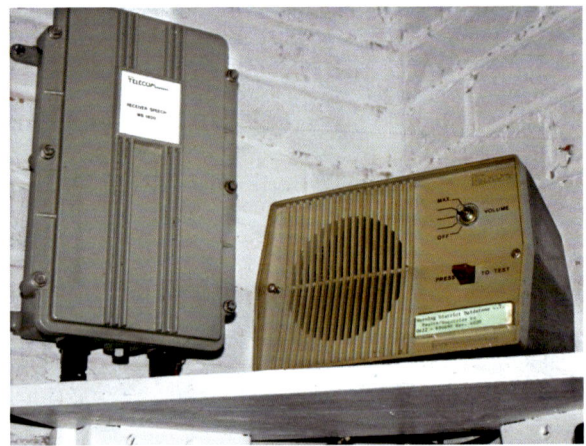

Above: Detail from the UKWMO leaflets showing the earlier WB400 and, *(right)* the later WB1400 Carrier Control Points in operation.

Below: The No.21 Preston Group Headquarters at Longley Lane had originally been an RAF Sector Operations bunker which was adapted by the ROC. The bunker was significantly larger than the purpose-built ROC Group Headquarters and was remodelled internally to become the Western Sector Headquarters in 1973. The bunker was subsequently extended in the mid-1980s with the addition of a new plant room, seen here, and became the UKWMO Standby Headquarters. The peacetime UKWMO Headquarters was in unprotected accommodation at Cowley near Oxford.

Above: No.8 Coventry Group Headquarters at Lawford Heath near Rugby, illustrating the typical external profile of one of the purpose-built semi-sunken protected group headquarters. This photograph was taken in the late 1990s just before the building was extensively remodelled to become part of a satellite uplink station.

Below: No.17 North Wales Group Headquarters at Borras in Wrexham, an example of the surface blockhouse type of purpose-built group headquarters. The site consists of this building, a prefabricated office block, a large mast and ancillary buildings, all within a large, high-fenced compound. It is now occupied by Aerial recording studios.

Above: Detail of the Lincoln Group Headquarters and Midlands Sector Control at Fiskerton. This was the first of the semi-sunken headquarters to be completed and was modified internally when it became a sector control.

Right: All the group headquarters acted as posts in their own right and had full sets of post instruments including a ground zero indicator (GZI), a bomb power indicator (BPI) and a fixed survey meter (FSM).

Below: The GZI was placed on the roof with external stairs for observers to reach it. Some locations, including the Bristol Group Headquarters at Lansdown near Bath (one of the two modified AAORs adapted by the Corps), had railings to improve safety for observers changing the GZI papers.

UKWMO

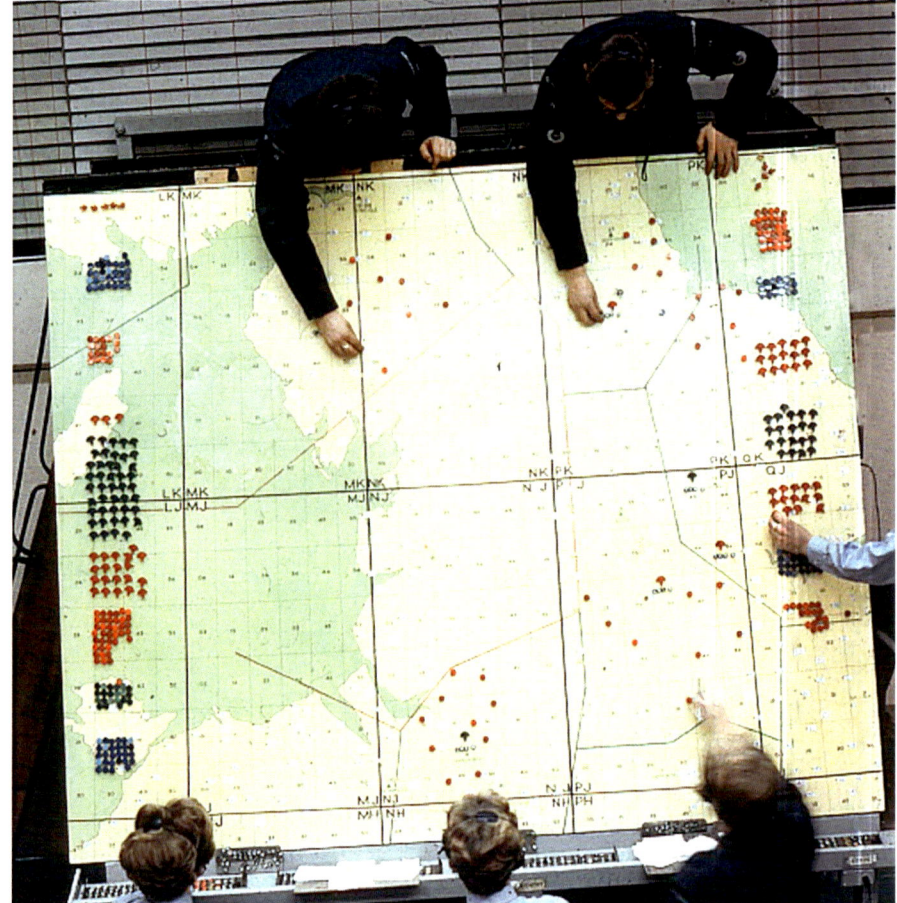

Right: The main control room in the earlier years of nuclear reporting was little different to that of the Second World War with the long-range board dominating the two-level operations room. This showed the status of the surrounding groups and warned the group of what could be heading their way.

Right: The main map table on the ground floor of the control room was of a large scale and was used to display the situation within the group itself. The photographs on this page were taken in the late 1960s at Preston Group Control.

Above and right: The advent of new data transmission technologies in the late 1960s meant a wholesale change in how the control rooms were set up. The long-range board and map table were replaced by transparent vertical displays on which fallout plumes and nuclear bursts were plotted. The post display plotters were relocated to the balcony and faced the plotter-tellers. Here they could write information from monitoring posts onto tote boards. These would be rotated so that the tellers could then distribute the information to the plotters on the ground floor.

Below: The triangulation team used the GZI and BPI data provided by the posts to calculate and then plot the position of a nuclear burst and determine its type and strength. This team also operated the post instruments that were located in the group headquarters. Twelve of the group headquarters had an additional instrument installed that could detect the optical and electromagnetic signatures of a nuclear explosion. This was known as the Atomic Weapons Detection Recognition and Estimation of Yield Device, or AWDREY. Later these instruments were supplemented by another device which gave bearing information so that the location of a burst could be determined.

Below: The rotating tote boards and post display plotter positions on the balcony in the York Group Headquarters at Acombe.

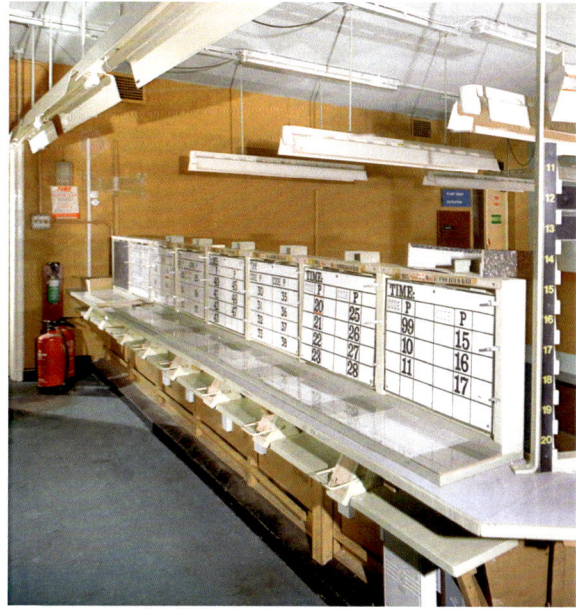

UKWMO

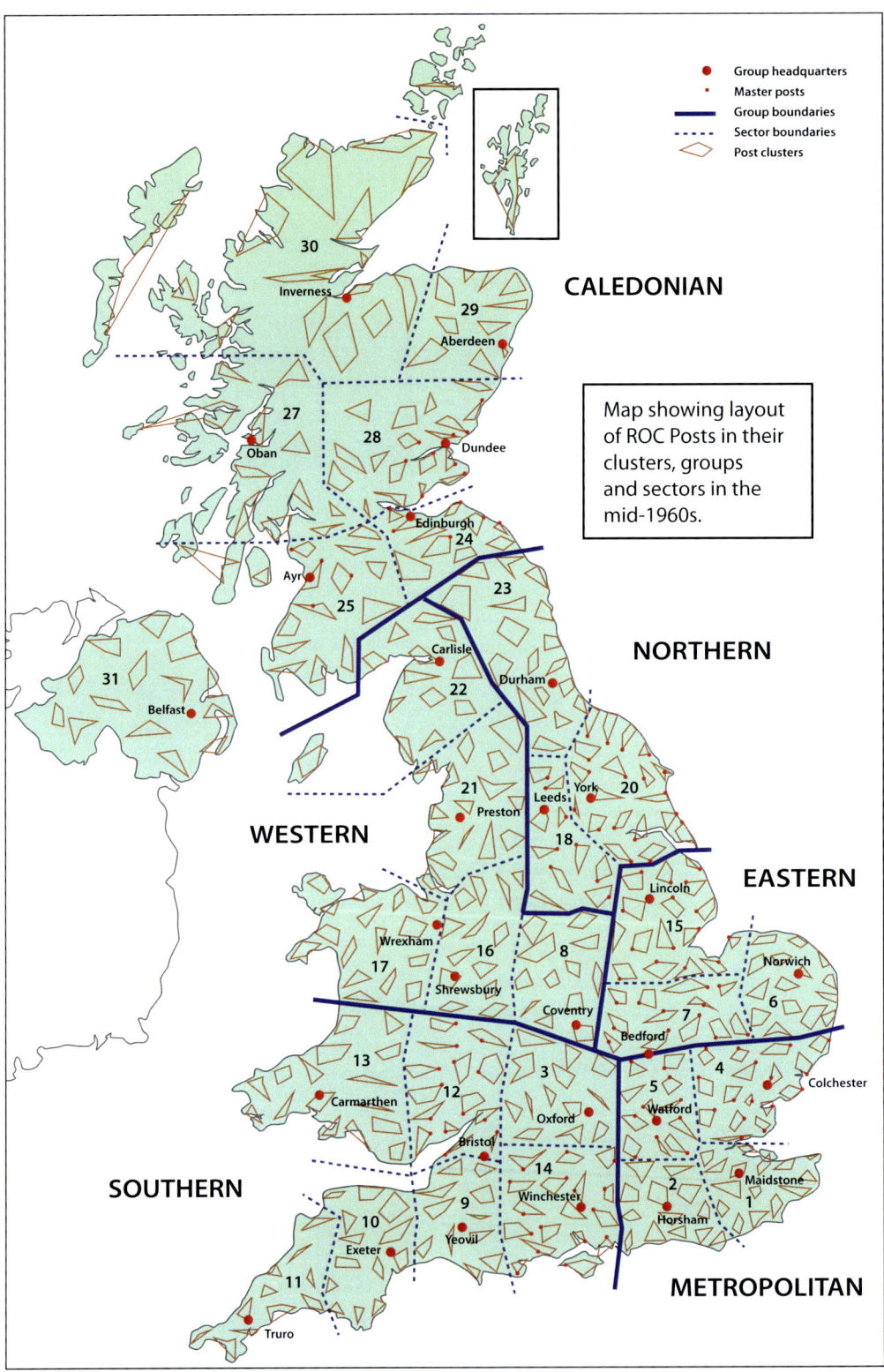

Above: This map shows how the country was split into sectors, groups and clusters of individual posts. The network changed significantly in 1968, 1973 and 1982. This map shows the organisation in the mid-1960s.

The Underground Monitoring Post

The existing above-ground posts were vulnerable to blast and had little fallout protection. A nationwide programme was therefore implemented that resulted in the entire network going underground. Before such a programme could commence, however, a suitable type of structure had to be developed which would protect the crew and allow them to undertake their duties effectively.

It was decided that locating the new posts underground would do much to enhance the survivability of the crew. The surrounding earth would provide good protection from radioactivity, and blast waves would pass over the top of the structure. Instrumentation could be placed at the surface but readings could be taken from the safety of the underground post. With these ideas in mind, a prototype post was constructed at Farnham in Surrey. This design, with a few modifications, became the standard underground post that was built throughout the country. The building programme started in 1957 with the intention of completing 250 posts a year. They were usually sited approximately eight miles apart and were grouped into clusters of two to five posts for operational reasons, with one post acting as a master post. Posts were linked with the group headquarters over the telephone network. Later, some posts would use VHF radio as a back-up to this system.

By 1965 the majority of the new protected headquarters and underground posts were on-line but only three years later there would be huge upheaval. In 1968 most of the volunteer forces were disbanded as a cost saving exercise. The ROC survived but it had to close over six-hundred underground posts and two group headquarters in order to maintain an effective service on the reduced budgets available.

While the Corps had seen large changes during the 1960s, the 1970s was an era of consolidation and a relaxation in Cold War tensions during the period of Détente. The Soviet deployment of SS-20 missiles in 1977 changed this and a resurgence in the ROC's fortunes followed with the vast expansion in Home Defence instigated by the Thatcher administration in the early 1980s. This resulted in new equipment being developed and new initiatives being taken to improve living and working conditions in the posts. These programmes continued for the rest of the decade and into the early 1990s before the dissolution of the Warsaw Pact, which effectively saw the end of the Cold War. As a direct result of this, the Corps was stood down on 30 September 1991. The underground monitoring posts were decommissioned on this date and the remaining full time staff closed the group headquarters in March 1992. A few hundred ROC members continued until 1995 operating as Nuclear Reporting Cells (NRCs) for the armed forces until they too were stood down.

Chapter 3

THE UNDERGROUND MONITORING POSTS

The Underground Posts

The first drawings for the new underground posts were produced in July 1955 and the first prototype example was built at Farnham in Surrey in 1956. This prototype established the basic structure that all subsequent posts were built to. The prototype was used for both equipment trials and experiments into underground living conditions. For example, trials conducted in September 1956 resulted in two ROC members spending thirty hours manning the underground post.

This initial trial was deemed a success and further, more scientific, experiments were subsequently conducted. These culminated in December 1959 when the post was manned by Home Office and ROC personnel for forty-eight hours with long periods conducted with the ventilators in their closed position.

Right above and below: The original split-hatch on the Farnham post had a rudimentary external counterweight. The casting line in the concrete around the top of the entrance shaft, clearly visible in the top photograph, indicates that the hatch was added after the main body of the post was built.

The overall success of the trials proved that the concept of crews living and operating underground for extended periods was tenable.

The posts were constructed of concrete reinforced with metal bar. The dimensions of the rectangular concrete box were 19ft by 8ft 6in by 7ft 6in. The walls were six inches thick and the roof consisted of a seven-and-a-half-inch-thick concrete slab for overhead protection. Internally, the structure was divided into two rooms. The larger room was known as the monitoring room and was approximately fifteen-foot-long. This contained all the instruments and facilities required to work and live underground.

The smaller room was known as the chemical closet or toilet cubicle and, as the name suggests, contained a chemical *Eltex* toilet similar to the wartime *Elsan*. This room was also used to store tools and various other items of equipment, including the Petrol Electric generating set.

Both rooms had doors which opened off an access shaft that rose to a surface hatch approximately three feet above ground level. Access was via a nineteen-rung steel ladder bolted to the shaft wall. Also attached to the access shaft wall was a hand-operated semi-rotary pump and outflow pipe which allowed water that had collected in a sump at the base of the ladder to be pumped out to the surface.

Adjacent to the access shaft was a ventilation shaft that ran from the surface down to a vent inside the toilet cubicle. A second ventilation shaft ran from the surface to the rear end of the monitoring room to provide additional ventilation. This was sometimes referred to as the 'turret' ventilator. Both ventilation shafts had protective louvres fitted to them to deflect any debris away from the shaft entrance. These were originally made of wood, although a metal design later became available. The shaft running to the rear of the monitoring room was dog-legged to prevent any surface debris falling directly into the room from above.

A three-foot-deep earth layer was placed over the structure and levelled off so that only the access

Below: The interior of the prototype post at Farnham in Surrey. The large bellows were used as a rudimentary air replenishment system during trials in 1959. The beds are standard RAF issue. The large floor-to-ceiling cupboard was replaced in service with a smaller waist-high unit. The sink was another innovation that did not make it into service in standard posts, although a few crews did introduce them as a local modification later.

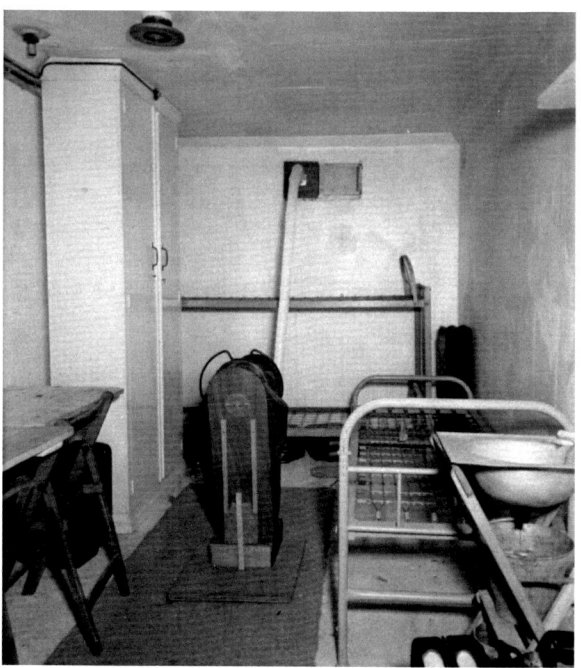

Below: This detail lists the drawings required in the construction of an underground monitoring post along with some of the subsequent modifications.

shaft entrance and the louvred ventilator stacks were visible above ground. Two pipes extending from the ceiling of the monitoring room to the surface were also put in place during construction. The smaller pipe was known as the 'blast pipe' or 'BPI pipe', the larger as the 'probe pipe' or 'FSM pipe'. In addition, cable access for a telephone line was included. Initially a three-inch-square hole was provided in the side of the entrance hatch for this purpose but was soon replaced by a conduit which ran from the monitoring room to a surface connection point and then, usually, onto a telephone pole.

The posts were initially very bare. The interiors were finished with screed and then received two coats of approved white cement paint. Interior metal fixtures were painted with an aluminium gloss, wooden fixtures with a white gloss.

The two internal doors were timber-built with their lower sections containing expanded metal vent louvres to allow airflow through the rooms. The doors originally had simple latches but these were replaced with doorknobs and mortice locks in 1959. At the same time the doors were strengthened by increasing the dimensions of the timber framework.

Furniture consisted of a cupboard, instrument shelf and fold-down table. All were made from timber and were painted with three coats of oil paint and a white gloss finish.

A few canvas chairs were provided for seating and three beds were supplied, comprising a double bunk bed and a single bed. Lighting was by means of a single 6 watt bulb run off a 12 volt battery. Improvements to both equipment and living conditions continued for the rest of the service life of the posts.

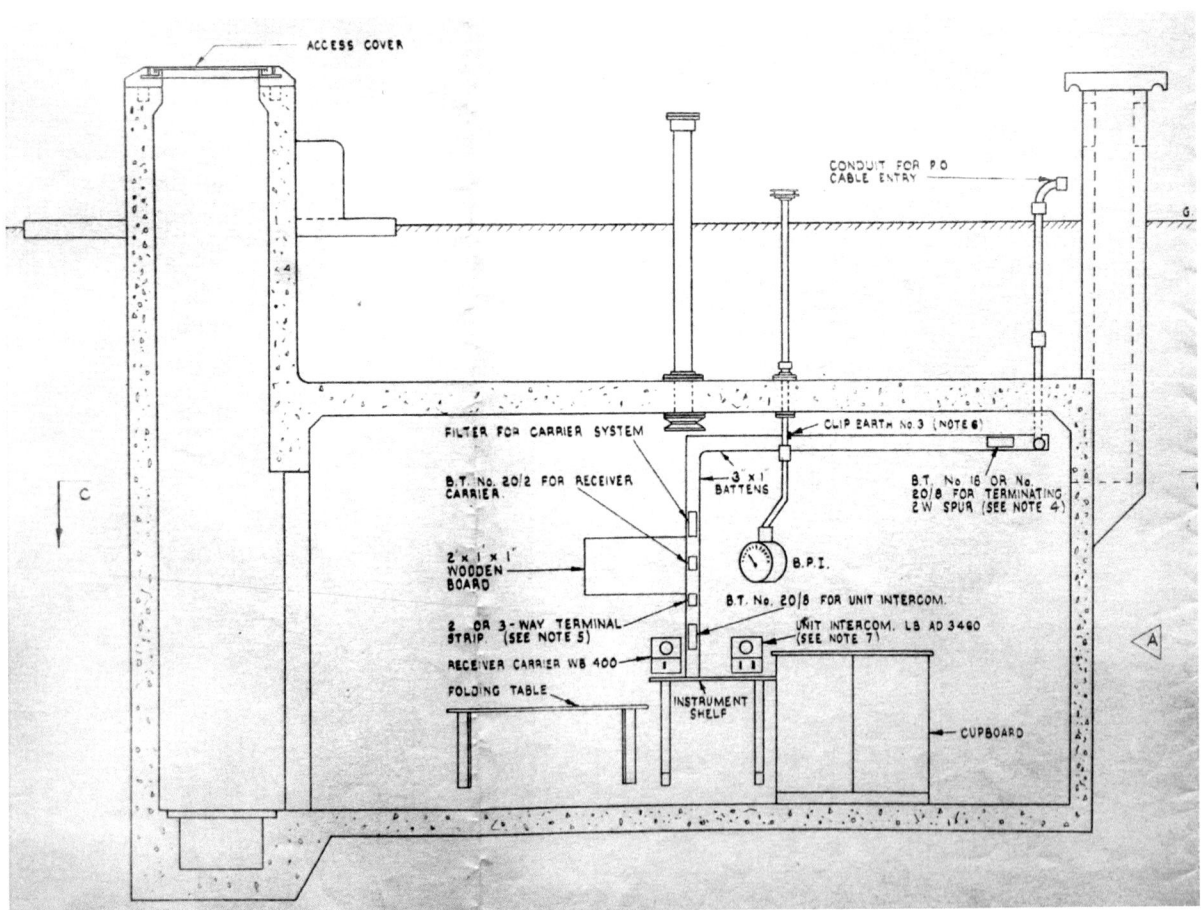

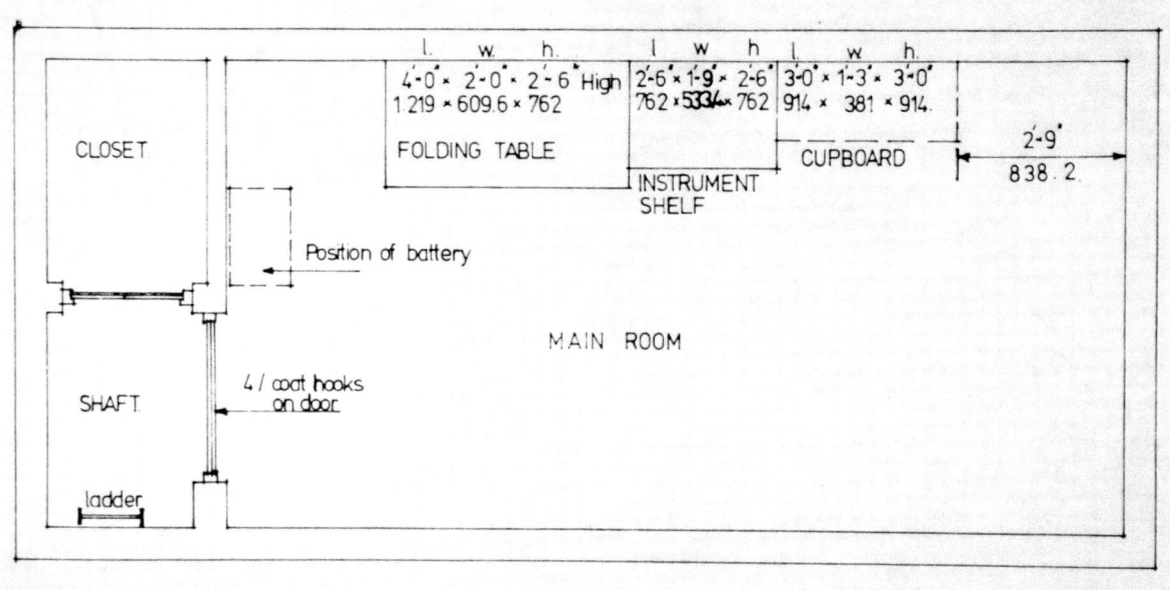

Above: This plan shows the overall layout and location of the principal internal fixtures and fittings. The bunk beds would have been placed widthways next to the cupboard at the right-hand end of the drawing. The single bed was placed along the wall opposite the furniture.

Below: Detail from a GPO cross-sectional drawing dated 1960, showing the general arrangement of the various instrument pipes and the telephone conduit into the post.

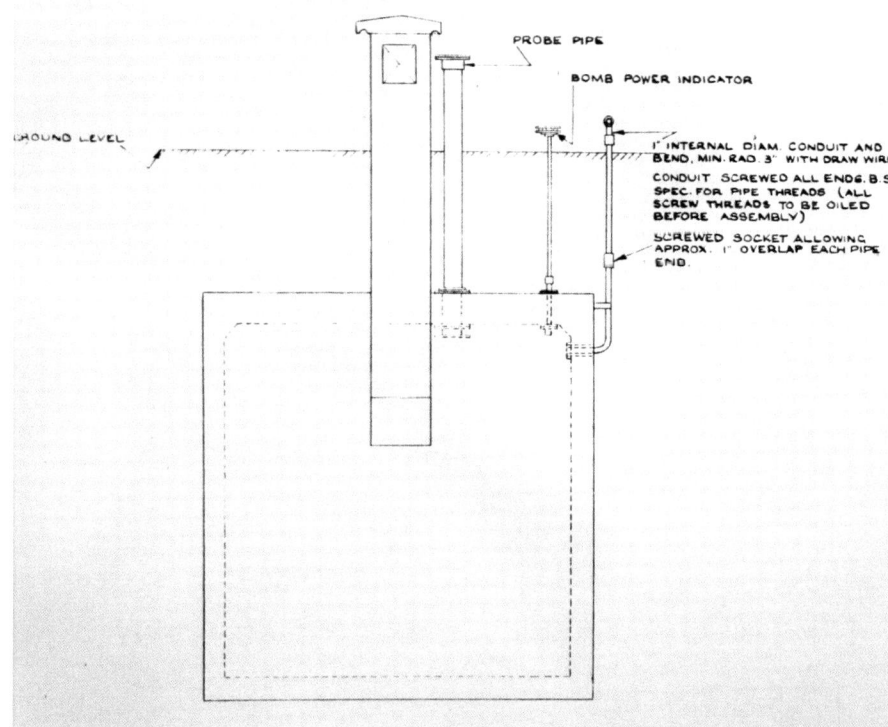

Opposite: This 1964 GPO longitudinal cross-section was drawn-up to detail the modifications required to install the AD3460 Teletalk, but is useful in that it shows the general arrangement of the post structure and its contents.

Right: The probe pipe was designed with a deliberately wide diameter as the actual size of the FSM probe head was unknown at the time. Some contractors installed pipes which were too long and had to be cut down. In one incident a contractor installed two probe pipes at the same post. The pipes were made from mild steel and hot-dip-galvanised for corrosion protection.

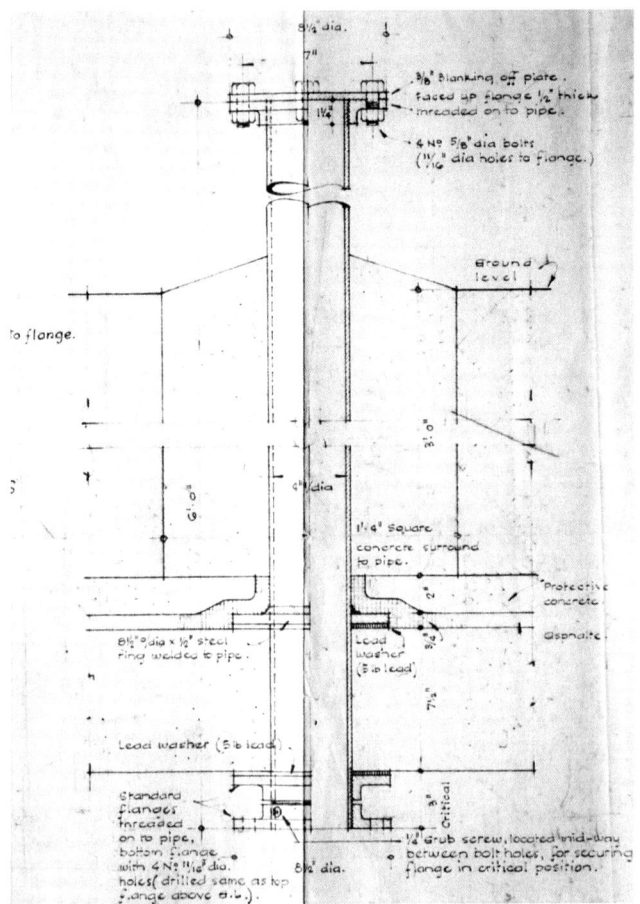

Below: This drawing shows the position of the waterproofing around the structure and states that "This drawing shows detail of Asphalt tanking which is to be incorporated into the construction if considered necessary by the Superintending Officer". Many surviving posts are now flooded. Allowing the tanking to be optional during the original construction may be one of the causes of this.

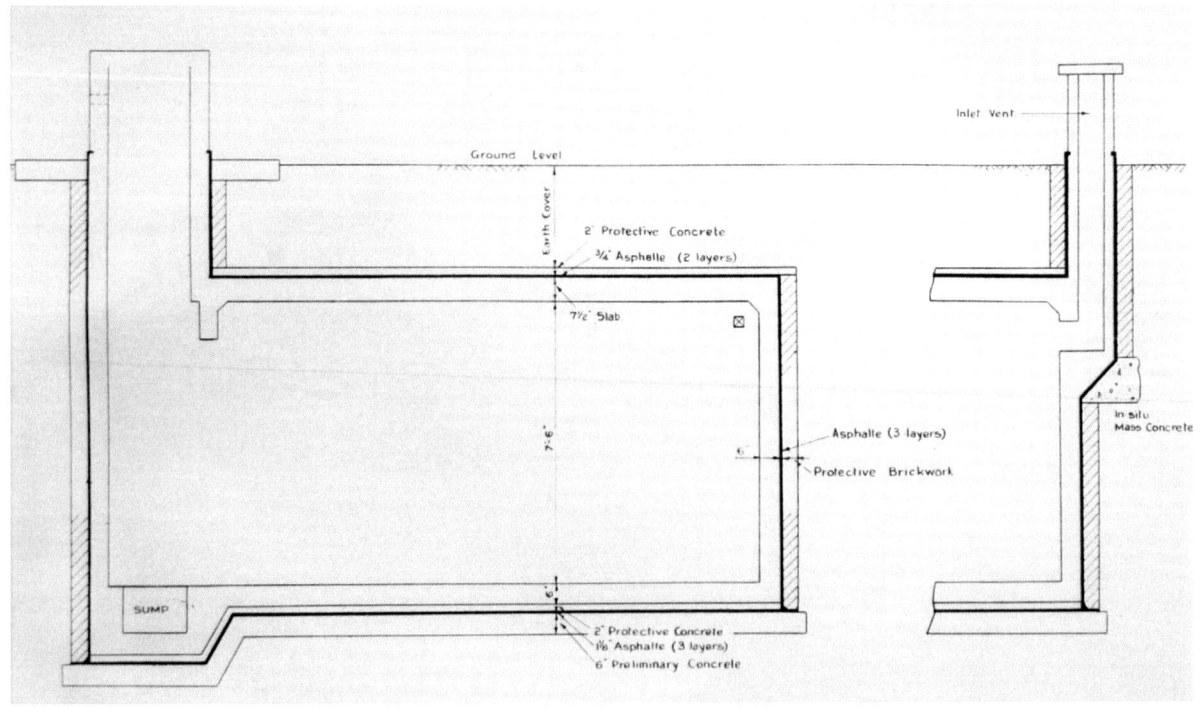

Building the Posts

Local contractors were employed to build the posts, working in conjunction with the ROC and Crown Land Agents to site and subsequently sign off the finished work. The basic criterion for siting the new posts was to have a minimum area of level ground fifty feet in diameter with no nearby features to obstruct the instruments. The land had to be available to buy or rent for a minimum of twenty-one years, with a right of access via a three-foot-wide path to the nearest public road.

As the existing system of aircraft posts had, in the main, already been sited on high ground for good visibility, it was relatively easy to position many of the new underground posts at the same locations. However, there were also many places where the land was unsuitable and sites had to be relocated, often nearby. For example, the underground posts at both Leominster in Herefordshire and Dalry in Scotland are within sight of earlier *Orlit* aircraft posts but were built on new sites.

The benefit of using existing sites was that they were already owned by the Crown so there were no usage issues. Difficulties did occur when new sites had to be found, with some landowners not being particularly receptive to losing a piece of their land and having to allow ROC crews access. Thus, efforts tended to be made to site posts close to public roads or public footpaths so that access issues were reduced. It has been suggested that posts that were less accessible tended to be chosen for closure in 1968.

Inevitably, with so many posts being built by many different contractors up and down the country, some mistakes were made. The most common mistake was to build a 'mirror image' post. This meant that as one faced the monitoring room, the toilet cubicle was to the right rather than to the left and all the furniture and equipment in the main room was also on the right-hand side.

Other mistakes included building the entire post underground, including the access shaft, so that the hatch cover was flush with ground level. Another mistake was to get the dimensions wrong so that the post visibly tapered along its length.

The total number of posts built is usually given as 1,563

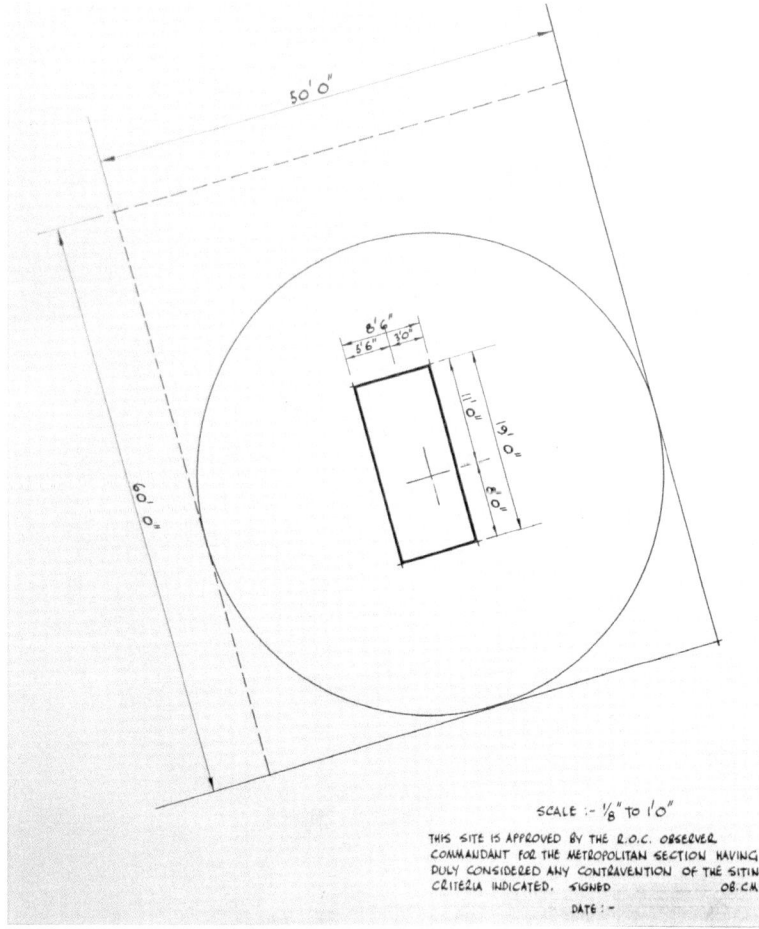

Left: A basic siting plan for an ROC post. This is part of the documentation for Littlehampton post in West Sussex which was built on the airfield at RNAS Ford and still exists today.

although several were demolished during the life of the Corps, due to road building and other civil engineering works. In some cases replacements were built (the major change being a doubling of the original six-inch wall thickness). The official number in operation at any one time was recorded in the ROC's *Schedule of Posts*. On 1 January 1966 this was given as 1,560. Ten years later, following the 1968 closures, this number had dropped to 869. Many 1968 closures were subsequently reopened to replace posts which had to be closed due to issues such as vandalism or water ingress. Thus, the number of operational posts varied throughout the life of the Corps, with the total number built at the end of the original programme incrementally increasing until well into the 1970s.

This series of photographs shows Hogs Back post in Surrey under construction in 1957.

Right: The concrete floor has already been laid, with timber battens keeping the basic shape. The outline of the monitoring room and toilet cubicle can be seen in the positioning of the reinforcing bars. At the extreme bottom left it is just possible to see the edge of the drainage sump set into the floor.

Right: Timber formwork is used to create the external shape of the post in preparation for further pouring. The machine on top is a 'poker' designed to vibrate the aggregate to ensure that it is evenly distributed within the mix.

Right: The finished concrete post with the formwork removed. The probe and blast pipes can be clearly seen. The pipe nearest the camera allows GPO lines to enter the monitoring room.

Right: Asphalt tanking has now been added to waterproof the structure. Note that the areas where the pipes enter the post have also been tanked.

Right: The bricks seen in the background of the previous photograph have now been used to line the exterior of the post. This protected the waterproofing layer from damage when the hole was backfilled. The waterproofing on the roof was protected by a two-inch-thick layer of concrete.

Right: The signing-off ceremony. An ROC Officer would officially take over a post and all parties including the contractor, works directorate and the ROC would have to sign the document. Note that there is only a temporary wooden cover where the hatch should be.

Lower right: The post is painted in a dark green shade and this aligns with Note 14 of the *General Arrangement & RC Detail* drawing "Exterior finish – concrete, steelwork and woodwork to be toned down to colour shade most like drab." At around the same time, anti-flash white paint schemes were appearing on the RAF V-bomber force with the intention of reflecting some of the thermal effects of a nuclear explosion. Some posts and group controls adopted this scheme. By the early 1970s there were fears that improved satellite imagery could detect the white painted structures so the posts were toned down to dark green and olive drab schemes. By stand-down most posts were in dark shades although examples could be found in white, black, camouflage and even desert pink.

Above and opposite above: These pictures show the building of Stratford post in East Ham, London in 1960/61. The internal timber formwork can be seen as well as a pile of bricks for the shuttering. Whereas Riseley post *(opposite below)* appears to have been built upwards in stages, this post has had one end completed prior to extending the building down the length of the structure.

Below right: The internal walls nearing completion – note the timber formwork. A third photograph in this series, not shown here, shows no evidence of a pipe for the telephone wires being in place. It has been suggested that letting in lines to posts after they were built resulted in water ingress due to the tanking not being properly repaired.

Below: This photograph, and the one to the right, show the post at Riseley in Bedfordshire being built in 1963/64. The floor and sump can be seen, along with the footings of the internal walls.

ROC POSTS

Above: Once the basic post had been built and accepted, the ROC then had to get the fixtures and fittings in place and also work with the GPO to get the lines installed. This could prove problematic. In one case the GPO engineer missed the post and wired up a nearby local reservoir building instead. These pictures show the GPO connecting an unknown post site to the telephone network.

In-Service Development

The following series of photographs, taken during Exercise 'Double Blank' on 23 April 1961, show the post at Springwell Colliery in Durham.

Below: Observer Ernie Guy leans against the entrance shaft. The early split-hatch design and external counterweights can be seen. The post was built on an old colliery waste tip.

Below: L to R Observer Peter Dockerty, Observer Tommy Cairns and son. It can be seen that the concrete GZI well has been added onto the ventilator after the post was completed. At the bottom of the well was a thin slate bed which would have been levelled. This would have allowed the GZI mount to be set up accurately on a flat datum. Posts were to be checked for levels and bearings every two years. Although the mounting well was provided on this post, no GZI was ever issued.

Above: Obs Ernie Guy with Springwell post in the background. The outflow pipe from the sump pump can be seen jutting out over the waste tip. The post hatch was never replaced and the split-hatch was retained until closure as part of the cost cutting measures in 1968.

Above: This post in Northern Ireland looks superficially similar to the Springwell post. However, the counterweight legs have a smoother profile and it appears that there are only two of them. The split-hatch opens at 90 degrees to the Springwell post thus avoiding hitting the GZI when mounted.

Below: Observers Peter Dockerty (foreground), Ernie Guy (headset), Tommy Cairns and son. The post is very basic with only a connection for the head and breast set. Early exercises were largely paper-based until the new instruments were developed and issued.

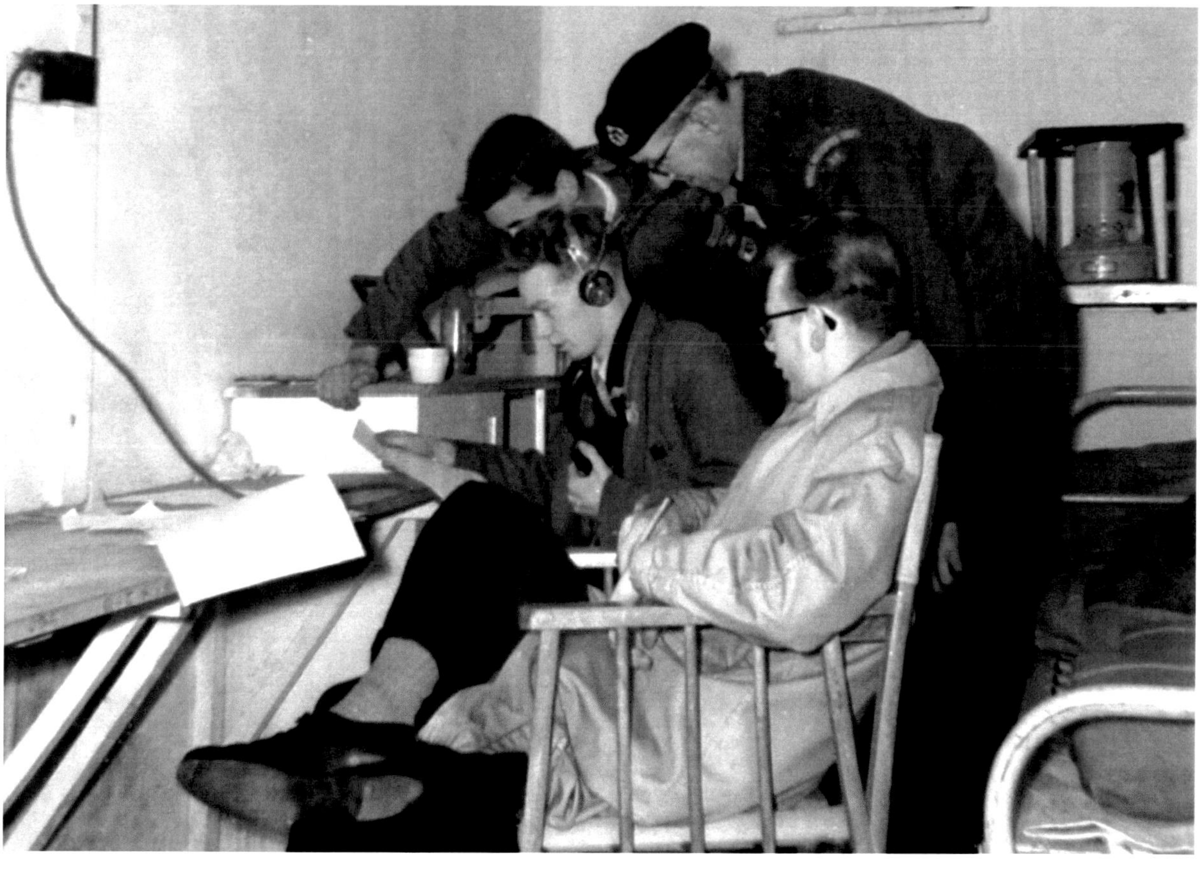

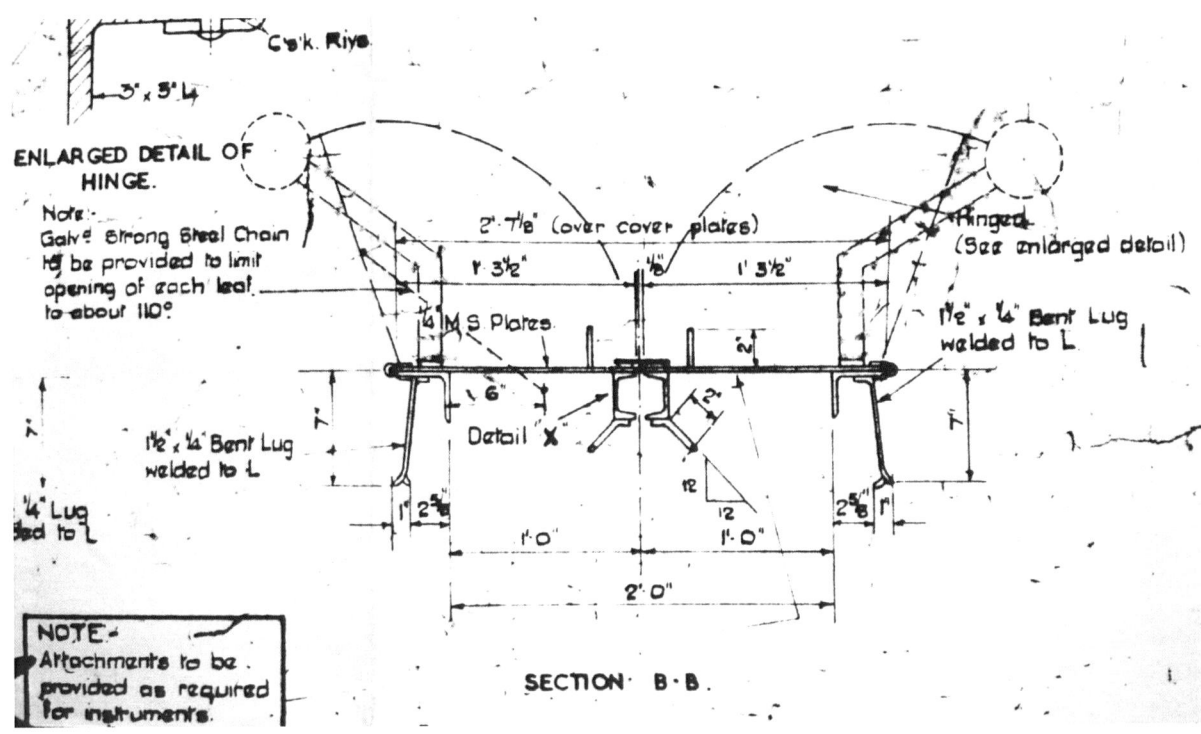

Above: These details from the *Details of Steel and Timber Work* drawing issued in September 1956 shows the original split-hatch with a two-leg counterweight design.

Below: A year later the hatch cover had changed to a four-leg counterweight design and each leg was now made from a single piece of bent metal tube. The Springwell and Northern Ireland posts illustrated overleaf appear to have elements of both the 1956 and 1957 designs with neither actually conforming to either drawing.

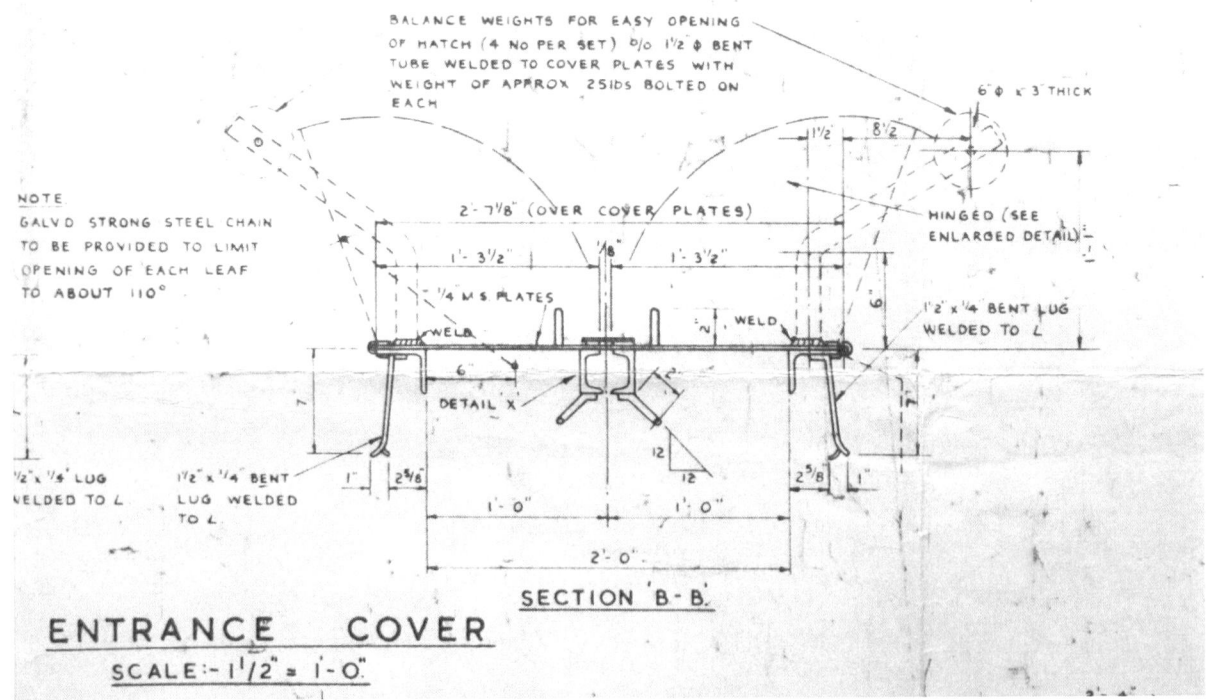

Above: The official opening of Winkleigh post in Devon in 1962. The hatch has now changed to a one-piece design with an internal counterweight.

Below: The internal counterweight design. The downside of positioning the counterweight inside the shaft entrance was that observers continually hit their heads or caught their backs on it. Eventually warning signs were fixed to the hatch and at the bottom of the ladder to remind observers to 'Mind your Head and Back'.

Below: With the exception of radio posts and the security measures of the 1980s, the final major modification undertaken was the addition of an extra vent at the top of the entrance shaft. The drawings for this new design became available in 1969 so the modifications were only made to posts that had survived the 1968 cutbacks.

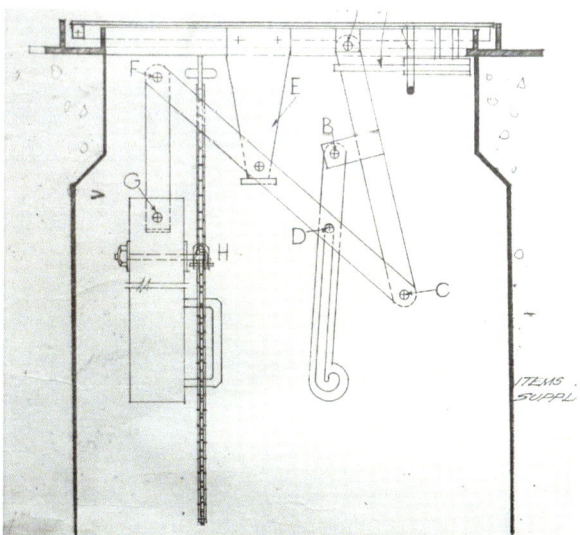

Above: With the introduction of the GZI, some posts had to be modified to raise the instrument above local obstacles so that a weapon burst would be captured on the photographic paper. This post at Modbury in Devon has had the mount extended and steps added to allow access. The black solar panel attached to the base of the mount is a much later addition.

Chapter 4

POST EQUIPMENT

As the Corps transitioned to the nuclear role it became obvious that a new range of equipment would be required. Training for the new role started in 1955 but the only equipment initially available was that already in use by the Civil Defence organisations. This primarily consisted of individual dosimeters and Radiac Survey Meters. Properly equipping the posts and training the observers became a priority.

The Radiac Survey Meter (RSM) No.1 was used initially, but was replaced early on by the RSM No.2, which was quickly adopted by the Corps as its principal radiation measuring device. It was soon relegated to a secondary role following the widespread introduction of the Fixed Survey Meter (FSM) in 1960. The Bomb Power Indicator (BPI) also became available in 1960 and this was followed by the Ground Zero Indicator (GZI). Measurements taken from the BPI and GZI allowed the power, location and type of bomb burst to be calculated. These three instruments, plus the communications equipment that allowed reports to be made, were key to the Corps execution of its role.

While most of the equipment was updated with the passage of time, the BPI and GZI remained unchanged. They were simple, robust instruments which were easy to use and maintain. The success of their design can be judged by the fact that they were still in service at stand-down in 1991, over thirty years after they were introduced.

Communications in the early days of the nuclear role used the existing Second World War era headphone and breastplate microphone arrangement. This continued until 1964 when a new 'Teletalk' unit became available, although this still used the existing telephone landline network.

It was recognised that overhead lines were vulnerable to attack so a supplementary reporting method using VHF radio was developed. Radio communications were trialled by the Winchester Group in 1961 and the ATE *Countryman* radio was subsequently chosen. This equipment began a slow rollout process across the Corps which continued well into the next decade.

Warnings of imminent attack, fallout and the all-clear were broadcast on the Carrier Warning System. The posts were equipped with WB400 Carrier Warning Receivers from the early 1960s onwards. Hand-operated sirens, similar to Second World War air raid sircns, were provided at posts to warn of attack, and explosive maroons were developed by the Royal Armaments Research and Development Establishment to provide warning of fallout.

The resurgence of the Cold War in the early 1980s resulted in the entire warning network being revitalised. British Telecom introduced the WB1400 Carrier Control System and replaced the old WB400 desk units in posts with a new wall-mounted receiver. They also replaced the old Teletalk units in the posts with a more compact unit which did not require battery changes. The hand-operated sirens remained but a new type of maroon was developed and introduced.

In addition to the improvements in the warning network, a new equipment development programme got underway. The Home Office contracted electronics giant Plessey to produce a new lightweight radiation meter to replace the existing RSM and FSM. The old single-channel VHF radio unit was also replaced by a new Burndept multichannel radio system.

The overall welfare and survivability of post

crews were also re-evaluated during this period. Attempts were made to reduce the effect of cold in the posts and an experimental ventilation system, the Luwa system, was trialled which would allow the posts to draw in uncontaminated air during fallout conditions.

The initiatives instigated in the early 1980s took years to roll out across the organisation and many posts operated a mixture of equipment for the rest of the life of the Corps.

Towards the end of the 1980s further attempts were made to improve the posts by trialling mains-capable generator sets. These would have allowed the possibility of microwave ovens to be used for heating food and there was talk of using combined TV/VCR units for in-post training purposes.

The late 1980s also saw a widespread review of the whole attack warning system. Automated blast and radiation detection systems were considered, with the 1988 introduction of the Radiation Incident Monitoring Network (RIMNET) showing what was possible.

Within the Corps it was felt that a further reduction in numbers was inevitable as technology superseded the old equipment. Ultimately, the end of the Cold War and the subsequent stand-down of the ROC meant that these new technologies were never implemented.

Radiation Detection and Monitoring

The task of detecting and monitoring radioactive fallout was the primary function envisaged for the Corps when a nuclear role was first suggested. The Corps had developed an infrastructure for reporting and tracking aircraft movements which was now becoming obsolete but which could be modified with new equipment and training to report on radiation plumes rather than aircraft.

To do this, new devices were developed which could give accurate readings, be simple to use and which could sustain the rigours of post life.

Two principal radiation detection devices were provided to post crews, the Fixed Survey Meter (FSM) and the Radiac Survey Meter (RSM). The FSM remained inside the post and was connected to an ionisation chamber which could be raised to the surface. In this way, radiation at the surface could be measured from inside the safety of the post. The ionisation chamber was fixed to a telescopic rod which was used to push the chamber upwards through a large diameter pipe set into the ceiling of the post running to the surface. At the surface there was a PVC cover bolted onto a flange at the top of the pipe which protected the FSM pipe and sealed it from the outside elements. The pole, and hence the chamber, could be lowered partially into the pipe to provide shielded readings if the radiation was particularly intense and exceeded the limit of the FSM scale in normal operation.

The early units were relatively sensitive and had to be calibrated at the group headquarters. They were not kept at the posts and would only be issued during exercises or at time of war. This meant that crews had little regular familiarity with the equipment, so a more usable, less sensitive training unit was developed. This looked almost identical to the real unit but had no internal radioactive source which required calibration, and could be stored in the post for short periods of time.

The training unit was designed to replicate

Above: The FSM was stored and transported in a wooden case, containing the indicator unit, battery pack, cable and ionisation chamber.

POST EQUIPMENT

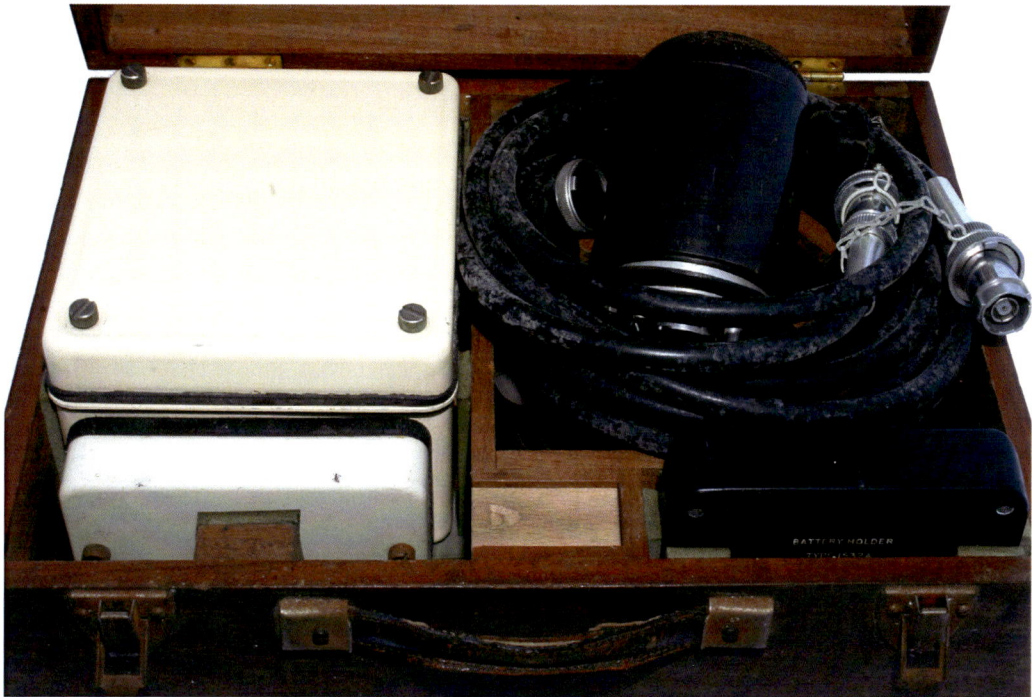

Above: The FSM indicator unit is on the left, the face being protected by a screw-down metal cover. The ionisation chamber is the large black domed unit to the right.

Right: The indicator unit with the protective cover removed, showing the indicator scale and controls. The metal cover at the base of the unit protects the battery pack. Underneath the black battery pack there is a screw-location hole enabling the unit to be screwed onto the monitoring room table so that it would be stable when operated.

readings that might be seen over several hours or more as radiation of varying intensity passed over the post and was detected by the ionisation chamber. This was achieved by using a roll of celluloid which was fed into the front of the unit and pulled through by a clockwork mechanism. The celluloid roll would be of varying width which would move the needle of the dial mechanically thus giving a range of readings for the observer to report. These rolls were issued for exercises so that post crews could get realistic practise in recording and reporting fallout.

The second radiation detection meter, the RSM, was also provided to posts. This was primarily designed for use outside the post but could also be used as a back-up instrument if the FSM failed. The RSM was provided with a protective weatherproof case and carrying strap, enabling it to be used more easily outside the post.

Between 1963 and 1968 master posts had the additional role of 'deposition', which required a fourth crew member. Trays would be used to collect fallout from outside the post and would then be brought into the hatchway. The trays would be placed in a rack in order of collection and measurements would be taken every hour using the RSM. These measurements allowed scientists at the Control to calculate actual deposition and decay rates.

The original FSM and RSM were both replaced by the much lighter Plessey-developed Personal Dose Rate Meter (PDRM), the former by the PDRM82(F) unit and the latter by the PDRM82. Both used standard batteries and had digital display readouts. They had strong, weatherproof polycarbonate cases. The FSM version could now be stored in its case in the post rather than having to be issued from group headquarters. The RSM version was provided with a plastic strap which could be placed over the neck to support the unit when used in a mobile role.

The FSM clockwork trainer now needed replacement and a new digital box was produced by Cambridge Instruments Ltd. Instead of a celluloid roll, the readouts were now held on an EPROM programmable memory chip. Complete exercises could be held on EPROM cartridges which could be plugged into a socket revealed when the top

Above: Also transported in a wooden carrying case, the FSMT did not require the batteries, cables and ionisation chamber of the FSM and so was smaller and lighter.

Above: The key for the clockwork mechanism of the FSM trainer was stored inside its protective metal lid.

POST EQUIPMENT

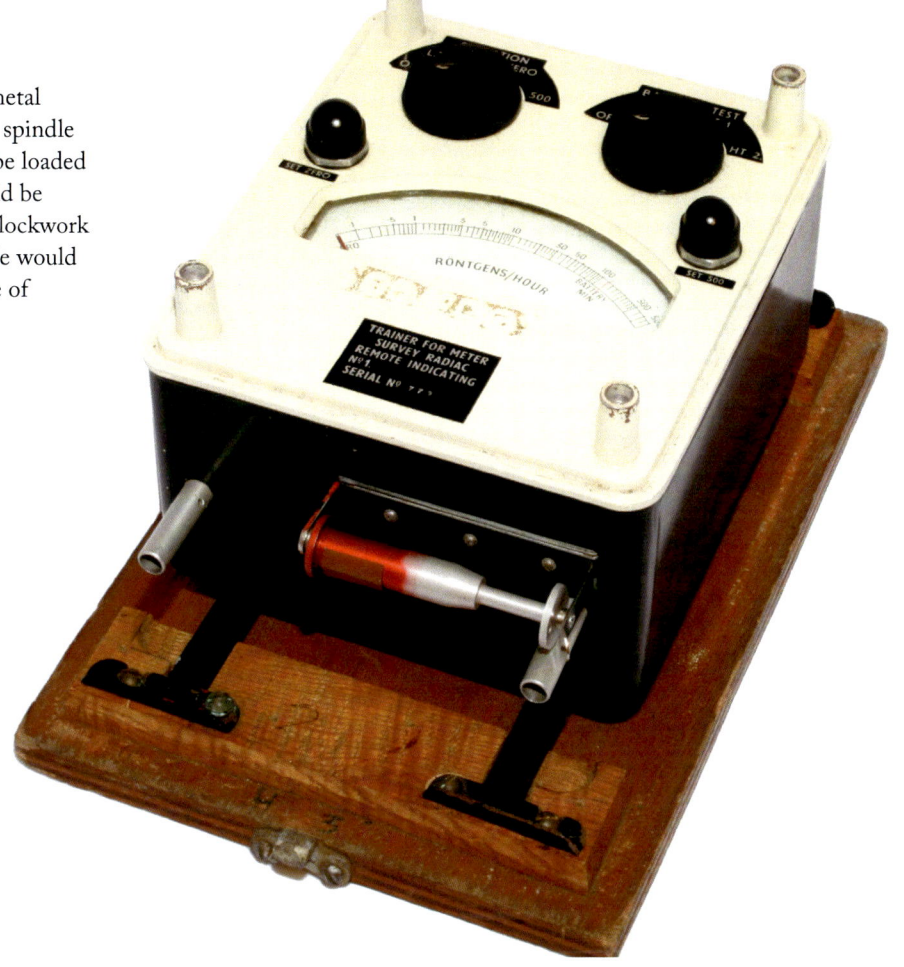

Right: The FSMT unit with metal protective cover removed. The spindle at the base of the unit would be loaded with a celluloid roll. This would be drawn through the unit by a clockwork mechanism and the dial needle would deflect to simulate the passage of radiation.

cover of the trainer was removed. In operation the trainer unit was connected to the rear of the FSM by a coaxial cable. When the trainer was switched on the digital display on the FSM would change over time indicating the detection and passage of radiation, just as the previous generation of equipment had.

A further item of radiation detection equipment employed in the posts was the personal dosimeter. This device was issued to individual crew members and was used to detect the accumulated radiation a specific individual had been exposed to. Its purpose was to ensure that crew members did not exceed a safe dosage in a particular timeframe. These devices had to be reset to zero using dosimeter charging units. Initially, the issued charger used a hand powered generator to produce DC power. Later versions were battery powered and were both smaller and lighter. The dosimeters were similar in size and shape to fountain pens and could be clipped onto crew members' uniforms or carried in their pockets. They came in several different versions with different dose ranges. The post crews largely used the No.3 and No.4 dosimeters, with the latter being the standard by the 1980s. If the dosimeters had been used outside in real fallout conditions then it was advised that they were covered by a small clear plastic bag to allow easier decontamination. Shortages of dosimeters within groups was not uncommon as they were easily misplaced and lost due to their small size and the fact that individuals carried them on their persons.

POST EQUIPMENT

Above and below: The Telescopic Probe Rod was used to position the FSM ionisation chamber above ground while the crew remained in the safety of the post. The Probe Rod Bracket *(below right)* was used to secure the ionisation chamber to the top of the Probe Rod. The rod was stored in the FSM pipe when not in use.

Above: The FSM dome consisted of a rubberised PVC cover which was bolted onto the top of the FSM pipe using a conical aluminium securing ring. The brown gasket was used to seal the securing ring to the pipe and stop water ingress.

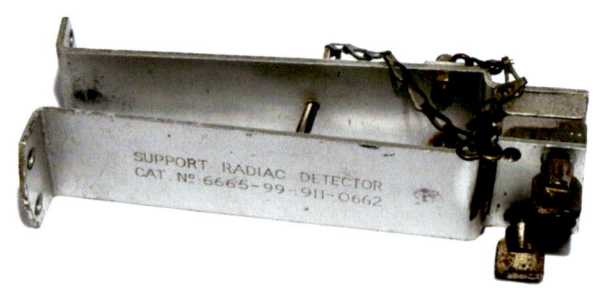

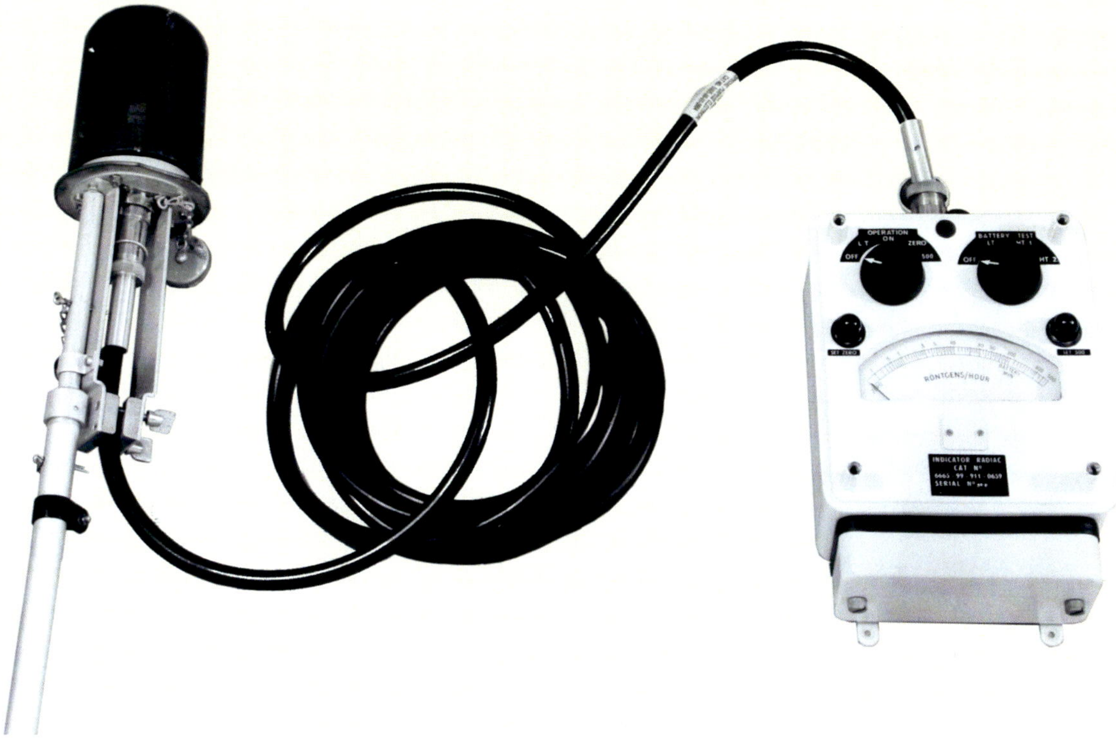

POST EQUIPMENT

Above: The Fixed Survey Meter ionisation chamber attached to the probe rod bracket. The cable connects the ionisation chamber to the meter and would have run down the probe pipe from the surface, along three hooks set in the ceiling and then down to the meter on the monitoring room table.

Left: The RSM No.1 was a larger unit than the RSM No.2 and was only in service for a few years. Many crews were never issued with it as the latter unit replaced it early in the nuclear period.

POST EQUIPMENT

Above: The Radiac Survey Meter No.2 was the first radiation detection device widely adopted by the Corps, but it required the readings to be taken outside. Once the FSM became available, the RSM was used as a back-up unit. It was also used when mobile monitoring was required away from the post.

Left: The Radiac Survey Meter No.2 in its waterproof carrying case. A transparent panel enabled readings to be taken without opening the case.

Above: The PDRM82(F) replaced the FSM in the mid-1980s. It was a much lighter unit that could be stored in the post in its plastic carrying case.

Below: The ionisation chamber (on the left) was much smaller than the previous unit and was connected by coaxial cable to the PDRM82(F) unit. The only external difference between this and the standard PDRM82 was that the fixed version had a coaxial connector at the base of the unit.

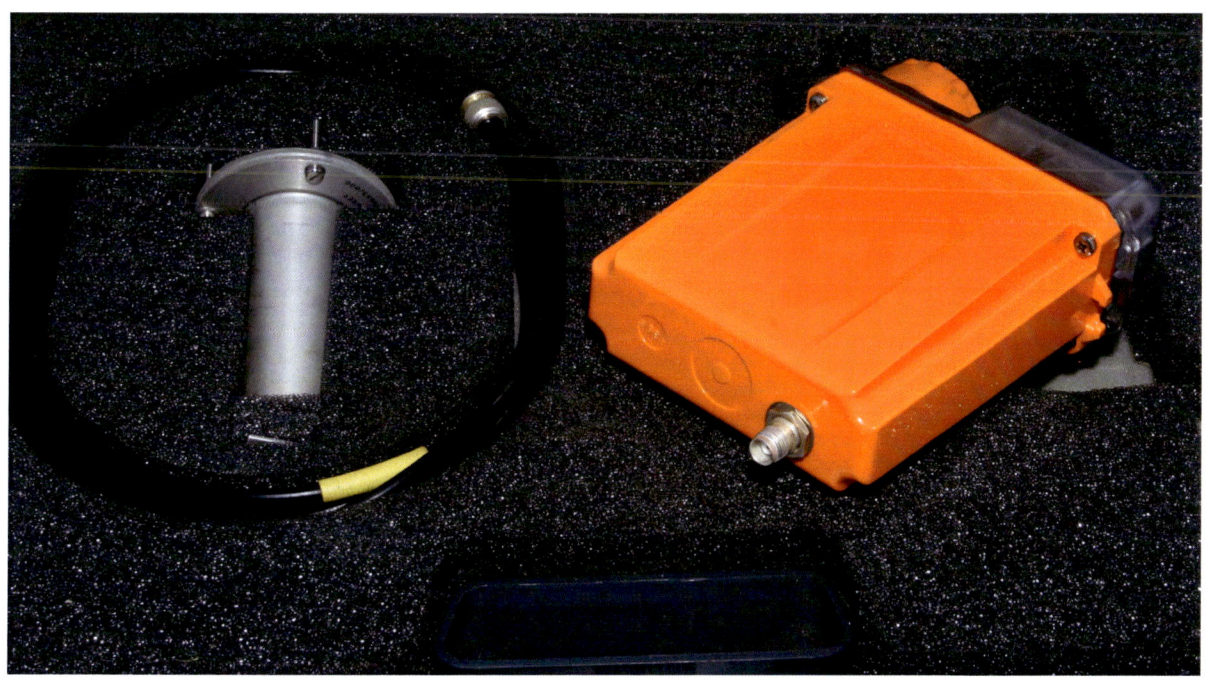

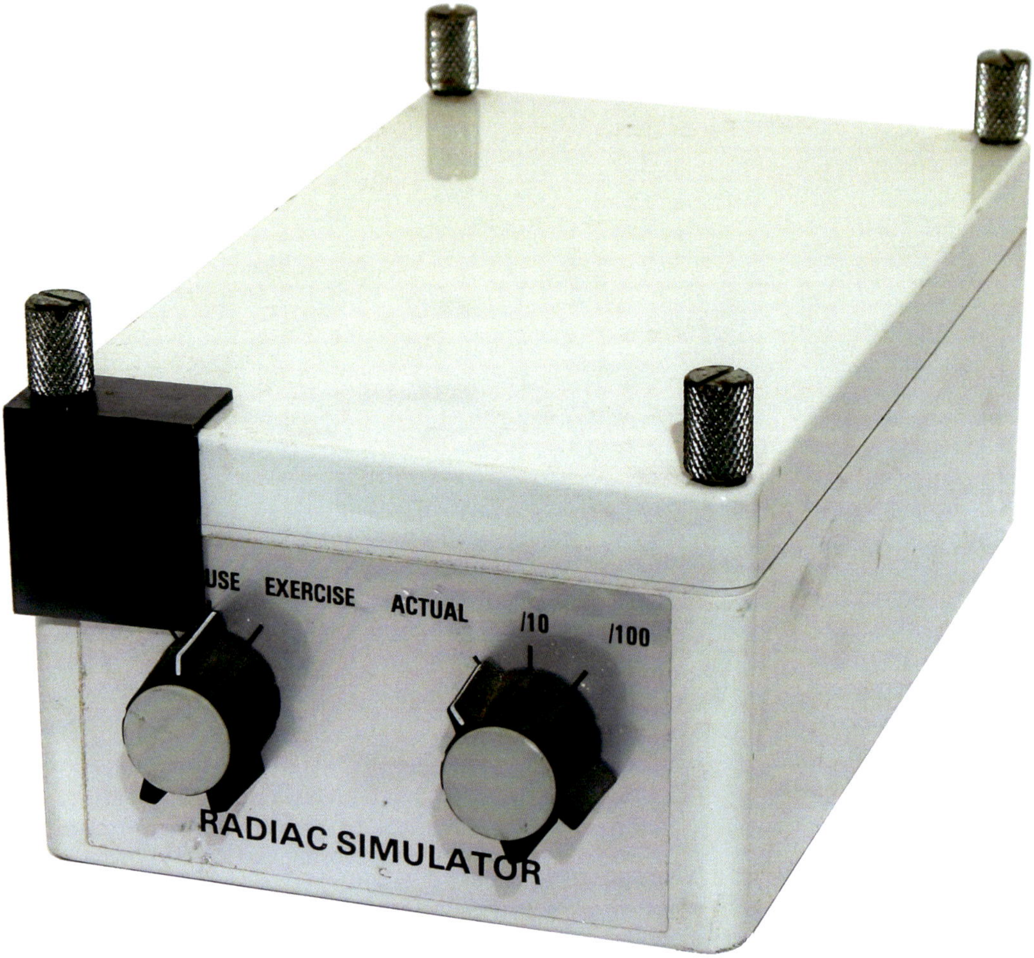

POST EQUIPMENT

Above: The Radiac Simulator replaced the old clockwork FSMT. The black plastic part on the top left of the unit was added after it was found that observers could accidentally turn the unit off when instructed to turn it to the 'pause' setting during an exercise. The new piece of plastic physically stopped this happening and saved many an observer from embarrassment.

Right: The EPROM memory module was used to simulate radiation readings for training purposes.

POST EQUIPMENT

Right: The PDRM82 is shown with its original packaging. The white plastic strap allowed the unit to be supported around the neck and the white lanyard secured it around the chest for mobile monitoring duties. The orange polycarbonate casings were surprisingly strong – the ROC team evaluating these units at Bentley Priory ran over one with a Landrover.

Above: The battery-powered type N105A dosimeter charging unit replaced the earlier Charging Unit No.2 in the 1980s.

Right: The Charging Unit No.2 used a hand-operated generator to supply DC power. Both this and the type N105A were used to zero the personal dosimeters that observers wore to measure cumulative radiation dose rates.

POST EQUIPMENT

The Ground Zero Indicator

The Ground Zero Indicator (GZI) was developed in the late 1950s as a simple and robust way of determining the position (the 'ground zero') and height above ground of a nuclear burst. Individual posts could use the GZI to determine the bearing and elevation of a burst from their post. Group control could then use information from two or more posts to triangulate the actual position and height of the burst.

The instrument was manufactured by General Radiological Ltd and consisted of a cylindrical metal cover which could be removed to reveal four concave faces. Each face held a piece of photographic paper in a cassette which consisted of a plastic sleeve marked with a lined grid in 5 degree increments. Each face aligned with a small hole positioned in the outer casing; this arrangement effectively being a pinhole camera. The GZI was positioned so that each pinhole camera aligned with a cardinal point on the compass.

When light entered the pinhole, the paper was exposed and spots of intense light, such as a nuclear burst, could be identified. The bearing and elevation of these spots could be read off against the cassette graticule and recorded.

If the spot was above the horizon-line then the spot was classed as an 'air burst'. If the spot was close to, or cropped by the horizon-line then it was classed as a 'ground burst'. Ground burst explosions would have carried the additional risk of fallout as irradiated debris would be sucked upwards and subsequently distributed across country before returning to earth as radioactive dust and particles.

The bearing, elevation and burst type would have been recorded on Form GZI by the post crew and then passed on to the group control.

In operation, the photographic papers would have to be changed on a regular basis as ambient light would slowly darken the paper. Replacement

Below: The instrument was originally supplied in a large cylindrical cardboard container and came with a cast metal mounting plate. This plate had three holes for mounting the GZI arranged so that the instrument would only fit onto the mounting plate in one orientation. It was therefore vital that the mounting plate was aligned correctly so that when the GZI was attached, the correct side would face the correct compass point. Once aligned, the mounting plate was concreted into position on the post ventilator, thereby ensuring that the GZI would always be correctly aligned in use.

Below: The Ground Zero Indicator.

POST EQUIPMENT

paper was kept in a light-proof box within the post. Papers to be used for immediate replacement would be loaded into a second set of cassettes and placed in a light-proof satchel. The No.3 Observer would then change the cassettes at predetermined times, when directed by control or, in a war situation, one minute after the BPI had detected a nuclear burst.

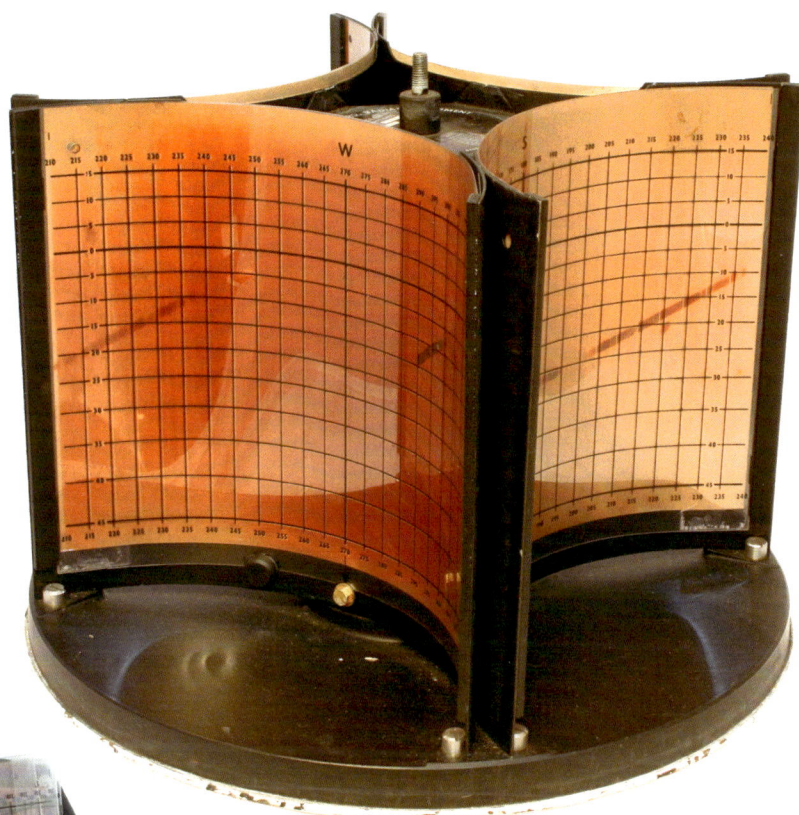

Right: The Ground Zero Indicator with the outer case removed. Each face contains a cassette which holds light-sensitive paper.

Below: The light-proof satchel was used by the No.3 Observer to protect new and used papers as he exited and entered the post.

Below: New paper was stored in a light-proof box in the monitoring room.

POST EQUIPMENT

The Bomb Power Indicator

The Bomb Power Indicator (BPI) measured the peak over pressure as a blast wave moved over a post. This information, combined with burst distance information from the GZI, could be used by group control to determine the power of the bomb. The instrument consisted of a large circular enamelled casing containing a bellows which moved a pointer on a dial when normal atmospheric pressure was exceeded by the pressure outside the post.

The instrument was usually fixed to an angled wooden board bolted to the monitoring room wall. It was connected to the outside world via a short galvanised pipe fixed to the top of the instrument. This was attached to the blast pipe running up to the surface. The pipe terminated in a baffle assembly consisting of two steel plates, the lower one with a hole in it to allow air to flow down the pipe and into the BPI. Baffle plates were removed and stored in the posts when not in use and a cap was screwed onto the top of the blast pipe to stop water ingress.

The BPI continued in use throughout the nuclear role, the only change being a move to reporting pressure in Kilopascals (kPa) rather than pounds per square inch (Psi). This necessitated a new 'Kilopascal' graduated dial being overlaid onto the existing face of the instrument.

Above right: This photograph shows the unit in service in the 1960s. The observer is displaying the protective end cap that would be fitted on the blast pipe when not in service.

Centre right: Detail of the underside of the baffle plate assembly.

Right: The Bomb Power Indicator and original packaging. Note the scale in Kilopascals.

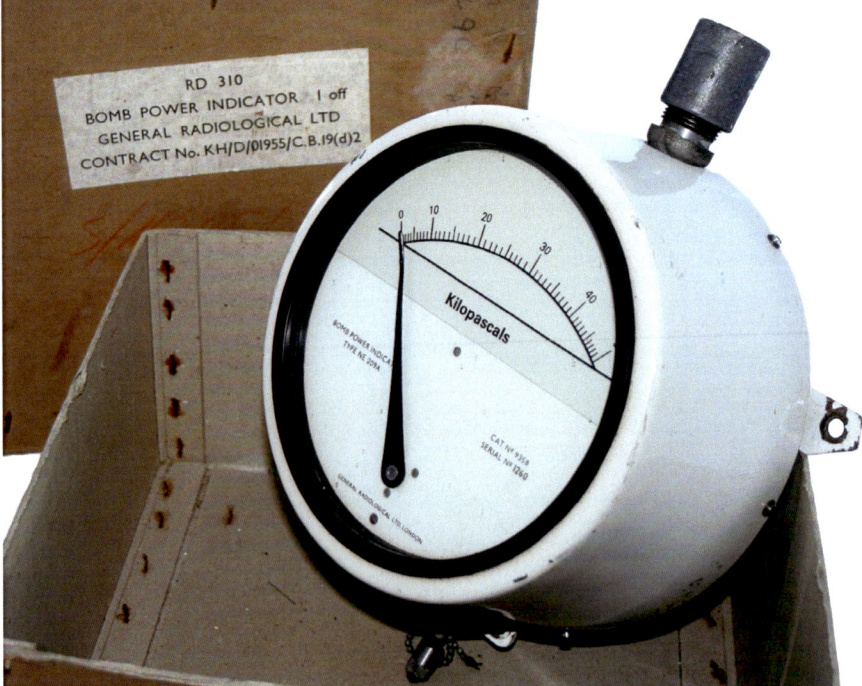

Communications

The Special Constables of the Great War used the public telephone network to communicate with control centres and this continued through the Second World War and into the nuclear age. The ubiquitous 'head and breast' set that was introduced in the late 1930s was still in use when the Corps went underground in the late 1950s and continued until the introduction of the first generation of Teletalk. The official description of this unit was 'Telephone portable for Observer Posts RAF Ref No 10G/125' and was also known as the magneto telephone. These units were initially used above ground in the existing aircraft posts and only allowed the operator to communicate. The rest of the post crew could only hear what was said into the breast microphone, not the response in the headphones. When the underground posts were built they were configured so that the magneto phone could be used above and below ground.

The introduction of the AD3460 Teletalk allowed the crew to communicate from the underground post and all were now able to hear the response from control. The downside was that the whole crew was continually disturbed if there was a lot of communication ongoing within the cluster and group. The Teletalk units had a 'call' button which was used by the post crew

Above: The terminals on the side of the box allowed the magneto telephone to be connected to the network both above and below ground.

Below: Behind the batteries can be seen an original wiring diagram.

Below left: The magneto telephone box in its closed position.

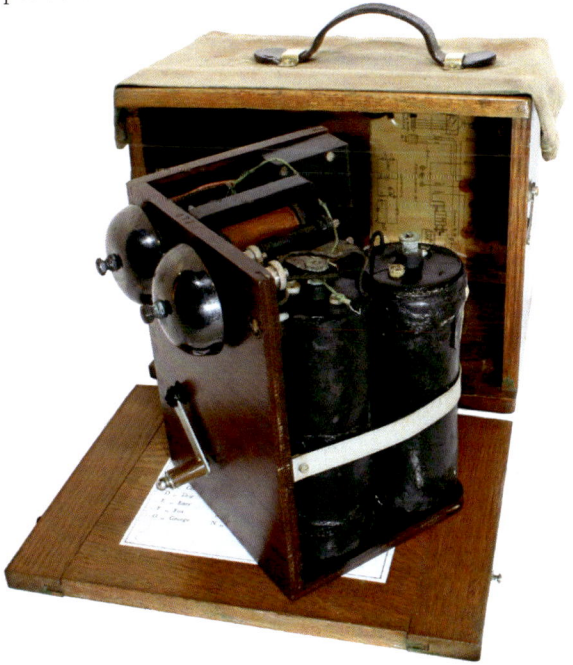

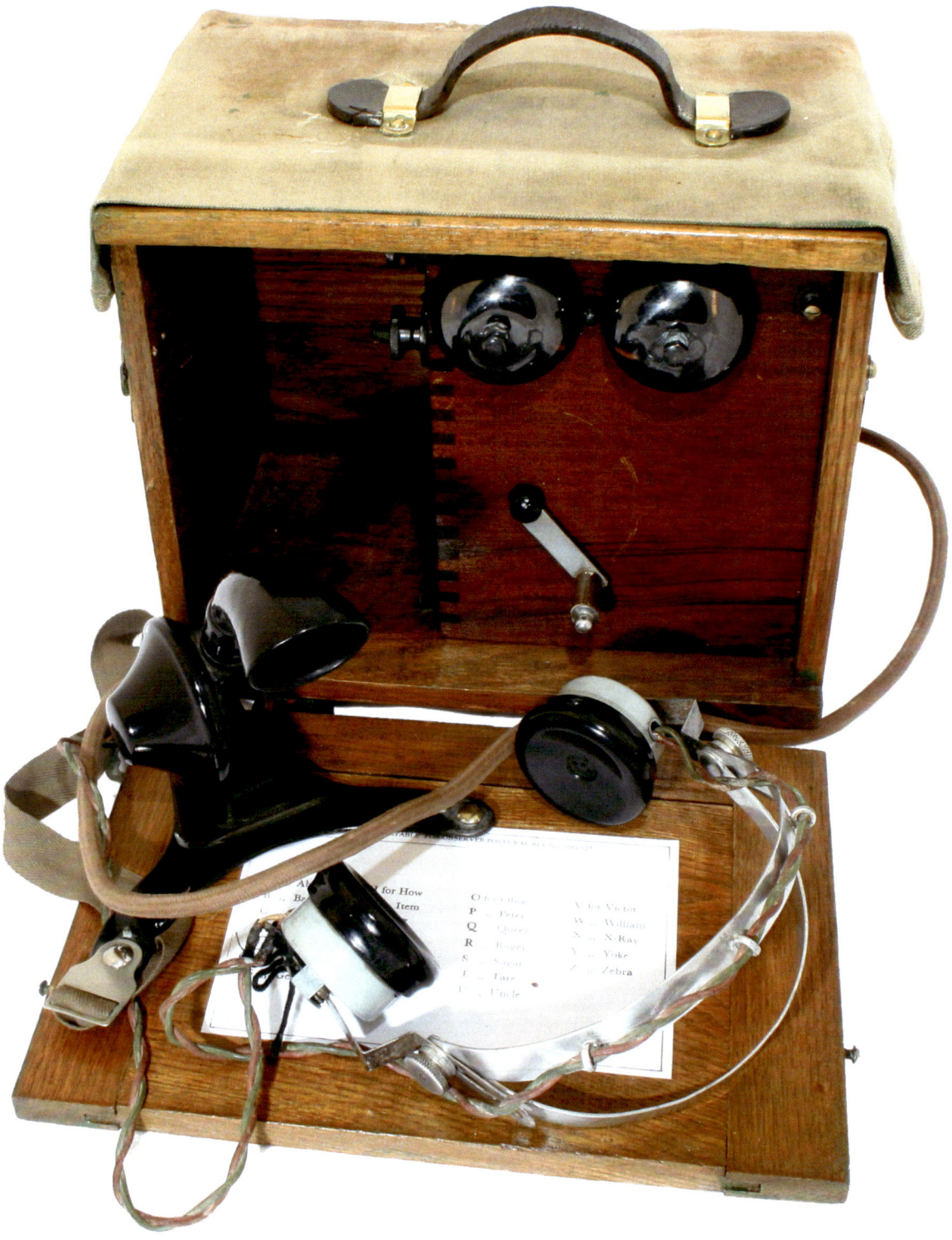

Above: The opened magneto telephone showing the 'head and breast' set with its microphone horn which was worn on the chest. Winding the handle on the front of the unit would ring the control room. The bells above would ring when control wanted to contact the post.

to draw the attention of the operations room at group headquarters, effectively ringing the control centre. The button would be returned to the 'listen' setting to allow the response to be heard. The 'speak' button could then be pressed to allow the post crew to pass any reports or messages.

The posts had dedicated private circuits linking posts to the local exchanges. At first this was a simple two-wire arrangement which also provided the WB400 Carrier Warning Receiver with its signal. The lines were usually carried on telegraph poles which made them vulnerable to blast damage and would have significantly reduced the effectiveness of the reporting network.

The system was complicated by the fact that a cost saving measure meant that the link from the local exchange to the group headquarters was carried over the public telephone system, the rationale being that if the ROC were not using the lines then they would not have to pay for them. Thus a complicated system of changing over these Emergency Circuits (EC) had to be implemented every time the ROC conducted an exercise.

This system was finally overhauled, starting in 1981, when the switched circuits were replaced by private circuits between group headquarters and the post exchange. This allowed posts in a cluster to talk to each other without having to be 'on exercise' and also independently of Group involvement. The number of wires into the post now doubled to provide a four-wire private circuit for the new AD8010 Teletalk. The equipment was also linked to a Test Box allowing British Telecom (BT) engineers to remotely test the post equipment. The new BT device was operated in the same way as the earlier unit but now had a clamshell lid that, when closed, would turn the unit off. The old unit was sometimes referred to as an intercom unit but, by the 1970s, training manuals were officially referring to the unit as a 'Loud Speaker Telephone' or LST, and this continued with the introduction of the AD8010. During this period an effort was also made to bury the phone lines at vulnerable post sites in an attempt to improve survivability.

Right: The AD3460 Teletalk. This was introduced in 1964 and replaced the Second World War era 'head and breast' magneto telephone.

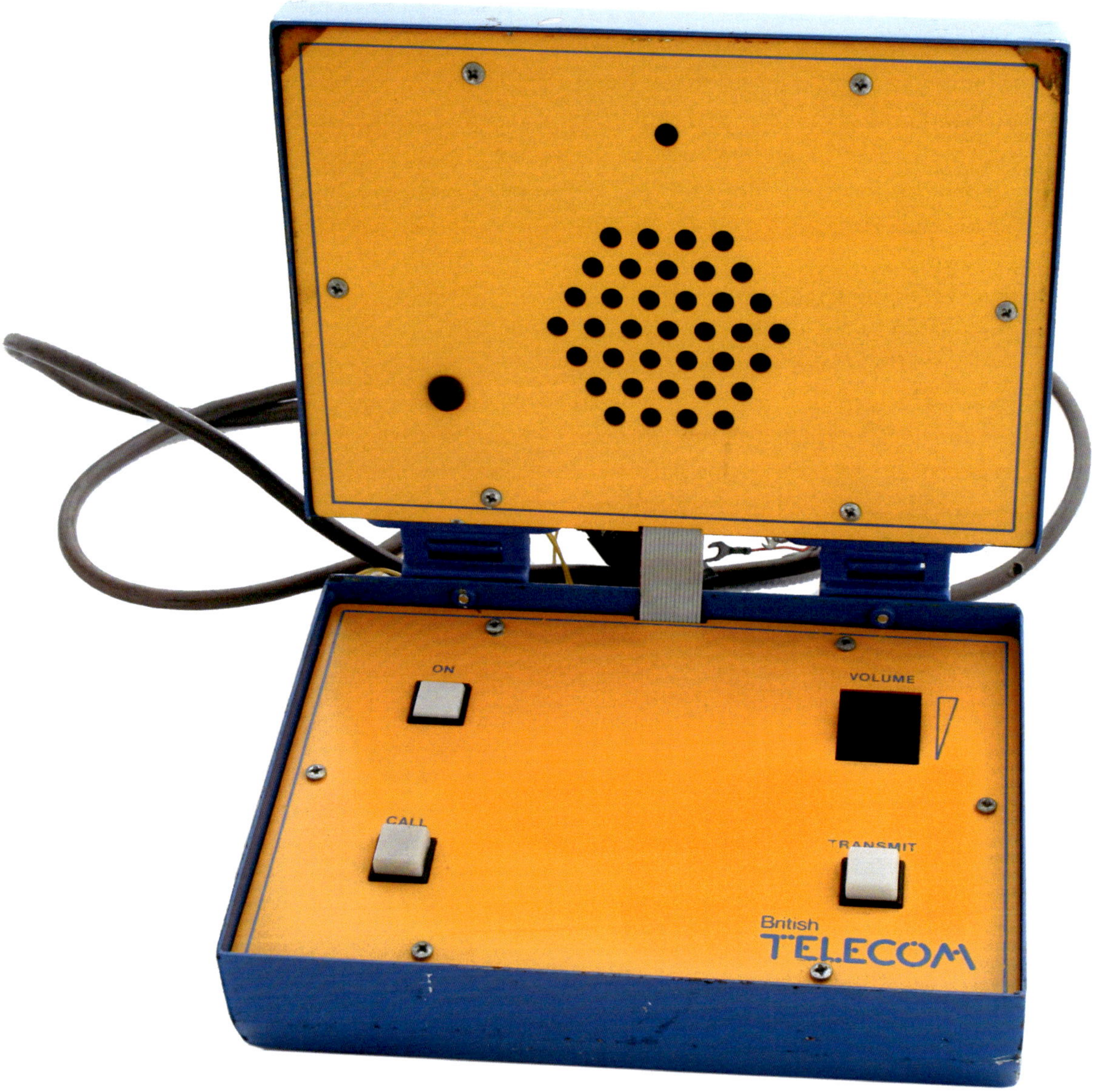

Above: The AD8010 Loud Speaker Telephone or Teletalk was used to communicate with group control and other posts within the cluster.

Right: The AD8010 unit in its closed position. Note the addition of rubberised handles on this example. These were a later addition as it was found that the clamshell design could snap shut catching an unwary observer's fingers.

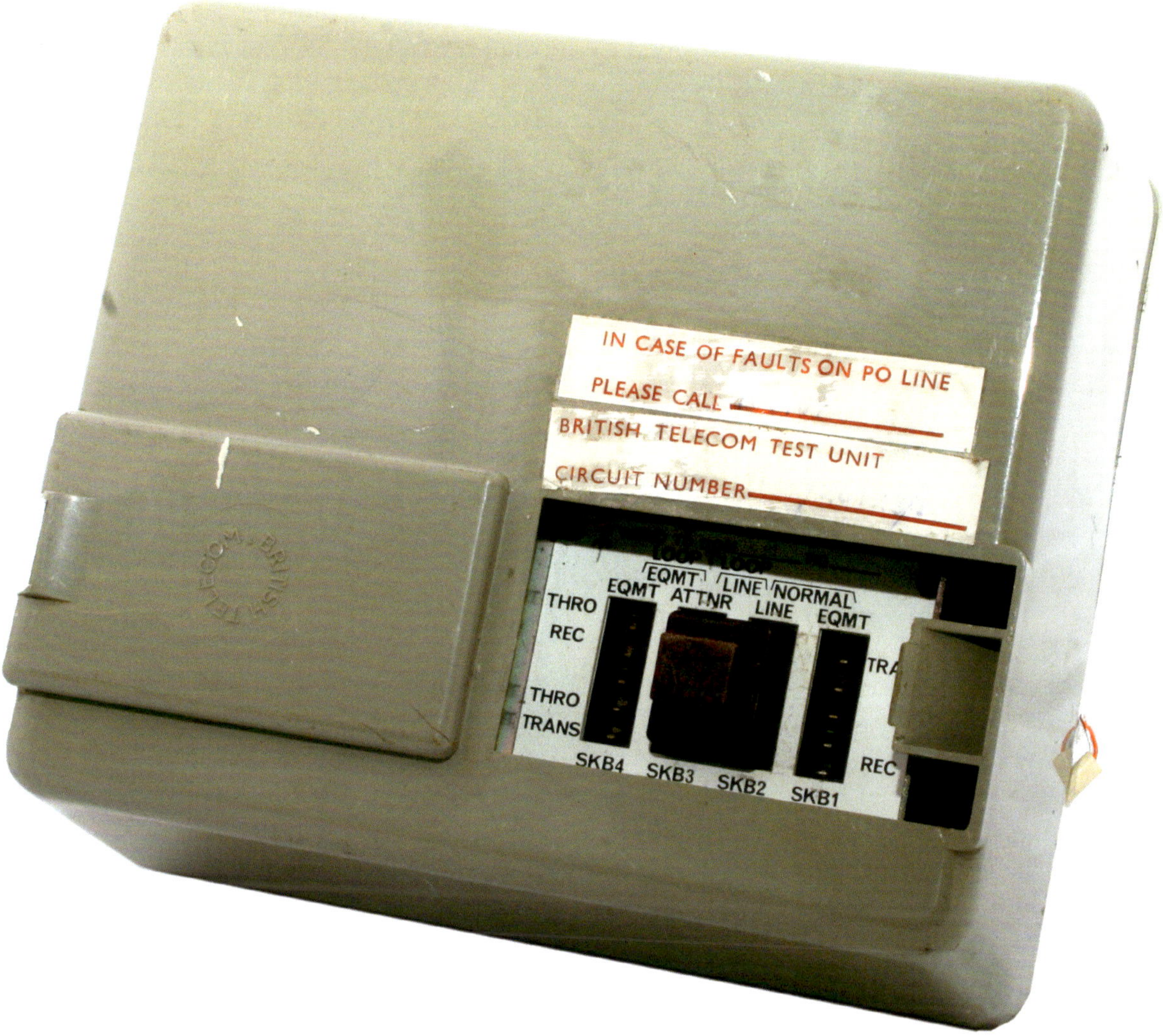

POST EQUIPMENT

Above: There were two different versions of the BT Test Box, but both allowed communications engineers to test the lines in and out of the post without it having to be manned. The brown plug in this 'Case 200' version is set in the 'line test' position which allows remote testing. On manning-up the plug would be moved to the right for 'normal' operation.

Right: Stocks of batteries were kept in the posts. These were used for the 1960s era Teletalk and Carrier Warning Receiver.

POST EQUIPMENT

Radio Communications

The use of overhead telephone lines was a recognised weak point in the communications system. If a line to a post was brought down then both its carrier receiver and its Teletalk would be disabled.

The cluster system provided some redundancy. Even if several posts had line damage, there was a chance that at least one was still connected to an exchange so that some information from that area of the group was still available. However, if the line back to the group headquarters was out of service then there was no way of relaying information.

The solution to this was to develop a radio system so that one post in every cluster had the ability to contact the group headquarters via a radio link. If landline failure occurred then one post could still provide information to the group control. That post could also relay information from other posts in the cluster that had lost their landline link with group but still retained a link to the other posts via the private Teletalk line.

Radio trials were conducted by the Winchester Group and the Automatic Telephones and Electric Company (ATE) *Countryman* radio was adopted by the Corps.

The ATE *Countryman* was a large, heavy, valve based, single channel VHF set. The weakness of this system was that the post crew could not talk to other radio equipped posts and, as each group operated on a different frequency, they could only talk to their own group headquarters.

The unit was wall mounted using bolts and a strong metal bracket. It was hung with the connection points facing downwards. This was not an issue as there were no user controls on the radio and volume was pre-set. The radio unit was connected to a spring-loaded 'push-to-talk' switch mounted on the underside of the monitoring room table. A combined microphone and speaker headset was provided for the operator.

The trials had started in 1961 and some groups, such as Winchester, were fully radio-capable relatively early. The equipment was demonstrated at ROC summer camps. A mock-up post ventilator was used at the summer camp in 1967 at RAF Coningsby to show how the aerial mast was attached

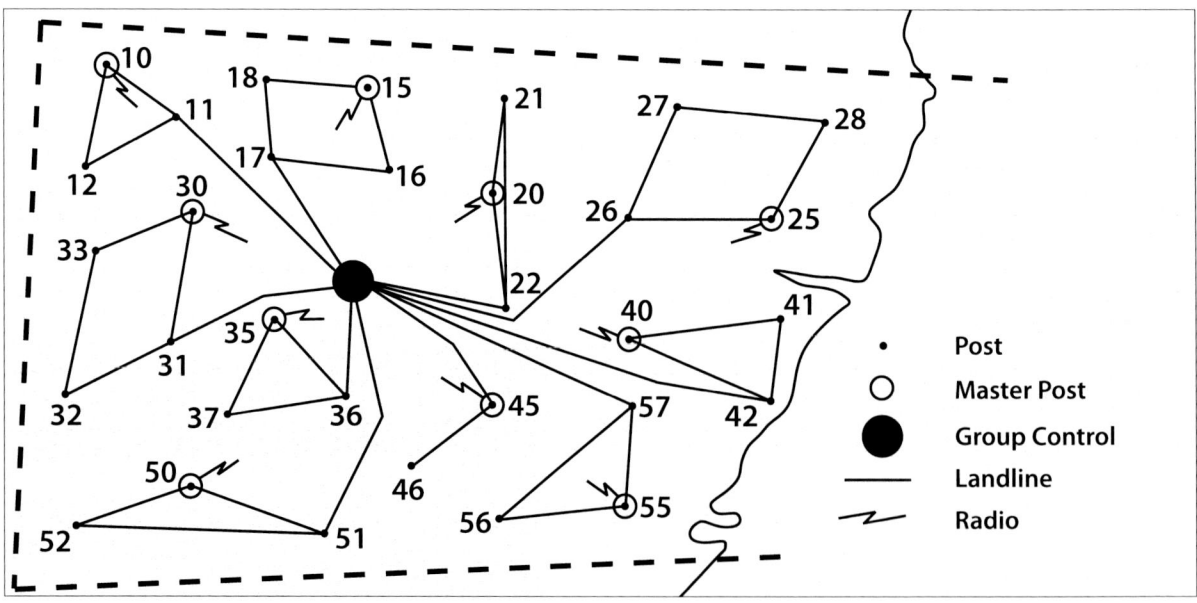

Above: Both the landline and radio links can be seen in this schematic diagram. The links between clusters and group were originally switched Emergency Circuits. These were converted to Private Circuits during 1981/2.

and erected. However, this was as close as many observers got to using the equipment as the rollout programme dragged on until the mid-1970s. In fact, the Northern Ireland Group were never issued with the first generation of radios and had to wait for the second generation equipment.

One of the key reasons why the rollout took so long, even when equipment was available, was the need to evaluate and trial each location designated for radio. The existing master posts within each cluster were the obvious place to add radio capability. However, some of these sites were not ideal for radio transmission and reception.

The radio range was limited to thirty to forty miles and local topography and position in relation to the group headquarters could result in poor radio reception. Posts distant from the group would require the use of several hilltop repeater sites to provide adequate transmission capability. Groups therefore had to determine which of their posts were best located for radio operations. Sometimes this could be within an existing cluster with the result that the newly selected radio post was redesignated as the new master post. Even more disruption was caused when groups of posts had to be rearranged into new clusters to make a radio post available per cluster.

Many of the shortcomings of the *Countryman* radio were overcome with the early 1980s introduction of the Burndept radio system. The Burndept BE525 unit was a modern transistor-based unit with a three-channel capability. With this system it was now possible to contact two other group controls if the parent group could not be reached. Also, other master posts within range could be contacted if necessary. The Burndept unit itself was mounted on the monitoring room wall in a metal *Serel* box. The box lid had a rubber seal and when opened the lid would act as a platform for the radio. The front panel now had user controls for volume, tone and channel selection and a handset with a 'push-to-talk' pressel switch. A tone switch was made available so that repeater stations could be used when posts were too far away to communicate directly with group.

A small loudspeaker was attached to the left side of the unit so that the rest of the crew could listen in as required. The new system was trialled in the Maidstone Group and then, as before, rolled out across the Corps. This took time and there is evidence that some Scottish posts were still operating the older ATE *Countryman* units into the late 1980s.

Above: Automatic Telephones and Electric Company (ATE) manufactured the *Countryman* radio. This was the first generation radio employed by the Corps at posts.

POST EQUIPMENT

Above: The front panel of the *Countryman* radio with connection sockets for power, aerial and the combined microphone/receiver headset.

Above: The 'push-to-talk' switch on the underside of the monitoring room table.

Below: Detail of the wall mounting.

Below: The operator's headset.

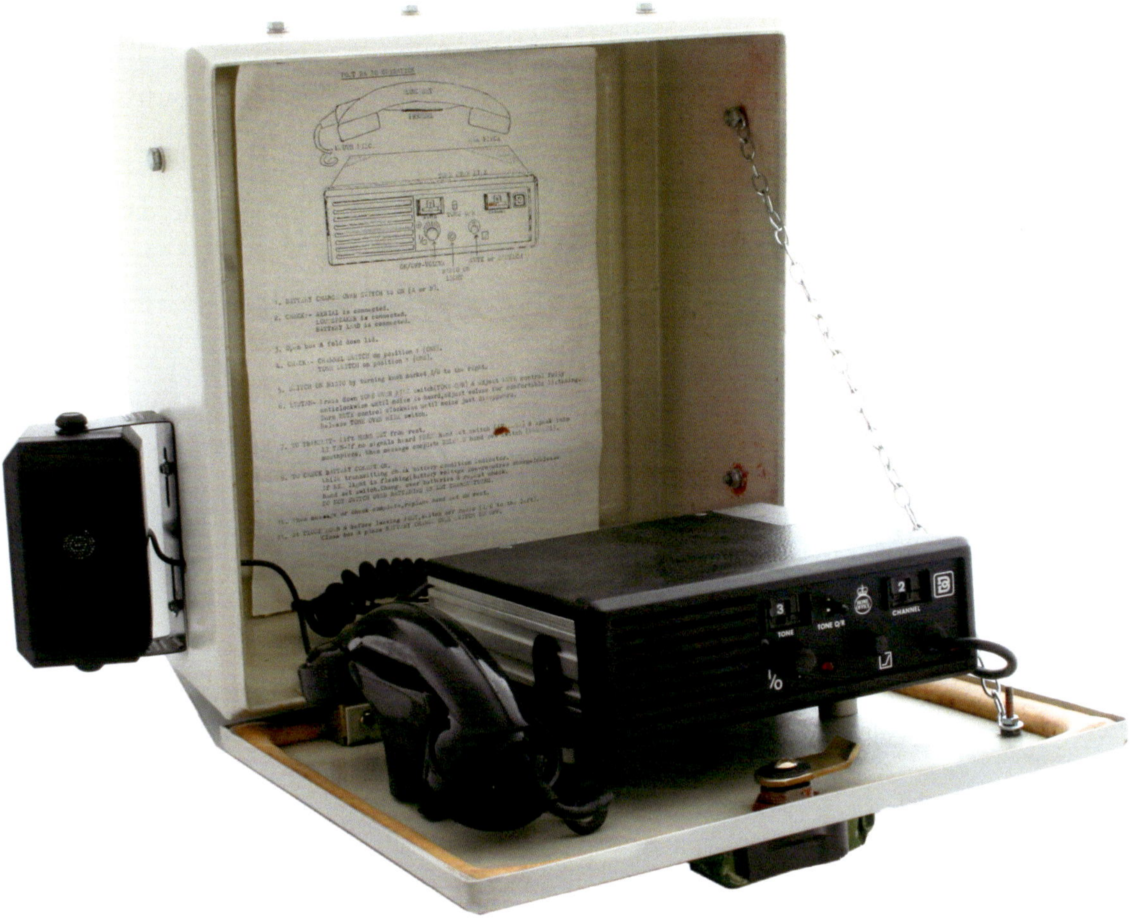

POST EQUIPMENT

Above: The Burndept 525 radio: The second generation radios were mounted on a tray inside a weatherproof metal box which was mounted above the cupboard in the monitoring room.

Below left and below: The *Serel* weatherproof metal radio box. The speaker allowed the crew to hear the exchanges with group and other posts. The example on the left, which is in a restored post, is decorated with RAF squadron stickers from the late 1980s.

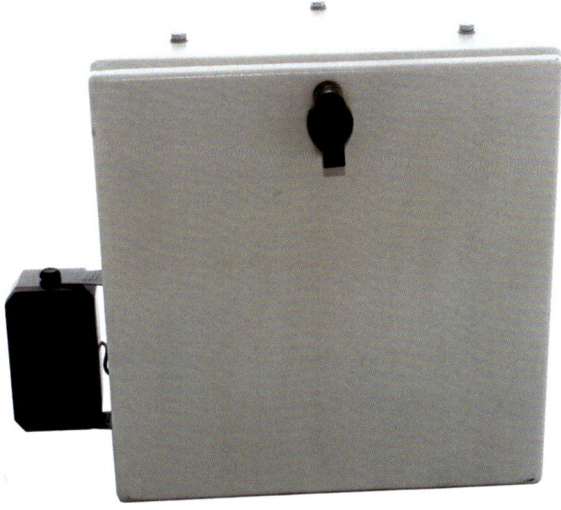

Attack Warning

In the early years of the nuclear era, public warning of pending air attack would have still come largely from police-operated sirens. By the early 1960s a new attack warning communications network, known as the Wire Broadcast (WB) system, had been developed. This enabled spoken word warnings and messages to be communicated quickly to warning points throughout the country, including the ROC posts.

Installation of the new Receiver Carrier WB400 units began at posts in 1963 and these were rolled out across the Corps, with nineteen posts of the Winchester Group having had the units installed and tested by September of that year. The WB400 consisted of a battery powered grey metal box, engineered to be robust to handling and environmental conditions. The interior contained a desiccant and the baseplate was sealed with cork. A stock of batteries was kept in the post for this unit and also for the Teletalk that was introduced at around the same time. The units were mounted on the instrument table in the post monitoring room. When turned on a 'confidence tick' would sound, indicating that the unit was operational. This tick would be interrupted and the volume would increase if a spoken voice message was transmitted to the receiver.

The whole system was replaced in the early 1980s by the WB1400 carrier system. The posts were re-equipped with new wall-mounted units consisting of a large metal box, the Receiver Speech WB1401, and a smaller Loudspeaker Unit WB1400. These units were armoured and weatherproofed and were designed to operate in environments harsher than the normal office. The WB1400 units were usually mounted on a single board which also contained a filter unit (WB1410). All the metal cases were earthed so that the effects of Electro Magnetic Pulse (EMP) would not disable the equipment by damaging the internal semiconductor devices. This secondary effect of a nuclear explosion had not been recognised when the WB400 system had been designed. The units were now permanently trickle-charged from the telephone exchange so that their batteries would not go flat. A few posts were equipped with the office version of the loud speaker unit, possibly due to shortages of the rugged post version.

Warning the Public

The ability of post crews to warn the public of attack and subsequent fallout was not addressed until the early 1960s. The introduction of the WB400 system gave sufficient warning to crews to then transmit that warning to the public. Distribution of hand-operated sirens to the posts started in early 1964. They could be used to sound the 'red' warning of imminent attack; and the 'white' warning for the all-clear.

The 'grey' warning used a broken siren note to inform the public that fallout was due in the next hour. This was discontinued in October 1968 and maroons were used for fallout warnings.

Two siren types were available, the Service Electric *Secomak* and the Gents *Carter*. They were issued in wooden crates and could be stored in the posts. The *Carter* siren had a tripod-style stand whereas the *Secomak* had a tubular design. The *Carter* was generally deemed to be more robust than the *Secomak*, which could strip its gear teeth if the handle was used to forcibly retard the rotating parts. The *Secomak* siren appears to have been issued in larger numbers than the *Carter* but both provided the same function.

Fallout warning was first given by gongs and whistles until pyrotechnic maroons were developed and issued. The Maroon 3-Burst No.1 kit was a large vacuum-packed canister containing three maroons. The canister was placed in a wooden crate designed to protect the maroons for ten years in a post environment. They were usually stored at group headquarters or in local police stations and would only have been issued in a war emergency.

POST EQUIPMENT

Left: The WB400 system was the network used to warn the population of impending attack. The unit shown here was installed at many warning points, including ROC posts, and would broadcast a 'tick' signal in normal operation. During an attack a spoken warning message would be transmitted and the crew would then sound a siren to warn the local population before closing down the post.

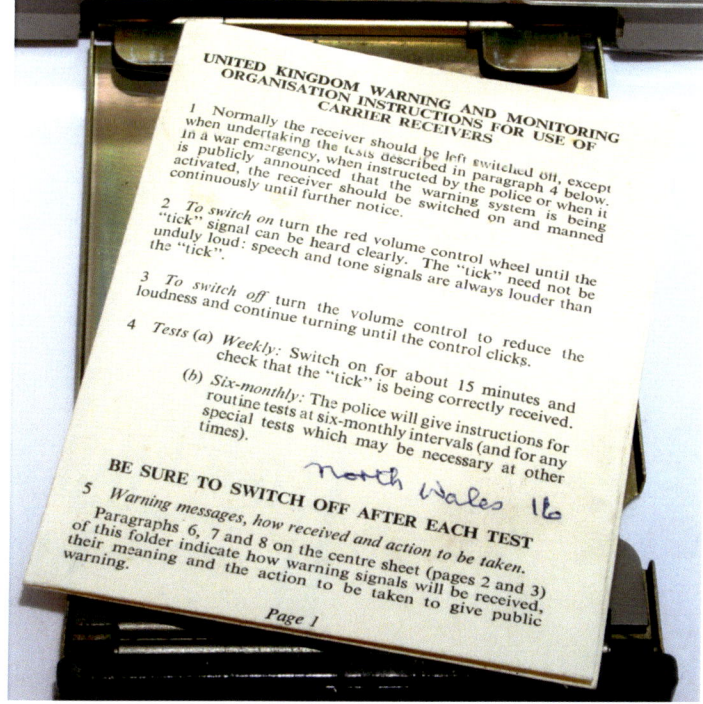

Right: A pull-out tray under the unit contained instructions for use, and listed the required responses to each type of message received.

POST EQUIPMENT

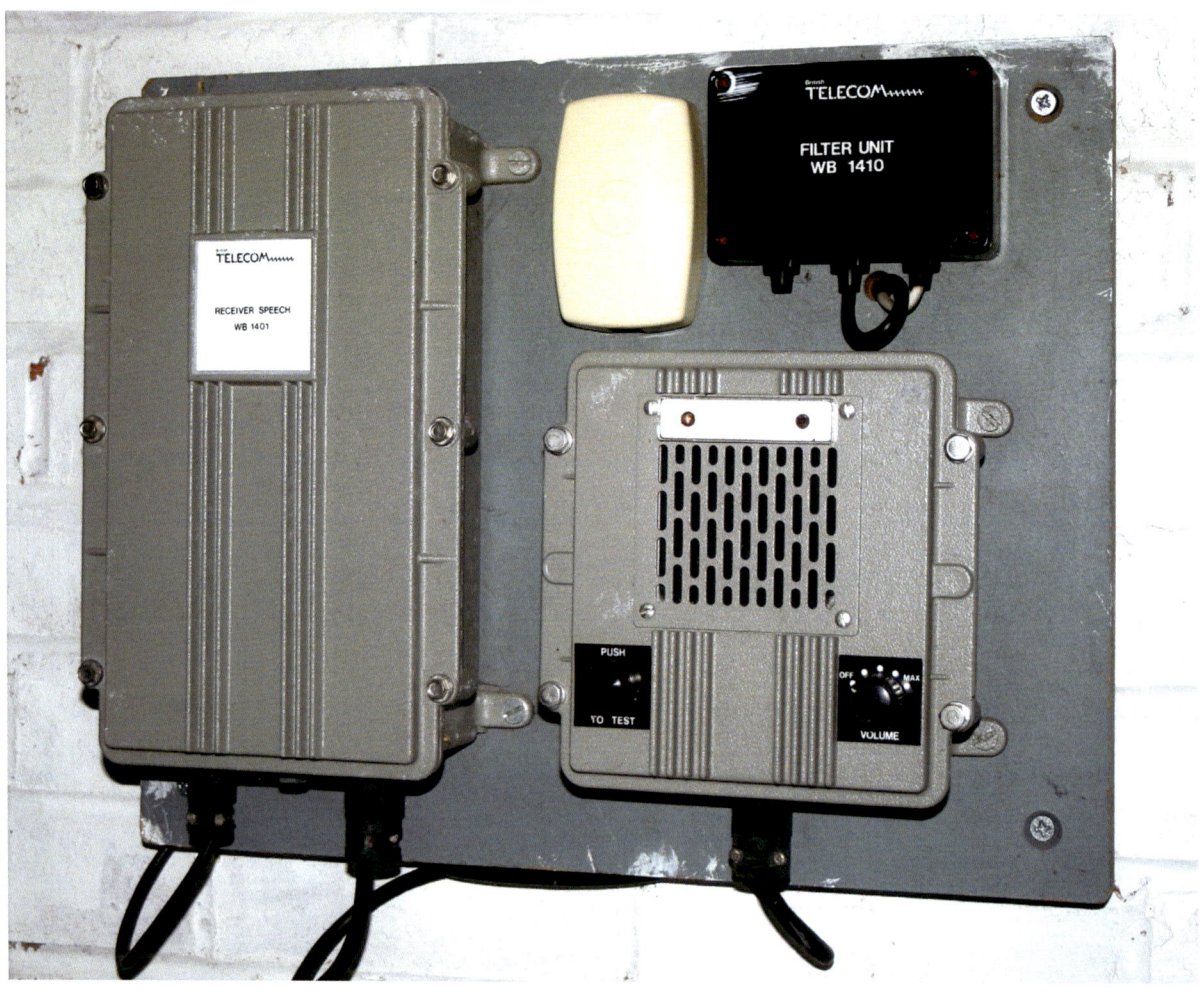

Above: British Telecom started rolling out the WB1400 system in 1981. This replaced the earlier WB400 system and was protected from the effects of Electro Magnetic Pulse (EMP). The loudspeaker unit is to the lower right of the picture and had a metal clip at the rear to hold the plastic instruction card.

Left: A double-sided plastic card replaced the paper fold-out instructions that came with the earlier unit.

Right: The WB1401 speech receiver could also be connected to this, less rugged, office loudspeaker. A few ROC posts were equipped with this loudspeaker unit.

Each maroon consisted of three tubes on a baseplate. When assembled, wires would be run from the front of the unit down the shaft to the post battery. The maroon was sited well away from the post and from overhead obstructions. The unit had detachable legs over which sandbags were placed for stability.

The maroon was fired from inside the post by attaching one lead to the post battery and touching the other lead on the free terminal. The subsequent three explosions gave a visual and audible warning to the public that fallout was on its way.

The No.1 kit was replaced by the No.2 kit in the mid-1980s at all the warning points including the ROC posts. By September 1984 5,000 of the 13,000 replacements kits had been issued with the rest to be issued 'soon'. The new kits also came in sealed packages but contained only two maroons. Sandbags were no longer provided in the kit as metal hoops were now used to stabilize the unit.

The firing device allowed operation with a single PP9 battery, although an adaptor was provided so that a 12 volt car battery could be used.

Training with live pyrotechnics was not considered a sensible option and so training kits were provided. These consisted of dummy maroons, with no explosive content, that could be set up so that simulated firing exercises could be conducted. The later, No.2, training kit was a more elaborate affair than its predecessor. This kit contained examples of the sealing and packaging the real units would come in and also contained the standard firing box, adaptor and a dummy maroon. It also had another dummy maroon which could be attached to a PP9 battery. The only difference to the real thing was that three lights would illuminate in sequence when 'fired', rather than three pyrotechnic explosions. These kits were rare and each group usually only had a few which could be made available for training post crews.

POST EQUIPMENT

The Secomak Siren

Above: The *Secomak* siren in its stowed position. The siren was originally supplied in a timber crate and was stored in the post like this until needed.

Left: The 'red' warning consisted of five fast rotations of the handle followed by five slow rotations. This sequence was repeated for one minute and resulted in the famous 'warbling' sound usually associated with the Second World War. The 'white' all-clear warning consisted of one minute of fast operation, which resulted in a continuous steady note.

POST EQUIPMENT

The Carter Siren

Left and below: Gents of Leicester manufactured the *Carter* siren. They also produced the large power-operated sirens usually mounted on buildings during the Second World War. The handle of both the *Secomak* and *Carter* sirens had a twist grip which could be moved to open and close the shutters at the front of the siren, thus damping the sound.

POST EQUIPMENT

Mk 1 Maroon

Pyrotechnic maroons were used to warn the public of approaching fallout.

Right: This training manual schematic shows how the Maroon 3-Burst No.1 unit would be set up for firing.

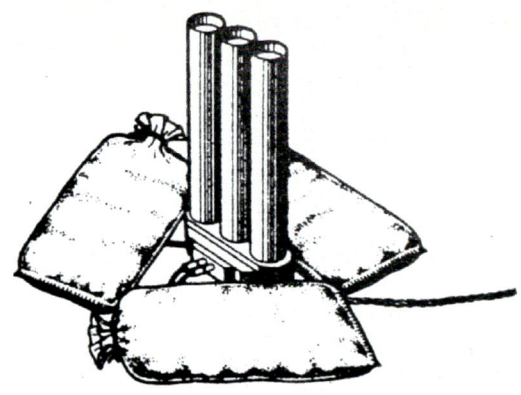

Setting up Ready for Firing

11. a. Stand the maroon upright in the selected firing position.

   b. Push the three stabilising legs into the holes in the base of the maroon and place a filled sandbag over each leg to hold it steady.

   c. Insert the two plugs fitted to one end of the firing lead into the sockets in the base of the maroon and drop the other end of the lead down the shaft. Leave the end of the lead coiled at the foot of the shaft; DO NOT take it into the monitoring room at this stage and particularly DO NOT connect either terminal to the battery until the maroon is to be fired (see Fig 3).

Fig 3
Maroon set up for firing

JUNE 78

Below left: The No.1 storage container held three pyrotechnic maroons under vacuum-sealed conditions. This rare survivor is on display at the ROC exhibition at Newhaven Fort.

Below middle: Exploded view from the training manual showing the contents of the No.1 storage container.

Below right: A dummy training version of the No.1 maroon. Note the connections for the firing cable on the base.

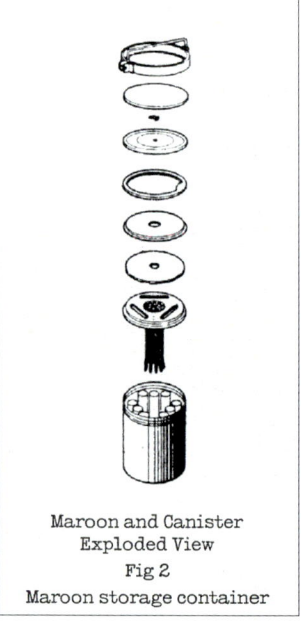

Maroon and Canister
Exploded View
Fig 2
Maroon storage container

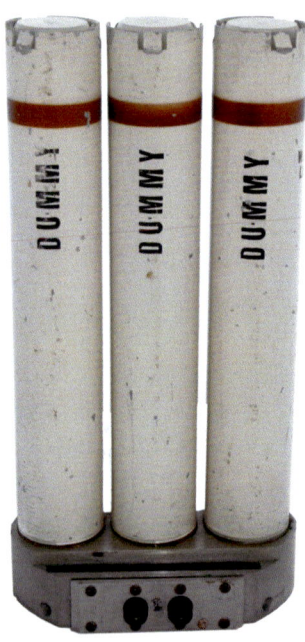

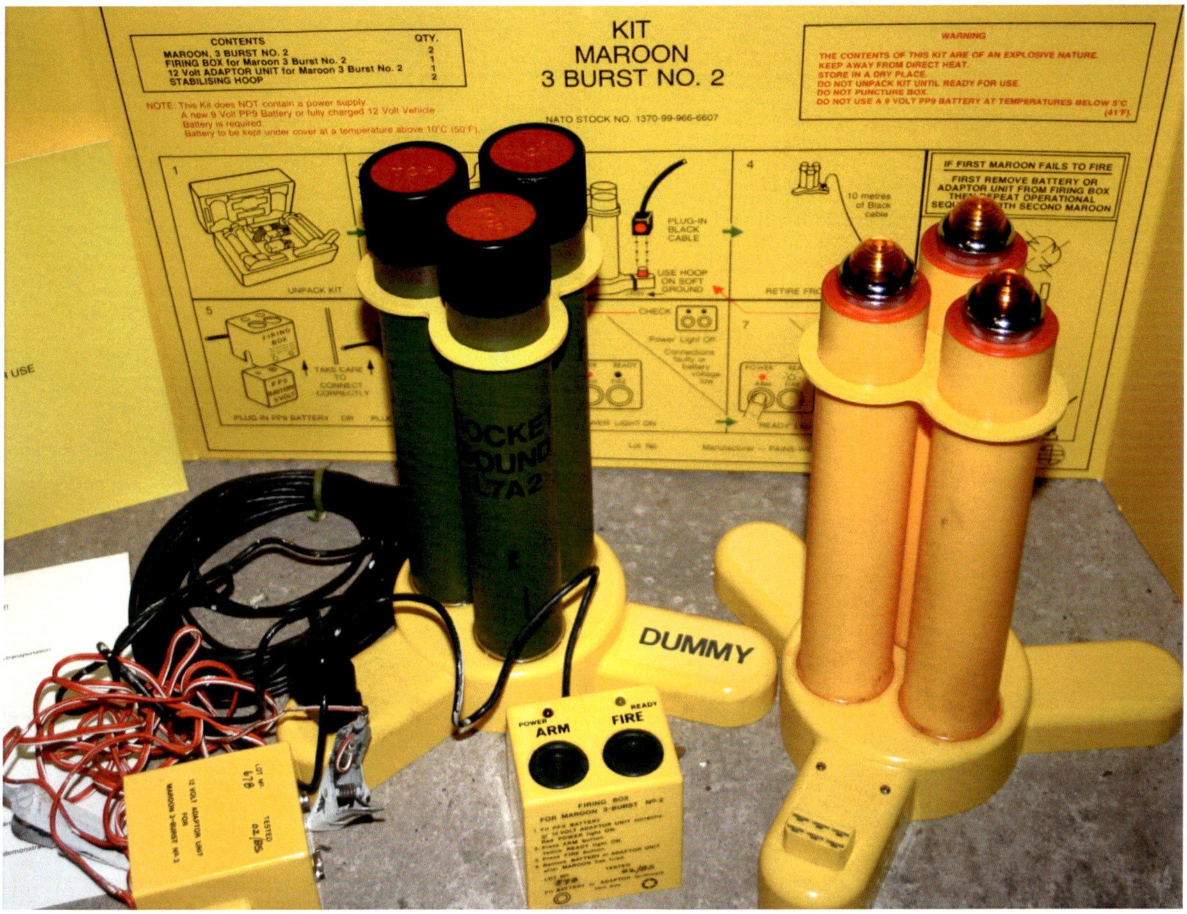

POST EQUIPMENT

Mk 2 Maroon

Above and below: The No.1 maroon was replaced by the No.2 maroon in the 1980s. To practise the firing procedures, a training kit was produced by the Pains-Wessex company. The 'Fire' button set off a three-light sequence which was meant to simulate the firing of three maroons.

POST EQUIPMENT

Luwa Air Filtration

Posts would be closed down under fallout conditions but air changes would still be required. A post ventilation team based in the group headquarters would monitor the fallout plumes and advise posts when they could open their hatches and vents to replenish air. This would be controlled locally by the cluster master post so that only one post at a time was 'open'.

This was not regarded as satisfactory and a new air filtration system was trialled from 1982. The units supplied were manufactured by the Swiss Luwa company in late 1980 and were designated 'VA20'. As many as six posts in the Horsham Group were equipped with the system including the cluster containing Redhill, West Hoathley and Holmwood. Cranleigh and Horsham were also Luwa equipped although Fernhurst, the third post in the cluster, does not appear to have been. A further two units were supposedly supplied to each of the other sectors with Bardney in the Midland Sector and Joppa, in the Scottish Sector receiving units. Catforth post in the Preston Group was also Luwa equipped and Reeth post in the Western Sector appears to have been identified to receive the equipment, although there is no evidence it was actually installed. The unit on display at the museum at Hack Green was acquired from ROC Headquarters at Bath implying that Southern Sector was also supplied with at least one unit for trials.

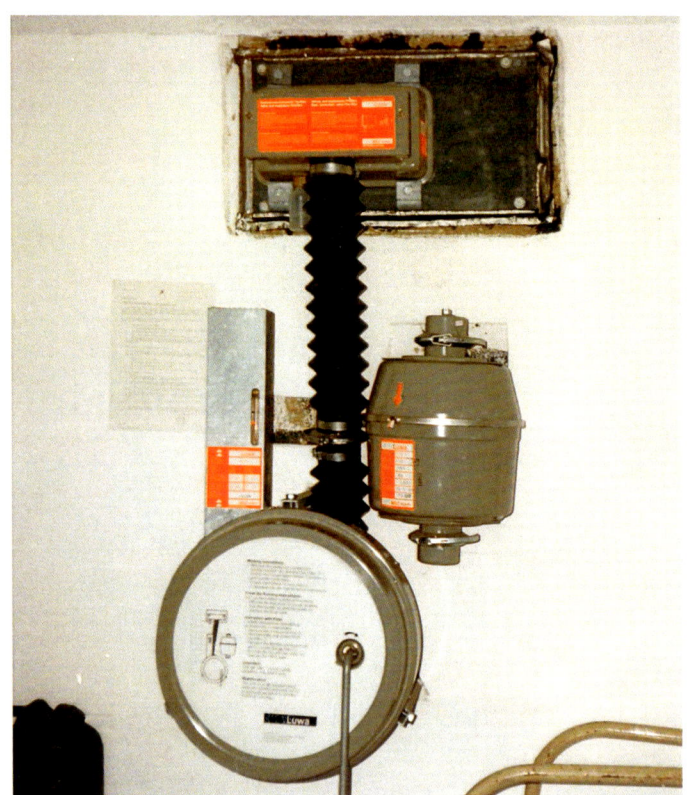

Above: The Luwa equipment installed at Bardney post. This was one of No.15 Group, Lincoln, posts and was part of the Midland Sector. The photograph was taken just after stand-down when Chas Parker was removing various items for subsequent display at Newark Aviation Museum. The Luwa kit seen here was saved and is now part of the excellent ROC display at Newark.

Right: A close-up of the operating instructions which were stuck to the unit. Observers who used the system remember having to wind the handle for about ten minutes in every hour to bring fresh air into the monitoring room.

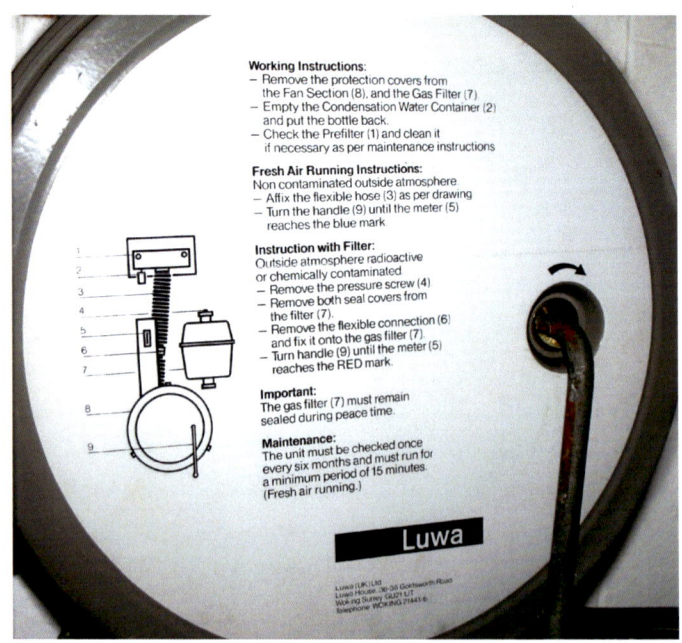

POST EQUIPMENT

Prototype Teletalk

Above and below: These prototype Teletalk units were developed in the early 1960s and appear to be very similar in design to the WB400 carrier receiver units that were introduced in 1963. Ultimately the AD3460 went into service rather than this design.

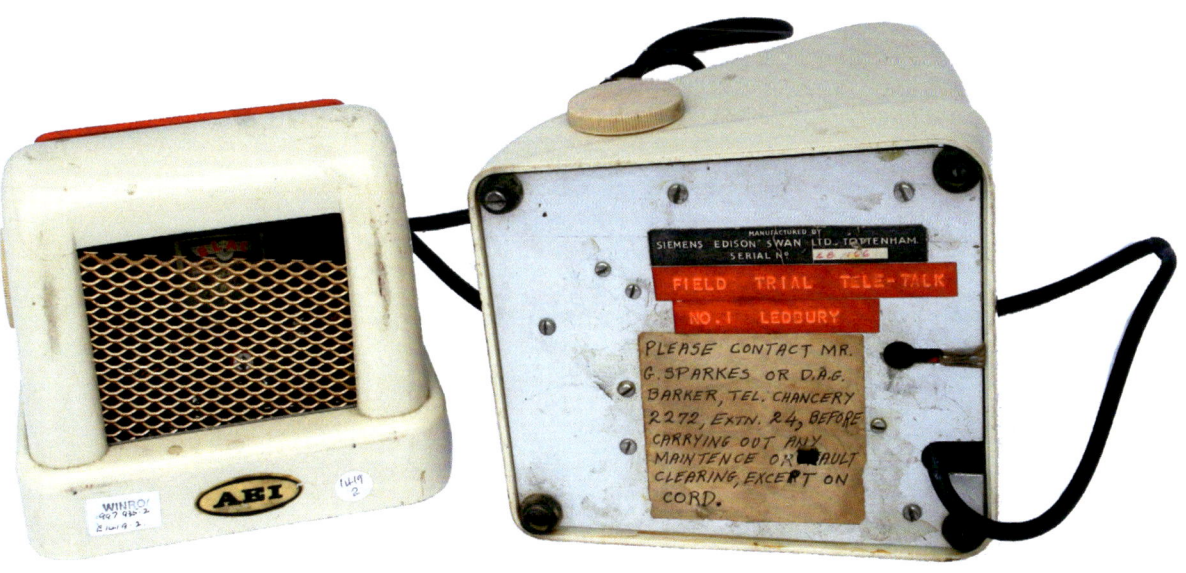

POST EQUIPMENT

Prototype Ground Zero Indicator

Right: This GZI unit does not have the standard three-bolt arrangement for fixing, but rather a threaded hole. It is not known when this unit was developed, but it is fully adjustable and can be revolved and also tilted, suggesting that this GZI was developed as a mobile unit that did not require a pre-aligned mounting plate.

Below right: This view of the underside of the GZI shows the three adjustment screws that allow the unit to be tilted. This prototype along with the prototype Teletalks above were given to the Royal Observer Corps Museum when the ROC Headquarters building at Bentley Priory was cleared out after the final stand-down in the mid-1990s.

Below: This view shows in detail the mechanism that allows the whole unit to revolve. Once the unit has been revolved to the correct orientation, the handle is used to fix it in position.

POST EQUIPMENT

Right: Pre-production versions of the GZI were originally trialled at Farnham in June 1958. The unit differed from the production version in that it had a socket at its base that allowed it to be pole-mounted. A simple bolt holds the cover on.

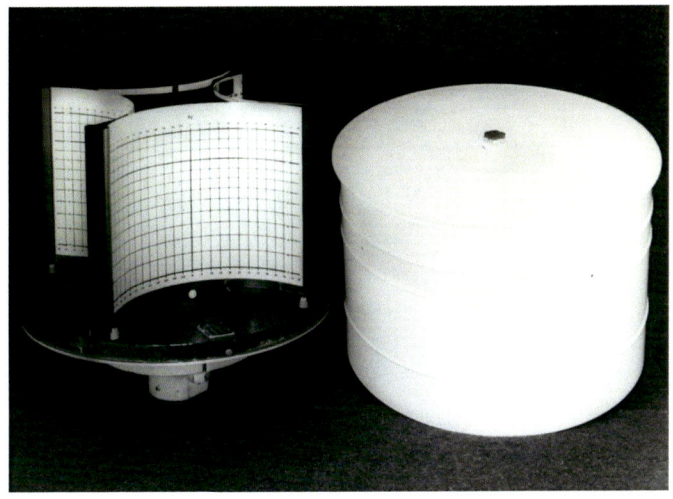

Prototype Telescopic Probe Rod

Above: It was not only the major instruments and communications equipment that went through several phases of development. These photographs show an early version of the Telescopic Probe Rod. Both the handle and the probe bracket were further developed before final production.

Marconi Radio Unit

Below: Trials of the Marconi RC530H radio system at a Maidstone Group post in the early 1980s. Both observers are using the old-style *Countryman* headsets. The Marconi radio has been mounted on an adapted *Countryman*-era wall bracket. Ultimately, this system was not chosen and the Burndept radio was adopted by the Corps during the 1980s.

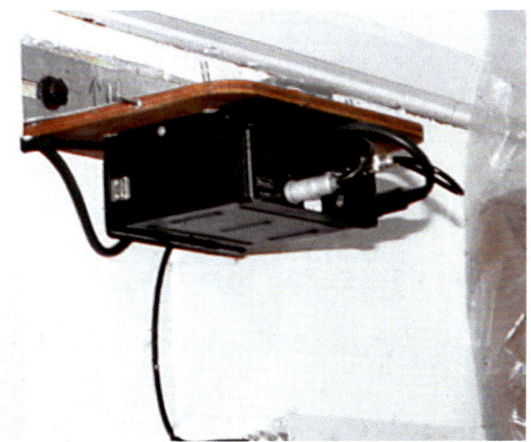

Chapter 5

LIFE IN THE ROYAL OBSERVER CORPS

Recruitment

When the Corps was re-established in 1947 many ex-wartime observers rejoined, but the poor state of the infrastructure and lack of equipment meant that the organisation had to cope with low morale. Recruiting and keeping sufficient personnel was particularly difficult in rural areas and it was also difficult to maintain numbers when many members had full time jobs that had to take priority.

To tackle this problem, the Corps refocused its training to be much more practical and much more 'hands-on'. It also targeted members of the Armed Forces Reserves as potential recruits.

Membership suffered following the demise of aircraft reporting as volunteers resigned. The 1968 cuts reduced the required official total from 22,500 to 12,500, but as manning was down at 17,500 at that time, the real losses were reduced. By the mid-1970s the Corps' strength was approximately 10,000 and this remained fairly constant until stand-down.

When potential recruits did come through the door they were asked to attend several meetings to get a feel for the organisation and the role it played before signing any paperwork. Some elementary training and a basic test were then required before the issue of the uniform. Men and women aged sixteen to fifty-five were eligible for recruitment

Below: This stand was put together for the *East Ham Leisure Time* exhibition in 1963 and was probably used to recruit crew members for the recently built Stratford post.

and at one time there was a minimum requirement of three years' service expected. There was no pay for volunteer members but expenses for travel were provided.

Cinema and TV films were used to both recruit and explain the role of the ROC. An early 1950s cine film makes it clear that people from all walks of life could volunteer for the ROC, including the 'Butcher, Baker and Candlestick maker'. Films such as *The Royal Observer Corps – To-Day* from the early 1960s, tended to use archive footage from the Second World War as an introduction to the Corps' proud tradition before talking about the nuclear role. Cine film shorts, again made in the early 1960s, talk of saving millions of lives and ask the question of the cinema audience "Can you afford to spend an hour or two a week to protect your family? Can you afford not to?"

The ROC also featured in UKWMO information films which used dramatised war situations to explain the function of the warning and monitoring organisation. *The Hole in the Ground* from 1962 and *Sound an Alarm* from 1971 both showed posts in action within the wider context of the entire organisation. 1991's *Forewarned is Forearmed* was developed as a recruitment film for the ROC but became a eulogy after it was apparent that the majority of the Corps would be stood down in that year. Some groups also produced their own promotional material, for example, No.15 Group produced and released a recruitment video in June 1991 which featured operations at posts in the Lincoln Group and the sector control at Fiskerton.

There were also many local initiatives and events which raised awareness of the Corps, with ROC members manning floats on parades, running stands at air shows, participating in charity events and parading at Battle of Britain and Remembrance Day parades.

Below: The modern version of the recruitment stand. This is C/Obs Terry Tracey manning the Royal Observer Corps stand at Liverpool docks in September 1989.

LIFE IN THE ROC

Above: These ROC recruitment leaflets cover the years *L to R* 1959, 1966, 1970, 1979, 1982, 1989 and 1991. These tended to be distributed around military, reserve and volunteer civilian organisations to encourage interest in the Corps.

Right: This detail from a 1959 recruitment leaflet shows the emphasis placed on the social aspects of being a member of the Corps.

Below: Probably from the 1970s or 1980s, this sticker implies that there was more to going underground than just taking fallout readings.

There is a good deal of fun and social life working with the ROC. Keen yet friendly rivalry exists in various contests between posts and operations rooms. Observers also experience the good companionship of training evenings, when they get to know each other and meet members of associated organisations concerned with defence.
But the highlight of the annual programme is the week which all men and women of the ROC can spend at a summer camp as guests of a RAF station. At these voluntary camps, a full-time entertainments officer ensures that Observers combine their practical training with a real holiday atmosphere — complete with dances, concerts, film shows and prize-winning competitions.

Training

Top right: The first complete ROC manual did not become available until August 1949. These manuals had two separate hard-backed covers held together by two threaded bolts. This allowed the covers to be removed and supplemental or replacement pages to be added. This style of manual was used up until the 1980s. The examples shown are the original 1949 issue, a 1958 edition and a 1978 edition.

Right: When the new nuclear reporting equipment became available, booklets were provided for the individual items of equipment. This information was soon collated and added into the standard format training manuals.

Below: Photographs of the equipment were taken by various RAF photographic sections and by Bentley Priory staff. This shows one of the original card-mounted photographs used to produce the training manuals. These are for the RSM2 and are dated 1970.

LIFE IN THE ROC

Above: At the most local level, training was conducted by the Chief Observer and the Leading Observer; the latter designated the Post Instructor and being officially responsible for the training role. Post meetings tended to be held at the post in the summer but were usually held at a crew member's house or somewhere else in the warm during the winter. This picture of the Ashwell post crew was taken at a post meeting at Observer Hugh Jarman's farm in 1985. *Rear L to R* Obs Hugh Jarman, Obs Charles Revells, C/Obs Peter King, L/Obs Trevor King. *Centre* Obs John Dowling. *Front L to R* Obs Bob Hitcham, Obs Alan Watkins and C/Obs John Shere (Bedford Headquarters).

Right: The crew at this post at Stottesdon in Shropshire managed to obtain a caravan to act as above-ground accommodation on training evenings. Many crews erected huts near their posts for the same reason or maintained the old aircraft posts for above ground use. If at all possible crews used some form of above-ground toilet facility rather than that in the underground post.

LIFE IN THE ROC

Above: Crew members from the Great Ayrton, Chop Gate and Redcar cluster meet in the late 1980s. Cluster meetings were less frequent but usually brought together the crews of five or six posts plus the Group Officer responsible for the posts. These meetings would take place in function rooms at pubs, schools or churches and would be a way of passing on the latest news and also allow the latest equipment or training methods to be discussed and demonstrated. Training also took place at group headquarters and at the annual summer camp.

Right: With the influx of new equipment in the early 1980s, Bentley Priory had to rewrite large parts of the training material. It was decided that the old manuals were no longer suitable and that a standard A4 paper size and ring binder would be used. This removed the tedious need to unscrew the bolts holding the old manuals together every time a new page needed to be added.

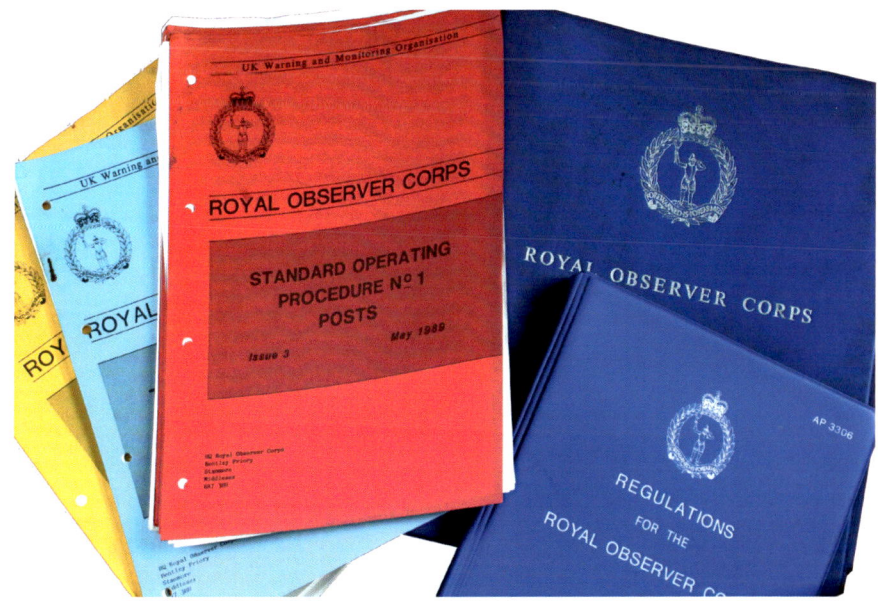

Page 71

LIFE IN THE ROC

Operation Hornbeam

Due to the increasing number of Soviet ships entering British ports in the early 1980s the Ministry of Defence initiated a scheme, known as Operation Hornbeam, which encouraged civil servants and members of the armed forces to report such sightings to the Intelligence Service.

Right: Members of the ROC were included in this scheme and their co-operation was requested via this notice in a 1981 edition of the *ROC Journal*.

REPORTING WARSAW PACT SHIPS

In view of the large numbers of Soviet and Warsaw Pact merchant and fishing vessels now visiting United Kingdom ports, the Ministry of Defence has introduced a scheme to encourage reports of sightings of such vessels.

Because Royal Observer Corps membership includes a number who are either involved professionally in maritime affairs or live in coastal areas we have been asked to canvass the Corps for members who would be prepared to assist. Very little effort is involved as it entails simply making a telephone call to a FREEPHONE number on each occasion of sighting such a vessel.

Anyone prepared to contribute to this important scheme is asked to write (quoting their Group and ROC number) to the Regional Intelligence Officer, Maritime Headquarters: Mount Wise, Plymouth, PL1 4JH; or Pitreavie, Dunfermline, Fife, KY11 5QE, depending on which side you live of a line drawn between the Mersey (north of Liverpool) and Humber (south of Grimsby).

Below: This two-sided card was supplied with a freephone number to which sighting reports could be filed. The back of the card carried a simple key to the Cyrillic alphabet.

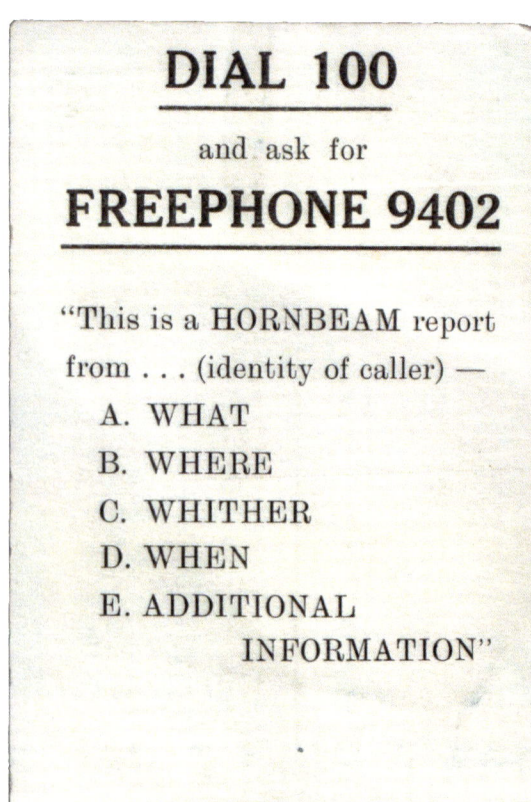

Right: Don Brereton served in the Corps for twenty-six years, first at Crosby post and finally as Chief Observer at Woodvale. Don's day job was with food company John West, and his work frequently took him to Liverpool's docks. Don responded to the request published in the *ROC Journal* and subsequently became involved in a little known aspect of the Corps' history. Don reported on over 100 Eastern European ships during the operation, always from a public telephone box to avoid traceability.

Dear Mr. Brereton,

Thank you for your very kind offer to assist in Operation HORNBEAM. I hope that as well as reading the article in the ROC Journal you will also have seen DCI(RN) 245/81 which has been issued to all ROC Area and Group HQs.

What we are asking is that if you should sight a Soviet or other Warsaw Pact Merchant or Fishing vessel entering/leaving/in a UK port or off the coast then please telephone MHQ Plymouth with the details, using the Freephone service. Ideally we need to know:-

    a. Name of the vessel - as well as Russian alphabet name plates fore and aft they usually show an English transliteration on boards each side of the bridge.

    b. Where it was sighted and, if underway, an idea of course and speed.

    c. Time of sighting.

    d. Any other information you may consider useful e.g. deck cargo, unusual activity of vessel or crew etc.

Many people find it convenient to report in the format given on the attached card. Don't worry if all of the information is not available, every little helps.

If you have any queries please do not hesitate to give me a call on the Freephone. During the day I or one of my colleagues try to answer personally but outside working hours we have a 'friendly' answering machine, please don't be put off by it.

Please excuse the typed proforma reply — made necessary by the very good response of ROC members. We get quite a few Eastern European ships visiting Liverpool and although most are reported by the Customs, some do slip the net. Hence any reports that you are able to telephone through will be most welcome.

Thanks again for your interest.

Yours sincerely,

Bernard Davies

LIFE IN THE ROC

Hunting Bears

Right: On 17 May 1990 Nos.40 and 41 post crews from No.8, Coventry, Group ROC were looking forward to a trip on a 101 Sqn VC-10 tanker aircraft flying from Brize Norton. The trip was to be a regular air-to-air refuelling exercise off the coast of Lincolnshire. Soon after take-off there was a change of plan and the tanker was tasked to refuel a Quick Reaction Alert (QRA) Tornado fighter off the west coast of Scotland.

Below: These crew members of No.41 post had the experience of a lifetime being part of an operational Cold War intercept. *L to R* Obs Albert Wright and Obs Chris Fletcher, L/Obs Pete Owen and Obs Nigel Bassett; Obs Dave Peace was also present. Five years later the Cold War was over and the now ex-observers were able to climb aboard a Tu-95 'Bear' bomber at the Fairford International Air Tattoo and explore it to their hearts' content.

Below: This QRA Tornado fighter was scrambled to intercept two Russian Tupolov Tu-95 'Bear' turboprop bombers which were flying in international airspace to the north of Scotland. Here we see the Tornado being refuelled by the VC-10 before the intercept.

Above and below: Much to the delight of the ROC members, the VC-10 crew decided to continue flying north after the refuel to intercept the slow-flying bombers themselves. The Russian bomber crews were extremely skilful and by flying at lower airspeeds managed to break formation with the VC-10 after these photographs were taken.

The RAF and Summer Camp

The annual summer camp was usually held at an RAF Station and was run by a cadre of full time Officers with help from spare time Officers on a rotating basis. As many as five, week-long courses would be run in the earlier days of the Corps and around 3,000 ROC personnel could be put through the annual camp during this time. Practical training was a major part of the camp programme.

Left and above: Observers learn about the FSM training unit and the GZI. This is the summer camp at RAF Newton which took place in July 1964 when these instruments were still new to many observers.

Right: More general training was also provided at camp. This is a First Aid class being held at RAF Cosford in 1978. The annual camp was also held at Cosford in 1977 and 1979. The ROC would try to re-run the annual camps at the same venue for a number of years as many of the administration issues would have been resolved and contacts made after the first year.

Above: Air Commodore Broughton inspects a morning parade at summer camp, RAF Leeming, in 1985. Although drill was not on the national ROC training syllabus, parades were conducted at camp and groups did tend to have small drill flights so that observers could be trained to acquit themselves well when parades were required.

Below: The ROC had a close affinity with the RAF and visits to operational stations were always appreciated. Here Observers Ernie Guy and John Meglenn examine a Valiant jet bomber at RAF Middleton St. George. This was the first of the V-bombers and the type that dropped the first British atomic and hydrogen bombs in 1956 and 1957 respectively.

Above: A big incentive for many observers to attend camp and visit RAF stations was the chance to fly in RAF aircraft on Air Experience Flights. Here observers from No.10 Group, Exeter, climb aboard an Anson at RAF Chivenor in the 1960s.

Below: Observers disembarking from a Beverley transport aircraft at RAF Middleton St. George in the early 1960s.

LIFE IN THE ROC

Above: Members of No.16 Group after a flight in a 115 Sqn Andover from RAF Benson. C/Obs B. Waldron standing on the left, Group Officer Peter Broom is on the right holding a bag, and Obs Flory is on the far right of the picture. The aircraft copilot is leaning against the handrail, the aircraft captain is sitting on the bottom step and the Nav/AEO is sitting on the top step in front of the door. The lady in the centre was a Major in the US Air Force based at West Drayton Air Traffic Control Centre. Other people in the picture were regular RAF and also observers from other groups.

Below: There were regular aircraft recognition competitions in the Corps, including a national event. In this picture Air Commodore Howe, ROC Commandant from 1977 to 1980, presents an aircraft recognition trophy to a Chief Observer from No.16 Group.

Above: The crew of this post took up the RAF tradition of 'zapping' – sticking calling cards to anything they could get away with when visiting RAF stations.

LIFE IN THE ROC

Left: The 1986 summer camp was held at the University of Newcastle-upon-Tyne, rather than the traditional RAF station. This 'first' caused some dissent within the observer community. However, a positive first also came out of this as the camp became the venue for the first all-female banner party in ROC history.

Above: VIPs sometimes attended camp and gave keynote speeches or lectures. Here, Home Secretary Douglas Hurd addresses a parade at RAF Scampton in 1983.

Right: Observers listen intently to an address given at annual camp at RAF Scampton in 1984.

During the 1980s the Corps also held camps at West Raynham, Leeming, Waddington and Watton. Other famous RAF stations that accomodated the ROC in earlier times included West Malling and Tangmere, and the Cold War fighter bases at Binbrook and Wattisham.

Chapter 6

MANNING THE POSTS

All the procedures required to operate a post were laid down in *Standard Operating Procedure No.1 Posts* which detailed the various operational stages that would occur from initial arrival of the crew at a post, through a war situation and into the post-attack phase.

The three-man crew would be assigned as No.1, No.2 and No.3 Observer on arrival at the post. They would each have a different role in preparing the post for operations and also in the subsequent operation of the post.

During the manning-up phase, when the post was being prepared for operations, the No.1 Observer would be in charge and would check the carrier receiver and LST and report to control that the post was manned. The No.2 Observer would prepare the below-ground instruments, the maroon and siren, while also helping the No.3 Observer, who had the job of setting up the above-ground equipment. When all the instruments and communications were operational a further report of 'instruments ready' or 'stage-one operational' would be made to the control centre. 'Stage-two operational' would be reported once a shift pattern had been established and fuel, food and water stocks were adequate.

After the initial manning-up, the crews would go into a regular pattern of instrument and communication checks. If the 'stand-to' period continued for some time then food and water stocks would be checked and replenished and the batteries recharged as appropriate. There would also be regular crew changes every eight hours or so, depending on the manning status of the post.

If the 'attack warning red' message was received over the carrier receiver, then the main actions fell to the No.3 Observer who had to go above ground and sound the warning on the hand-operated siren

The following series of photographs was taken at Girvan post in 1989/90 by David Ross and were originally to have been used for training purposes.

Right: Removing the blanking plate from the FSM pipe. In the foreground it can be seen that the BPI baffle plate has already been set up.

before closing the post. If the post was a master post conducting radio operations, then the radio mast had to be retracted and placed on the ground before the crew could retreat to the safety of the post.

During the attack, any reading above 0.3 pounds per square inch, or 2 Kilopascals on the BPI would be regarded as evidence of a nuclear burst and would be reported using the code word 'TOCSIN' to control. One minute after the last reportable BPI deflection, the No.3 Observer had the unenviable task of going outside to retrieve the exposed GZI papers and replace them with fresh ones. The bearing, elevation, type and spot-size determined from the GZI papers would then be communicated to control following the code word 'nuclear burst'.

Following a nuclear attack, crews would be warned of subsequent fallout by control sending a 'fallout approaching' message. The 'fallout warning black' message would be transmitted over the carrier receiver along with the warning districts affected.

If the post was within the effected warning district, then the crew would check that their dosimeters were zeroed and No.3 would prepare and fire the maroon. This would also be done if the FSM reading had reached a predetermined value of 0.3 roentgens per hour (0.3 rph) but no warning message had been received.

Below and right: Details of the underside of the FSM dome and the gasket.

FSM readings would be taken and reported at five-minute intervals, and when fallout was detected above 0.1 rph a 'first fallout' report would be made to control. If levels continued to rise and reached 400 rph then a 'shielded reading' procedure would be triggered. In this procedure the probe rod would be lowered in the FSM pipe (so that the ionisation chamber was shielded by the earth covering) until it read one tenth of the initial reading (eg 40 rph). These readings would be reported as the full (x10) value but with the note that they were 'shielded readings'. Reports of actual dose rates would continue until the level had dropped back below 0.1 rph as the radioactivity decayed.

The end of the attack and of immediate danger to the public would be signalled over the carrier receiver by the 'attack message white'. On receipt of this, the No.3 Observer would go above ground and sound the 'white' signal on the siren.

Right: The GZI being attached to the mounting point on the entrance hatch ventilator. Two of the three mounting legs can be clearly seen in this photograph. The nuts resting on the hatch surround secure the legs once they have been placed through the holes in the mount. A Scottish T-bar key also rests on the hatch surround.

Below: With the GZI in place, the nuts are attached and turned until finger tight. The post rope and net can be seen in this photograph along with a Yamaha generator.

MANNING THE POSTS

Above: Cloud charts were provided late in the life of the Corps to help classify the weather as part of METAR reporting, which had developed from the original SUPMET/ROCMET weather reporting system.

Above: Weather observations would begin during the 'stand to' phase until it was necessary to return to the post following 'attack warning red'. All posts provided basic weather information allowing the Corps to maintain fallout plotting in the event that information from the Meteorological Office was no longer available.

Left: This photograph shows an observer with an RSM No.2 in its carrying case ready for above-ground operations. Mobile monitoring was introduced in 1970. This was a secondary role and required observers to leave the post and collect fallout data from locations specified by sector or group control. In addition, observers were also tasked with reporting on the local infrastructure within a ten-mile radius of their post. Had roads been blocked? Were bridges still up, and so forth? Crews were instructed to use their foul-weather gear as rudimentary protection against fallout on these missions and very basic decontamination procedures are referred to in the training manuals. On exercises observers were paid a mileage allowance when they used their own vehicles for these tasks.

MANNING THE POSTS

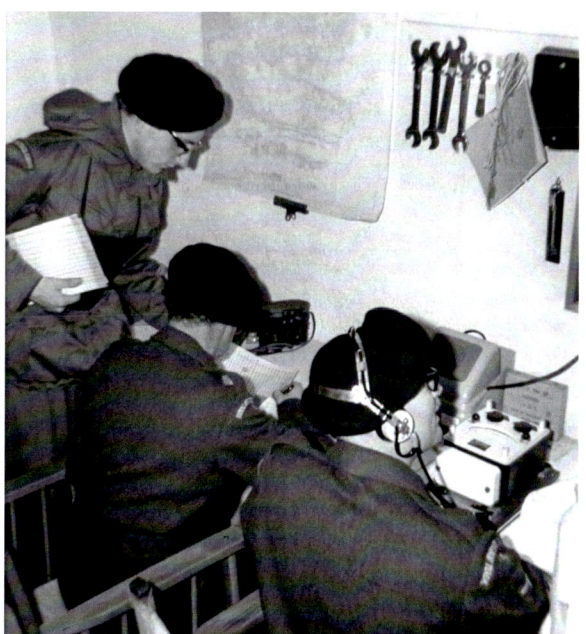

Above: This photograph taken at Stratford post, London in the mid-1960s shows No.3 (Obs Michael Goodey) changing the GZI papers in an operational simulation. Note that he has protective clothing and his hood is up to offer further protection. Well-practised observers could change GZI papers and get back into the safety of the post in under a minute, although training manuals did request that they note details of the mushroom cloud if they happened to notice it.

Left: Once back in the post the No.3 Observer would hand the papers over to the No.1 Observer for assessment. This information would then be reported by the No.2 Observer to group headquarters – No.2 Observer having taken responsibility for landline communications during the 'stand-to' phase.

MANNING THE POSTS

Above: The four photographs on this page were taken at Speke post, near Liverpool Airport, in 1967. Here the GZI has been secured in the post net and is about to be raised to the surface. This first generation rope net was replaced by a nylon version in later years.

Above: The GZI printing out paper had to be pre-exposed so that the graticule lines and numerals could be read. Here an observer stands at the bottom of the shaft and exposes the paper held in a cassette.

Below: No.3 Observer places a new cassette into the GZI. Note the light-proof satchel on the observer's chest.

Below: The No.3 hands over the GZI cassettes to the No.1 Observer for assessment.

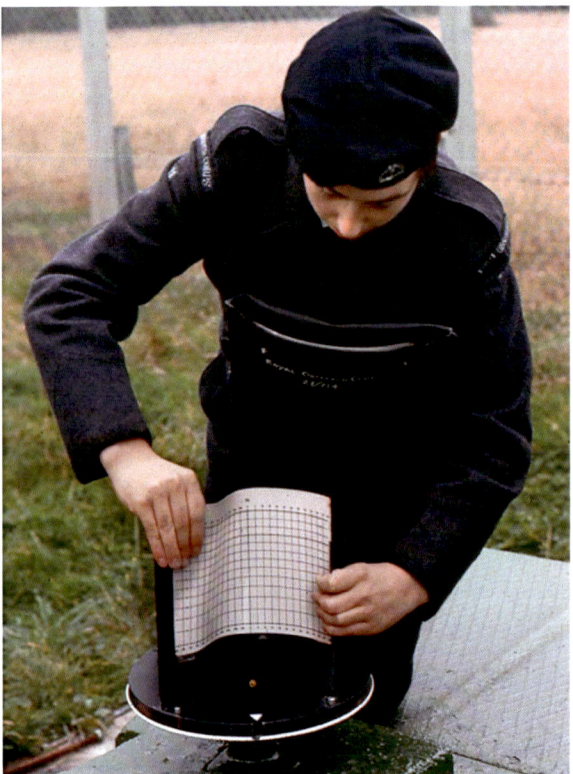

MANNING THE POSTS

Above: This series of photographs was taken in September 1990 at 15 post at Hoo in the Maidstone Group for use on the cover of the *ROC Journal*. The observers were photographed demonstrating a number of operational tasks. Here the Burndept radio is being used. During operations it was the responsibility of the No.1 Observer to operate the radio.

Below: The FSM would be monitored and all readings recorded in the post log. During fallout conditions the cumulative dose rates of the observers' personal dosimeters would also be recorded to ensure that wartime emergency dose levels were not exceeded.

Above: Here the FSM probe rod is placed into the FSM pipe and will be pushed upwards until the handle is secured against the pipe flange set into the ceiling. The bracket attached on the left side of the flange was used to clamp the rod in place when it was retracted for 'shielded readings'.

Below: The siren was usually operated by the No.3 Observer and would be used for 'attack warning red' and 'attack message white'. Once the 'red' warning had been given the observer would lay the siren on its side before going underground and closing the hatch.

MANNING THE POSTS

Transition to War

It was envisaged that the run-up to a nuclear exchange would be well flagged by a deteriorating political situation and possibly some form of conventional warfare in Europe or elsewhere. This would allow for a certain amount of preparedness, although a surprise attack was always possible. In order to move the ROC onto a war footing, 'transition to war' orders were kept at group

---

TRANSITION TO WAR PROCEDURES

POST PERSONNEL

Specific duties during the early stages of Transition to War are as follows:

1. **Public Announcements**

    On hearing the public announcement eg. ACTIVATE UKWMO FOR WAR, you are to report for duty at your Post, as quickly as possible, in uniform with Identity Card and Small Kit.

    Note:- Chief and Leading Observers will be expected to notify as many of the Post members as is compatible with prompt arrival at the site.

2. **Preplanned Callout**

    On receiving the message MAN UP THE POST from your Group Officer, the Group Headquarters or from another authenticated source, you are to ascertain if you are the first member of the Post to be called.

    If so, you are to set in train the prearranged system for notifying all members of the Post and when satisfied the system is working, report for duty at your Post, in uniform with Identity Card and Small Kit at Annex A.

    If you are not the first member to be called and the system is under way, report for duty at your Post, in uniform with Identity Card and Small Kit.

3. **Further Action**

    On arrival at the Post, the Chief Observer or Leading Observer (or senior member present in their absence) is to ensure that the following actions are carried out in accordance with Standard Operating Procedures or preplanned arrangements.

    a. Prove line communications.
    b. Prove radio communications, if applicable.
    c. Set up Operational Instruments.
    d. Check and supplement Logistics Supplies.
    e. Make the appropriate Operational Reports.
    f. Set up a shift manning system to maintain 3 Observers on duty continuously, until stood down at Attack Warning Red is sounded.
    g. Set up the preprepared Family Safety arrangements.

headquarters and these detailed the necessary procedures required to call out the Corps. They also detailed what the wartime roles of all personnel were within Posts, Groups, Sectors and the Nuclear Reporting Cells.

Call-out would occur either via the broadcast media or by a group call-out plan. At a post level, Group Officers (who were typically responsible for five or six posts) would implement their pre-prepared call-out plan and Chief Observers would implement manning rosters at their posts when observers arrived. The Chief Observers also had to ensure that there was adequate water, food and fuel for a fourteen-day period and that, if possible, one car was available at the post site.

As part of the plan, selected observers from each post would collect operational equipment, spares and ration packs from the group headquarters before making their way to the post. Group Officers would inform headquarters of the status of the posts under their control and would make their way to their designated war location at one of the posts.

The welfare of those left behind was also considered and post crews were encouraged to explain their role and the expectations of them if they were called out. Some groups provided basic information on refuges for families and suggested that they should be relatively near posts so that off-duty crews could be with them. Information was provided as to what these families should do before, during and after an attack. The overall purpose of this approach being to reduce anxiety within the minds of the crews while they conducted their service in an emergency situation.

Opposite: Each observer carried an envelope which contained two letters. This, headed *Transition to War Procedures*, detailed the actions he or she should follow upon hearing the public call-out announcement.

Right: The second letter was the *Schedule of Small Kit*. By the 1980s it was recommended that observers bring enough food for forty-eight hours rather than the original one day's supply. Durham Headquarters' orders recommended a range of foodstuffs including Shreddies but not Cornflakes as "… they are too bulky".

```
SCHEDULE OF "SMALL KIT"

1.   The small Kit itemised below is a compromise between taking everything
that could possibly be taken, the carrying capacity of the individual, the
storage space available and constraints on use of water etc. Items already
supplied at the Post should not be taken. It may also be possible for
Posts to agree in peacetime on individual items that can by common consent
be used by all on duty and thus avoid needless duplication - however this
list is considered a guide to the recommended minimum.

2.   The list of recommended individual supply items is -

     a.   Holdall or small case - clearly marked with your name
     b.   Toilet bag with toiletries, combs etc and deodorants
     c.   Razor (Battery Powered preferable)
     d.   Towel
     e.   Handkerchief and/or tissues
     f.   Spare underclothing (3 changes)
     g.   Spare socks or tights (3 pairs)
     h.   Spare shirt              )
     j.   Spare trousers/Slacks    )   UNIFORM if possessed, otherwise
     k.   Heavy Duty Woollen pullover )   civilian pattern
     l.   Personal Medication - Advise Group Commandant via Post Supervisor
     m.   Spectacles, if worn
     n.   Outer clothing including gloves
     p.   Sleeping bag, if possessed
     q.   Thick woollen socks (eg. Sea Boot pattern)
     r.   Two favourite books.

3.   Additionally you should also bring with you at least one days supply
of food to supplement the official rations in the "stand to" period.
```

Exercises

Fortunately, the call-out never happened for real and the posts were ultimately never used for their intended purpose. However, crews continually practised and trained so that they would be ready in case a war situation arose.

Exercises in the early days were still heavily linked with the RAF and fallout reporting was conducted alongside aircraft reporting during defence exercises. The exercises were also used to test the RAF's ability to operate under fallout conditions and a system to provide a priority 'first strike' message was developed. The first continental fallout exercise was held in 1959. It was important to practise liaison with NATO allies to ensure that radioactive plumes moving towards the United Kingdom were identified and monitored. These international exercises (INTEX) evolved to include nuclear burst reporting and many of the larger exercises ran on weekends that coincided with major NATO field exercises.

Below: This entry in a post training diary refers to a common training session run in 1987. Group Common Training Sessions (GCTS) were run as evening exercises within groups every few months. Many of these re-used old exercise material as the availability of new material was limited. By the 1980s there were also usually two twelve-hour *Warmon* exercises each year which, by 1990, had been replaced with *Posthorn*, (*Posthorn 1* being run to test the 'transition to war' procedure). The major exercise of the year, INTEX, was a full test of the UKWMO and also its interactions with its equivalents in NATO. In this exercise posts were manned for up to twenty-four hours with group and sector controls being manned for several days.

COMMON TRAINING SESSION 10-2-87.

1945	POST MANNED. - HON DUTY - CARRIER RECEIVER OPERATING
1950	Time Checked
1951	MESSAGE RECIEVED FALLOUT STATE BLUE.
2010	STAGE ONE OPERATIONAL 8 MEN ON DUTY
2017	WITH EFFECT FROM 1000 HRS SECURITY STATE "BLACK SPECIAL"
2020	STAGE TWO OPERATIONAL MOBILE MONITORING FACS AVAILABLE
2027	GCTS. "ATTACK WARNING 'RED'"
2030	DUTY OFFICER STARTING 10 MIN READINGS
2145	SITREP No 1 RECIEVED FROM GROUP H/Q.
2230	SITREP No 2 RECIEVED FROM GROUP H/Q.
2245	REPORTED COMMUNICATIONS WITH CENTRE STILL NOT GOOD, BUT OTHER POSTS IN CLUSTER, O.K.

Stand-Down

During the late 1980s a government review into the country's air attack warning and monitoring system was conducted. This was completed in 1988 and concluded that the warning system was complicated to manage and costly to run. It suggested that modern electronic devices should be investigated with a view to using them for peacetime emergencies as well. It also recognised that the equipment for identifying nuclear bursts and fallout was nearing the end of its life and suggested that a small number of automated devices could give national coverage. The review also noted the fact that any change could take a considerable time to roll out and that the part played by the existing structure was of continuing importance.

The threat of a nuclear or conventional war against the Soviet Union diminished dramatically with the fall of the Berlin Wall in November 1989 and the huge changes that followed. Most people in the ROC realised that these changes, plus the recent reviews, would almost inevitably result in change and probably a reduction in the size of the Corps. For example, it was thought that a series of control centres could remain to operate the new automated equipment networks. However, this was not to be and by 1991 the British government had decided to disband the Royal Observer Corps. This was communicated by the Home Office to the MoD and to the Commandant of the ROC on 1 May 1991. News of this decision could not be cascaded to the personnel of the ROC until it had been announced in the Houses of Parliament, which it was on 10 July 1991. At the same time, previously-delivered sealed envelopes were being removed from group headquarters' safes and opened, to the shock of the Officers concerned. There was then a concerted effort to get the news out to ROC members as quickly as possible. Unfortunately, by the time meetings took place that evening and in the ensuing days, most members had already become aware via the media and not via the organisation itself. This in turn led to resentment with some personnel believing that group headquarters had pre-knowledge of the announcement but did not pass it on, which was not the case.

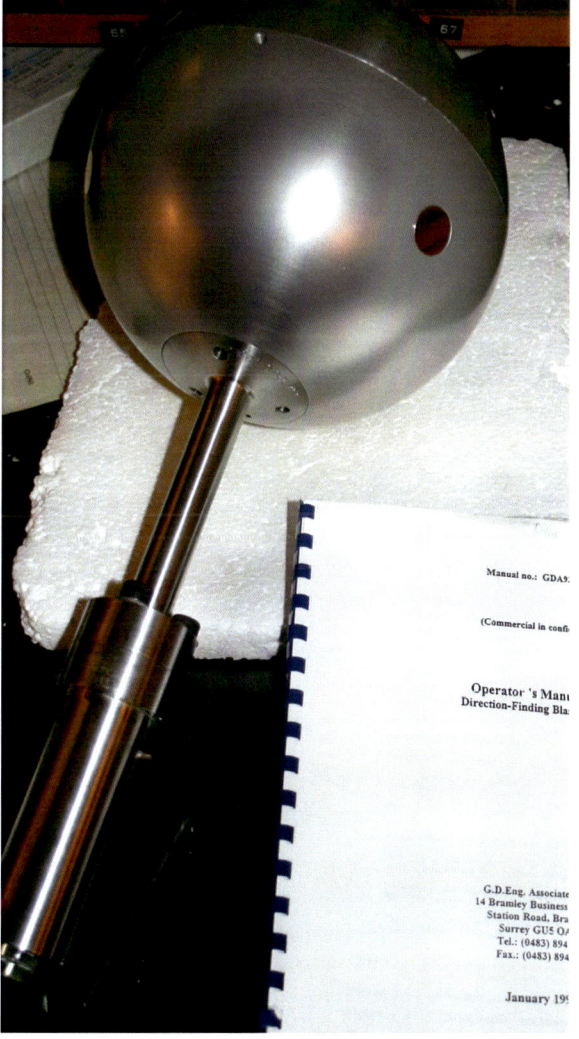

Right: This device is a Direction Finding Blast Gauge and is the type of technology that was being considered to upgrade the warning and monitoring systems. The sphere contained four pressure gauges and the direction of blast could be determined from measuring the time at which the blast wave reached each sensor. Several of these units could be linked together in a computer-controlled network to provide extended automated coverage.

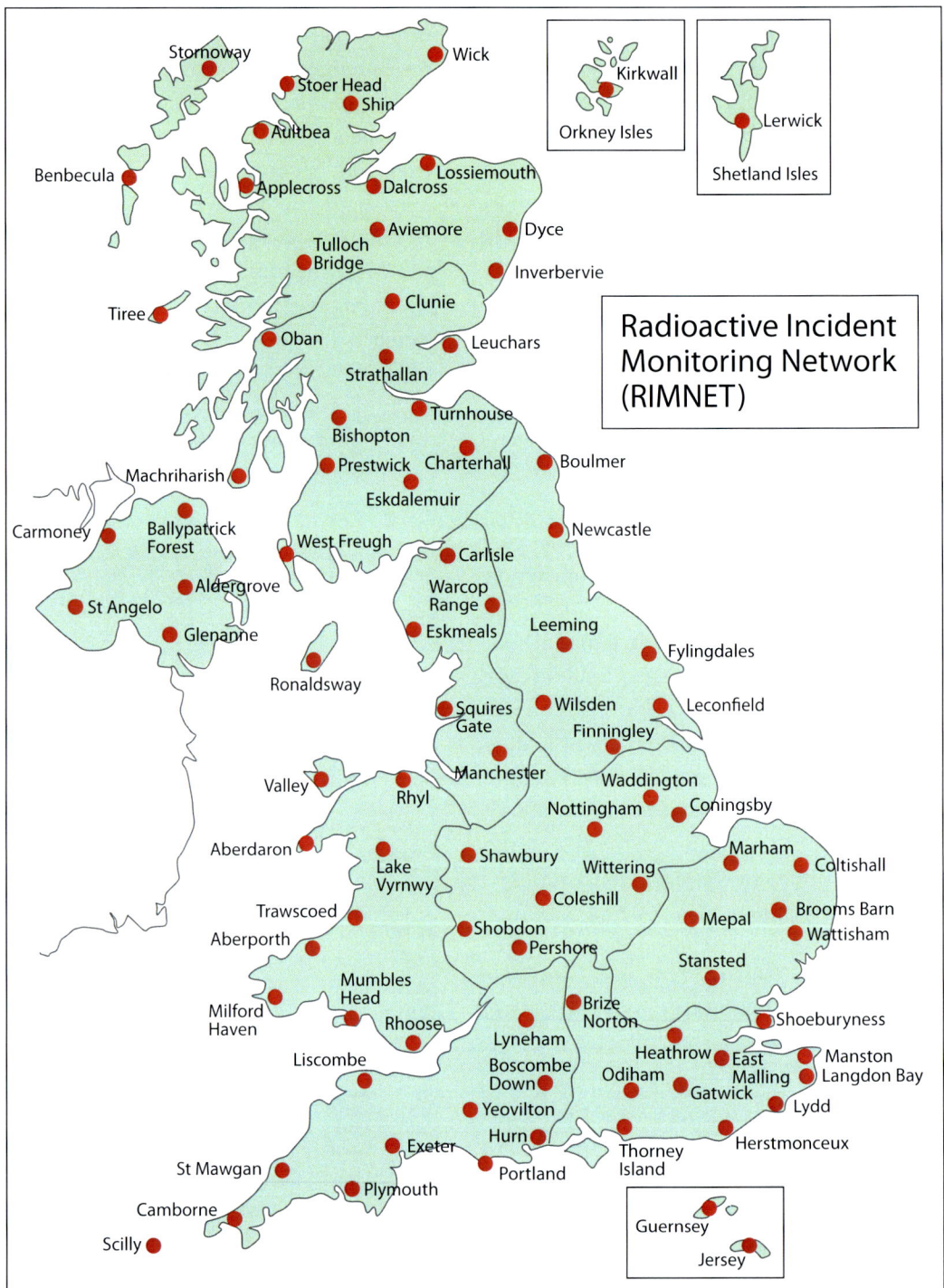

Above: The Radioactive Incident Monitoring Network (RIMNET) was established in 1988 in response to the Chernobyl accident of 1986. RIMNET measured background radiation at locations around the country using an automated system with sensors based at existing weather stations and MoD sites. Although unable to provide the level of fallout detail provided by the much more extensive ROC post network, it did highlight what was possible using new technologies.

Right: This excerpt from No.6 Group ROC HQ's Group Orders issued on 11 July 1991 breaks the news that the organisation was to be stood down. The 'body blow' referred to was made all the more painful by the rapid run-down expected. Training was to end in the same month and by 30 September 1991 all volunteers were to be stood down, with the exception of a few hundred Nuclear Reporting Cell personnel. Full time staff would stay on until March 1992 when they would effectively be made redundant.

Below: The reality of the end of the Corps can be seen in some of the grim faces at this final No.16 Group cluster meeting held in early September 1991.

GROUP ROUTINE ORDERS

BY

OBSERVER COMMANDER B H WATSON

HQ NO 6 GROUP ROYAL OBSERVER CORPS

ORDER NO 1 - ISSUE OF GROUP ROUTINE ORDERS

1. Officers and Head Observers are to take special care to ensure that the contents of this issue of Group Routine Orders are brought to the attention of all Observers.

ORDER NO 2 - MESSAGE FROM THE COMMANDANT

2. The Home Secretary is today advising Parliament of the outcome of his Review of Emergency Planning and Civil Defence.

3. As far as the UKWMO (including the ROC) is concerned the Home Secretary has decided that the arrangements for monitoring details of nuclear bursts and radioactive fallout in wartime must be restructured and that certain of UKWMO's functions in this area will be carried out by Central Government and integrated with existing local authority plans and responsibilities for monitoring in the field. The Home Office will be discussing with local authorities the implementation of these proposals but have concluded with regret, that they can no longer justify the continued use of the ROC and Home Department Volunteers for the monitoring task. Against this background the Home Office and Ministry of Defence have decided that there is no future role for the Corps in its present form. Hence stand down has become inevitable and in practice, this will mean that volunteer activity will end by 30 September 1991 and arrangements for stand down will be complete by 31 March 1992.

4. I know that the spirit of the Corps will continue through the Association and I hope that volunteers will seek to continue their service to the country in other ways. I recognise that this message represents a body blow to you all and I regret that I cannot lessen its impact. With the Chief of Staff and a representative of Civilian Management from the MOD, I will meet Senior Officers at Area HQ's in the next few days to amplify this order and to address the way forward. I am particularly concerned that as far as possible the chain of command should be used to advise our volunteers of the position accurately and quickly. Meanwhile I repeat the text of the Home Secretary's valedictory letter to the Corps.

MANNING THE POSTS

Above: The crew of Lytham post at the last post meeting on 22 July 1991. *Rear L to R* Obs Tony Morley, Obs Douglas Black, C/Obs Terry Tracey. *Front L to R* L/Obs Karen Sale, Obs Ann Clarke and Obs Irene Crosswaithe.

Left and below: The crew celebrated the passing of the ROC by cooking-up the remaining rations and by introducing a few bottles of wine into the proceedings.

MANNING THE POSTS

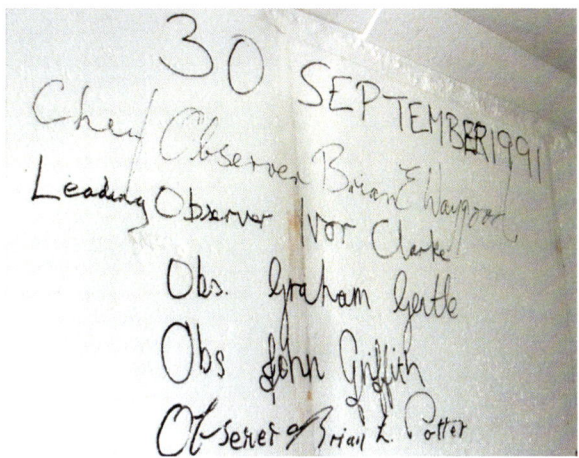

Above: Many post crews left farewell cards and notes or signed the hatch or walls, as in this post at Linton in Cambridgeshire.

Right: The betrayal felt by some ROC personnel can be seen in this poster found in Trumpet post in Herefordshire. Kenneth Baker was the Home Secretary at the time of the announcement and became the target of this 'Wanted' poster.

Below: There was a respite to the bad news with the running of the ROC Royal Review on 25 July 1991 at which the Queen presented the Corps with a new banner. 1,826 Observers and 175 Officers attended the event and the Garden Party afterwards. Observer Lieutenant Commander David Ross, Deputy Group Commandant of 25 Ayr Group, recalls that when asked by the Queen what he thought of the members of the Corps he answered – "salt of the earth ma'am".

MANNING THE POSTS

Top right: No.16 Group Headquarters Officers Obs Lt Cdr Anthony Foster and Obs Lt Adrian Cotter collect equipment after stand-down. It was left to the remaining full time staff to collect equipment from posts and this was all stored at the group headquarters. Most of the equipment collected in mainland Britain ended up at the Home Office stores at Marchington in Staffordshire. It remained at Marchington until sometime in the mid-to-late 1990s when it was reportedly scrapped with some of it going to landfill. For some years afterwards the car park at Marchington still used painted FSM covers as bollards until they were snapped up by collectors and post restorers.

Middle right: The official stand-down ceremony took place at St. Clement Danes, Central Church of the Royal Air Force in Central London on Sunday 29 September 1991. On this date, the 1966 Sovereign's Banner for the Royal Observer Corps was laid up and placed into the safe keeping of the Church.

The remaining full time staff stayed on until 31 March 1992 when the group headquarters were closed up for the last time. This photograph shows the ceremony performed at No.25 Group to mark the closure of the headquarters at Prestwick.

Bottom right: A few hundred ROC members carried on in Nuclear Reporting Cells, which were originally established to provide military command structures with bomb burst and fallout information and to interpret data from the ROC groups and sectors. The role was later expanded to include Nuclear, Biological and Chemical reporting. The sixteen remaining units continued to function until deemed non-essential and the NRCs were stood down on 31 December 1995. Observer Lieutenant Frank Alexander, as Officer in Charge of the Banner Party, hands the 1991 ROC Royal Banner into the safekeeping of the RAF at the laying up ceremony on 8 December 1995 at RAF Cranwell.

Chapter 7

ABANDONED POSTS

The posts closed down in 1968 have stood abandoned in farmers' fields for over forty years. Most have been open at some point during this time and many are now in very poor condition due to vandalism and the effects of the weather. These posts may still contain beds, furniture and sometimes items such as Jerrycans and the post battery, but little else. The reasons for this are twofold; when the posts were closed the ROC was still in existence and so equipment was removed for re-use elsewhere; also, at the time of the 1968 closures, the posts were largely unmodified and relatively bare anyway.

Those posts that closed at the end of the Cold War in 1991 have the potential to be more interesting as they were in service for much longer and incorporate all the improvements made during the twenty-three years of service following the 1968 closures. Many have been modified by their crews to improve the working and living conditions underground. This evolution of what was originally a standard structure meant that by 1991 many posts had unique features, with some of the crews displaying high levels of ingenuity in adapting the posts to better suit their needs.

The other key reason why some 1991 posts appear to be time capsules frozen at the end of the Cold War is due to the nature of the ROC stand-down.

That decision was communicated poorly and

ABANDONED POSTS

Barmouth

Previous page: Barmouth post on the North Wales coast is typical of a 1968 closure still in reasonably good condition. All the external features are still present, although the louvres are missing from the turret ventilator. The hatch locking mechanism has become detached, hence the need for a large rock to hold down the hatch cover.

Right: The floor of the post has been painted and a large amount of packaging remains. The prominent cylindrical cardboard carton is the original packaging in which the GZI was delivered. The package would have included the GZI itself and also the cast mount which was subsequently attached to the exterior of the post.

Below: Barmouth was part of No.17 Group whose headquarters by the time this post was built was in protected accommodation at Borras near Wrexham. The address on the wooden lid refers to the earlier Second World War era headquarters in Caernarvon. The old headquarters was retained for administration and training purposes until its closure in 1968.

Below: These boxes contained ROC jackets. Similar packaging can be found in other 1968 closures, many of which were only open a short time, (in this case only three years) and discarded packaging was left behind on closure.

many observers felt that they had been let down by the government of the day. When the posts were closed down there was sometimes little interest in clearing them out and in many cases paperwork and other items were left. The key items of equipment were removed by teams of Group Officers who stayed on until 1992 running down the Corps. Occasionally even these items were not retrieved due to various logistical issues and the odd piece of equipment can still be found.

The communications equipment was owned by British Telecom so, even when the ROC cleared out the posts, this equipment remained. BT did visit posts to remove equipment but in a large number of cases the kit was left in place as it had no re-use value and it generally was not worth the effort to collect it. In some cases BT maintained lines into posts long after stand-down and still do in some cases. In the last five years at least two abandoned posts have been found with Teletalks still connected and live. The 'on' light still pulsed and static could be heard over the loud speaker.

There are still many posts that are open and in good condition. Occasionally one that has been locked up since 1991 is reopened and, if lucky, another Cold War time capsule is revealed.

It is worth noting that the majority of posts are on private land and permission should be obtained to visit. There are various safety risks regarding these structures including air quality, hazardous substances and dangers of head and back injuries when entering and exiting posts.

Much Wenlock

Below: Much Wenlock in Shropshire is an example of a 1991 post that was locked until recently. Despite being untidy the post has many original features. The post has now been re-secured.

ABANDONED POSTS

Above and below: After a bit of tidying the Much Wenlock post looks more true to its operational days. The wooden chairs and metal cabinet are non-standard. The map is of the local area and marks the position of the cluster – Much Wenlock was in the same cluster as Church Stretton and Upton Magna.

Right: Candles and candle holders are often found in posts and were used as emergency lighting. Some posts even started training before electric lighting was available. The thirty-two Northern Ireland posts that took part in exercise 'Signal Fire' in April 1960 had to use candles as the post batteries were not delivered until three months later.

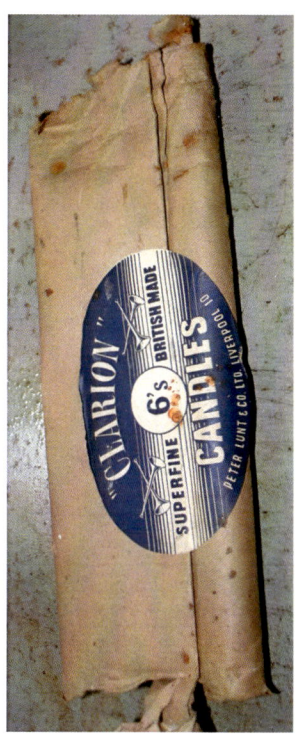

Below: Corroded batteries are one of the features of abandoned posts and care has to be taken in handling them. These would have been used for the Plessey PDRM82 and 82(F) units and the Radiac trainer.

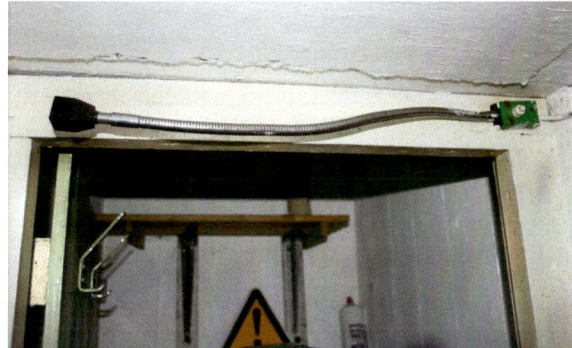

Above: This flexible light has been added by the crew. With the monitoring room door and entrance hatch shut, there was no provision in standard posts for lighting in the entrance shaft itself.

Below: The post at Much Wenlock has an array of tools stored in the toilet cubicle. The scythes were probably well used, since maintenance stopped, the post site has become extremely overgrown. The reason for the non-standard air pump is unclear as this post was not equipped with radio. Upton Magna was the master post in the cluster.

ABANDONED POSTS

Hawes

Above: This post at Hawes in the Yorkshire Dales is set in picturesque countryside but is close to housing.

Right: Unfortunately, although only closed in 1991, the interior of the Hawes ROC post is now in poor condition after being badly vandalised.

Keeping Out the Cold

While the overall temperature in the posts was relatively constant throughout winter and summer, the very nature of the crews' role could mean spending long periods underground with minimal physical exercise. As no heating was allowed in the posts for safety reasons, the cold, which was exacerbated by the bare concrete floor and walls, was a cause of constant complaint.

Many crews laid down mats or carpets to improve things and a few resourceful crews even built raised floors out of timber to create an insulating air gap. The Corps was aware of the problems and by 1972 was actively looking at providing polystyrene tiles as lining material for the post walls and ceilings.

Insulation of the floor was finally officially tackled when *Scandura* conveyor belting was issued in the autumn of 1984. In fact, the belting was surplus material from the National Coal Board.

The rubber belts were extremely heavy and five rolls were needed to insulate a post. The crew at Middlesmoor post in the Yorkshire Dales got round the problem of moving them over the rough access tracks by arranging for an Army Air Corps Gazelle helicopter to airlift the rolls in.

Buckden

Below: The surface features of the post at Buckden in Yorkshire.

Overleaf: Both improvements were made at the Buckden post; the polystyrene tiles can be clearly seen on the walls and ceiling while one of the sections of rubber belts has been removed to show the original concrete floor. The polystyrene tiles were a major fire hazard and were painted with *Decadex* firecheck emulsion to reduce the risk.

ABANDONED POSTS

Llanbedr

Above: The post at Llanbedr sits on a hill overlooking the old Royal Aircraft Establishment airfield on the north-west coast of Wales. The roll of rubber belting *(right)* was sitting unused in Llanbedr post when visited in 2008. It seems odd that after taking the effort to move the roll into the post, it was not laid. The rubber belts are stamped with 'NCB' for 'National Coal Board' and dated 1980.

ABANDONED POSTS

Hatch Design

Right: The original split-hatch was replaced by a one-piece hatch in the early 1960s. This was initially locked using a flat, metal locking bar. The locking bar slotted into a metal receiver at one end, with a slot cut into the bar at the other which fitted over an eyelet set into the concrete hatch surround. A padlock placed through this eyelet could then secure the post. This example at Lea in Herefordshire has a modified locking bar as well as the later padlock arrangement.

Left: There were variations on the same theme – this hatch cover at Aberangell in Wales (a 1968 closure) has the hasps welded to the hatch side with no provision for a locking bar. Note that the pattern on the hatch cover is of a different style to the 'cross hatch' pattern on the Lea example.

Right: In addition to padlocks, the hatches had an internal locking mechanism that required a 'T-key', more commonly referred to as a 'T-bar'. Different designs of T-bar key were manufactured with different numbers of lugs but essentially the mechanism and operation were the same. Two different types of T-bar key can be seen in this photograph as well as padlock and internal door keys. Both 51 and 52 posts were Durham Group posts which have since been demolished.

Top right: The T-bar key is inserted through a key hole on the outside of the hatch and, once engaged in the lock mechanism, can be used to turn an internal locking bar which will then release the hatch. In this photograph the internal locking mechanism is in the 'open' position. The locking mechanisms had a tendency to weaken over time and the chain was a safety measure to stop the mechanism dropping down the hatch if it became detached.

Bottom right: This general view of the hatch surround shows the standard arrangement of features after 1968. The hatch locking mechanism would be rotated by the T-bar key until it was positioned underneath the metal lug protruding from the bottom of the frame. This secured the hatch.

Above: The one-piece hatch and turning mechanism, known as the 'Broads Pattern' hatch, as described above, was the standard for the English, Welsh and Northern Ireland posts, and even the later security *Torlift* hatch had a similar type of operation. However, north of the border there was a distinct difference. Posts in Scotland had a completely different pattern of internal hatch mechanism and used what was known as the *Moran* design of hatch. Instead of a large rotating mechanism, the posts in Scotland had a simple two-lever latch. A T-bar key was still required but the lugs on the shaft were to a different design to those on keys from the other areas of the country.

ABANDONED POSTS

CND and Vandalism

The Campaign for Nuclear Disarmament (CND) first targeted the ROC in the late 1950s and early 1960s at the height of the Aldermaston marches. This was reignited in the 1980s as a result of the increased sabre-rattling from the Thatcher-Reagan axis and the corresponding Soviet response.

CND members would arrive at post sites and watch proceedings until dispersed by the police. Sometimes CND members tried to disrupt activities and in one incident a smoke bomb was tossed into a post temporarily incapacitating the observer below.

Above: The physical security of posts was largely dependant on the integrity of the hatch cover and, as has been shown, this developed during the 1960s until a good level of deterrence was provided. At post sites where it was felt that the hatch was not enough in itself, the security of the compound could be enhanced with high fences and barbed wire as in this 1960 photograph of the post at Letchworth which was built close to a large housing estate.

St. Ives

Below: St. Ives in Cambridgeshire was targeted by CND in the mid-1980s. A transit van was seen at the post and it was subsequently found that the padlocks had been sawn through.

Above: In 2008 the St. Ives post was reopened for the first time since stand-down and was found to be highly secure. Despite having the original keys and large amounts of WD40 it took around an hour to work free the rusted padlocks and jammed T-bar mechanism.

Below: The metal boxes are known as 'hasp protectors' and were added when it was realised that, although the padlocks themselves were hard to cut, (as they were made from hardened steel) the hasps themselves were not and were therefore much more vulnerable.

Below: The padlocks are Chubb No.1 *Battleships* – the originals would have been supplied with a padlock bar which was bolted and concreted into place so that it was embedded in the entrance hatch surround. The hasp is the hinged part that closes over the eyelet bolted to the hatch cover. This arrangement was to become the standard method of securing the hatch and instructions issued with these new parts stated that the old-style locking bar and its fitments should be removed during the work.

ABANDONED POSTS

Above: The interior of the St. Ives post. Unusually, the battery switching box has been attached to the main wall and not behind the door as was standard. The rectangular hole in the table in the foreground accommodated the PDRM82F. Although an official modification, it made the LCD screen difficult to read and many crew members made holders that tilted the unit so that it could be read more easily.

Right: Boxes for replacement padlocks, issued after the CND break-in, were still in the monitoring room.

Below: The interior doors could also be locked as a last line of defence against intruders.

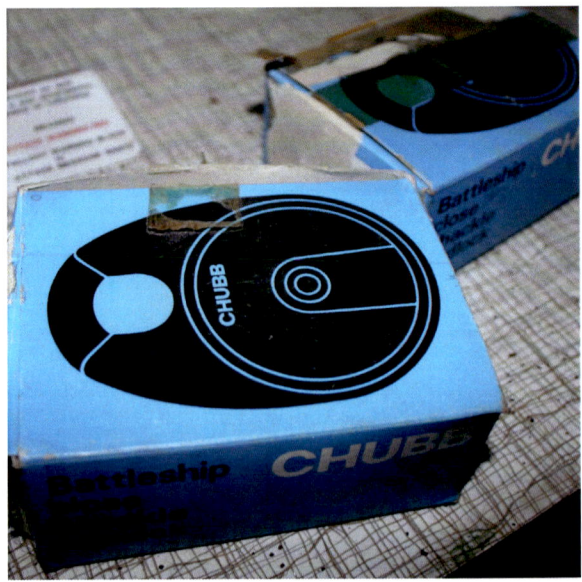

ABANDONED POSTS

Watton

Right: The post compound is easily visible from the A1075, the major route from Watton to Dereham in Norfolk. Its visibility is further enhanced as there is an elevated *Orlit B* aircraft post still on the site.

Below: While the rest of the Corps abandoned aircraft reporting in the early 1960s, aircraft posts that were around the cluster of V-bomber airfields in the east of the country were retained until 1965. The original corrugated metal roof covering was found stacked inside the post.

ABANDONED POSTS

Above: The interior of the underground post at Watton.

Below: Distressed signage at the Watton ROC post.

Below: A similar CND visit to that at St. Ives appears to have taken place at Watton, evidenced by this notice found pinned to the monitoring room wall.

Posts which were vulnerable to attack, either by CND or general vandalism, were modified with a new hatch design – the *Torlift* hatch. These hatches had no external hasps or padlocks which could be sawn through and the hole for the T-bar key had a security plug. This stopped any screwdrivers or other implements being used to force the hatch. A special tool was required to remove the plug before the hatch could be opened.

Trawsfynydd

Overleaf: While appearing to be at a remote location, this post at Trawsfynydd in Snowdonia is actually relatively close to housing. It is likely that for this reason the post was equipped with a *Torlift* hatch. The metal pole and grid structure attached to the GZI mount is believed to have been used as part of an apparatus to monitor radioactivity from the nearby nuclear power station after the post was closed.

Buckminster

Below and right: The underside of the *Torlift* hatch at Buckminster post in Leicestershire. This also has a grille over the entrance shaft. Two bolts were used to secure this from the inside of the post and it allowed the hatch to be open for ventilation while stopping unauthorised access from above. These grilles are quite rare and indicate that this post must have had persistent security issues.

Far right: The security plug is still in place in the keyhole, although it has been damaged by attempts to enter the post.

ABANDONED POSTS

Right: Even when post hatches resisted break-in attempts, vandals and members of CND realised they could unbolt the blanking plate on the FSM probe pipe and pour paint (or worse) directly down into the monitoring room. A new blanking plate was therefore devised which did not require external bolts. Note also the BPI pipe and behind that the GPO connection point for the communications equipment.

Below left and right: This flat plate was manufactured with a large hook on the underside. A long pole, fed through the FSM pipe to the room below, could then be screwed tight against the pipe flange in the ceiling of the monitoring room, thus securing the new blanking plate over the top of the pipe.

ABANDONED POSTS

Date	Organisation / Dept / Contractor + Reason for Visit
2.12.87	PSA Building Inspection
6.4.88	A J Dyson G0 4UW Raynet
6.4.88	Raynet Exercise
16.4.88	P.C. 3261 Lennon Checking Post Security
16.4.88	PC 3656 Flanagan - Checking Post
16.4.88	Sgt 1396 Osbourne Post Security
16.4.88	A/Insp 206 Kenny Post Security
16.4.88	A/PS 1797 Kheavis Post Security
16.4.88	SDO 623 P. McCarthy " "
12.6.88	PC 2272 J.V Goodwin. Tamworth Police (Security)
20.6.88	Jackie Edwards - New Recruit
20/6/88	Teresa Bull - New Recruit
20/6/88	Harbi Franik New Recruit
27/6/88	Harbi Franik New Recruit
27/6/88	Teresa Bull " "
27.6.88	Jackie Edwards " "
27.6.88	8080 Ex Obs Sandars. Old Recruit
29/11/88	Home Office DofTels Romsley Post Inspection
11/1/89	Home Office DofTels Romsley. Post Modification of Radio Equipment
12/1/89	" " " " "
13/1/89	" " " " "
17/1/89	H.O DofTels Post Mod.
17/1/89	PSA Coventry pwo
15/4/89	ROC visitor L/Obs 16 Gp
"	Police visit 2272 Goodwin 2345
7 Jun 89	DGC - 1) Replaced PE Set

Above: If vandals or CND visited a post site when it was active then group headquarters was informed. They would then in turn inform the police. At some posts which had been targeted previously, observers would be left above ground to act as a watch for any intruders on the site. Chief Observers were permitted to make their own arrangements with the local police so that patrols could visit the posts at regular intervals during exercises and times when the post was manned overnight. This page from the Harlaston post diary shows that six police officers squeezed into the Staffordshire post on 16 April 1988.

ABANDONED POSTS

Aircraft Reporting

Below: Many of the underground post sites still have structures close by from the days when the ROC was an aircraft spotting and tracking organisation. This is the post at Brassington in Derbyshire. The two-storey aircraft post behind the underground post is a Second World War survivor.

Right: The local Ashbourne ROC Association had been trying to get this structure listed by English Heritage since 2004. Success was finally achieved in October 2010 when the wartime building and the later underground post were both listed. One of the key points in favour of the listing was the fact that there were two distinct structures at the same location from two different historical periods.

ABANDONED POSTS

Above: Another example of a wartime ROC structure, at Burghill in Herefordshire. The left side of the building was open to the elements during operations so that the Observers could conduct their aircraft tracking duties.

Above: This *Orlit A* post at Leominster, also in Herefordshire, is essentially a 1950s prefabricated version of the Second World War post at Burghill.

Below: This post at Joppa in Ayrshire is the *Orlit B* variety – the structure is the same as the *Orlit A*, but raised on stilts to give observers clearer visibility over local obstructions.

Above: The aircraft role was retained in the eastern part of England until 1965. Some posts in these areas, which had not previously had facilities for aircraft reporting, had simple scaffold-type structures built. Observers could support binoculars on these and some of the structures could be rigged with tarpaulins to keep off the worst of the weather.

Right: A crew on duty in an aircraft post. Note the Very Pistol cartridges behind the Chief Observer. Very Pistols were issued so that crews could warn patrolling RAF fighters of low-level intruders. The Very Pistol cartridges, and the use of the post instrument, date this picture to the early 1950s.

ABANDONED POSTS

Above: The weathered ROC sign still visible on the door to the *Orlit A* at Bottisham post in Cambridgeshire.

Above: This metal box was used to secure the Very Pistol (and the ammunition) issued to the crews. These boxes were bolted to the floor in the small covered annex on the left side of the *Orlit* and some can still be seen in situ today. Very Pistols were only issued to posts in rural areas as firing such a pyrotechnic in a built-up area would have been highly dangerous.

Below: Inside the open working area was this square wooden pillar. The plotting table was secured on the metal mounting at the top of the pillar and the magneto telephone could be placed on one of the shelves when in use.

Aircraft Recognition

The reduction, and finally cancellation, of the aircraft reporting role was a major blow to the Corps, many of whom had joined because of their interest in aircraft and the strong associations with the Royal Air Force. Although the transition away from aircraft was gradual, many observers elected to leave the Corps when it became obvious that the days of aircraft reporting had officially ended.

There were various local attempts to re-instigate aircraft reporting, and trials at cluster-level were sometimes attempted by enthusiastic Group Officers. Observers were called on to support the RAE trials conducted in 1970 and 1971 which monitored the sonic boom produced by Concorde, although this was not strictly aircraft reporting. Larger trials, reporting low-flying aircraft, were conducted with the RAF starting in 1976 with Lincoln and Norwich groups participating. Although successful these were not adopted and the project was dropped in 1982.

Occasionally the Corps' expertise in aircraft recognition was utilised by the Armed Services. In 1981 observers were asked to support the RAF's Tactical Bombing Competition at the Otterburn range in Northumberland. The ROC members operated with Rapier missile crews and acted as observers and umpires during the competition.

This expertise also proved vital a year later when it was realised that no air recognition slides existed

Above: Anyone leafing through these magazines could be excused for thinking that the ROC was still primarily focussed on aircraft as virtually all the features were about how to recognise Warsaw Pact and Western aircraft, with usually only a small section covering the modern-day role. This did improve from the mid-1980s with some more rounded content, including features on defence policy and the Soviet threat. However, it is telling that virtually all the covers of the *ROC Journal* featured photographs of aircraft until 1986, when cover shots started to show the interiors of monitoring posts and group control operations.

of the Dassault Super Etendard and the IA58 Pucara – principal Argentinian aircraft-types that were likely to be deployed against British Forces on their way to retake the Falkland Islands. Ex-observer Eric Vine and observer Byron Scott were quickly contacted by ROC Headquarters as they were known for their model-making expertise. The models were delivered to Bentley Priory only two days later and were subsequently photographed by the MoD in Whitehall. The finished material was flown out to 63 Rapier Squadron, RAF Regiment, who were embarked on Queen Elizabeth II, just before she sailed. A further batch of material was subsequently produced and was used by all the air defence units in the Falklands.

ABANDONED POSTS

Right and below: Model-making and aircraft recognition remained a mainstay of the Corps throughout the nuclear period. Martin Cooke, Chief Observer at Stoke Golding post *(see Chapter 8)* won several model-making competitions at summer camps. Martin hand-made these wooden models from scratch and is holding a model of a Soviet Tu-22 'Blinder' bomber.

Food and cooking

If three crew members were to work and live underground for the stated two weeks then methods of heating both water and food had to be found. The official solution introduced in the late 1960s was to heat cans with Tommy cookers and later, in the 1980s with Centre Forge Mini Cookers. The cooking methods were not particularly effective and could only heat food and could not boil water. It was possible to eat these later rations cold and *Puritab* water purification tablets were provided to sterilise water for drinking.

Right: Typical British Forces rations used by the Corps at stand-down.

ABANDONED POSTS

Above: A locally-made Tommy holder. The *Meta* solid fuel tablets in the foreground were a more modern interpretation of the Tommy cooker idea.

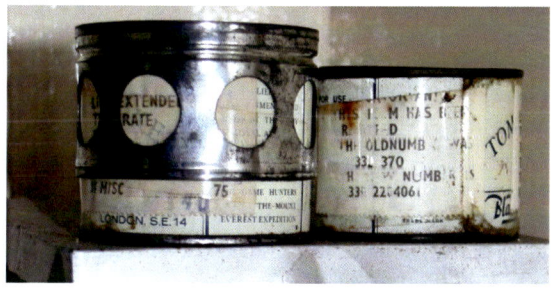

Above: Gel fuel for the Tommy cooker.

Right: Care was required when using Tommy cookers. They used a gel fuel and instructions stated it should only be used in the hatch-shaft with the hatch cover open. The more enterprising crews fabricated holders that could be placed on the post ladder in order to prepare a brew-up.

ABANDONED POSTS

Above: The official solutions were basic and many crews used additional camping stoves and commercially available cookers to heat food and water in the posts.

Left: This cupboard, at Reeth post, contains lots of non-issue cooking pots and utensils and is typical of the additions crews made to their posts to enhance the living conditions.

Below: The observers at this post (in Yorkshire) were keen on their tea. The brown teapot was the standard issue item.

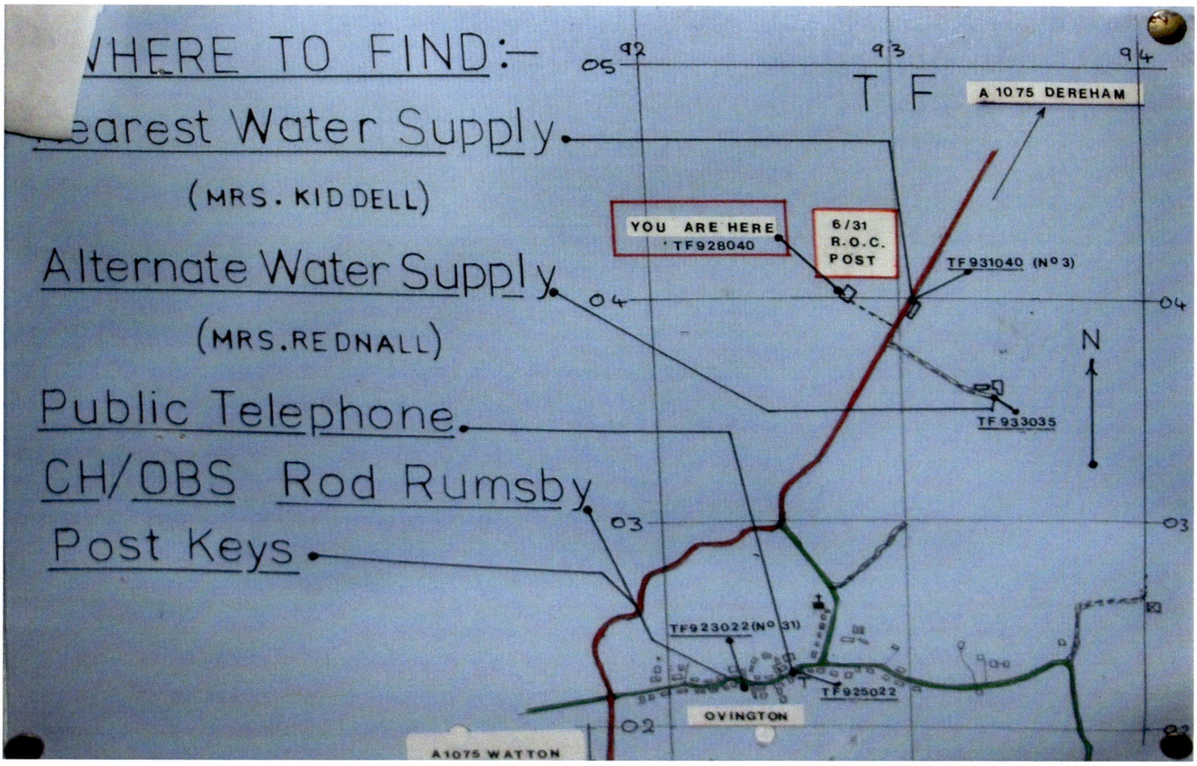

Above: Water supply and replenishment was a labour-intensive job and crews were expected to do water-changes on a regular basis. Some crews were able to run hosepipes from nearby houses if they were fortunate but many had to haul Jerrycans of water to and from the post site.

Health and Safety

Current Health and Safety standards would mean that the posts could never be built today to the design of 1956. There was only one exit and entrance, and that was via a narrow vertical shaft; there were a range of toxic chemicals used in the posts – the fluid for the chemical toilet being particularly nasty; there were potential air quality issues (high levels of radon gas were found in at least one post), and there were trip hazards above-ground (primarily the BPI pipe).

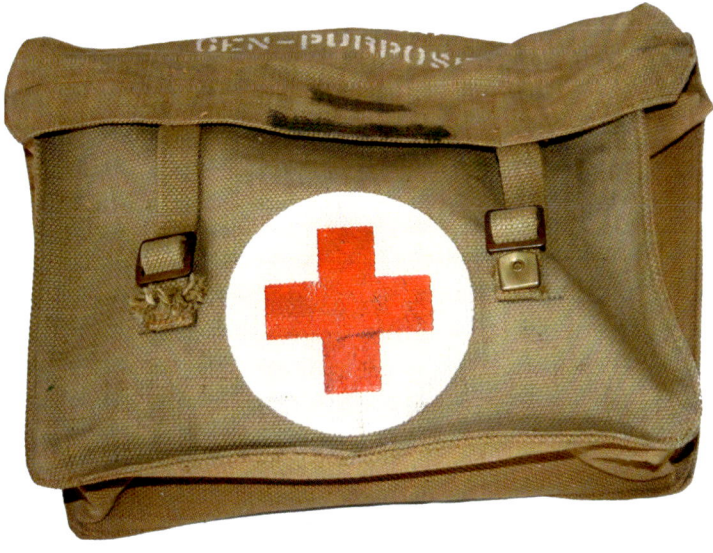

Right: The old wartime-style First Aid kit used in some posts. These were later superseded by a more modern green plastic-cased kit.

ABANDONED POSTS

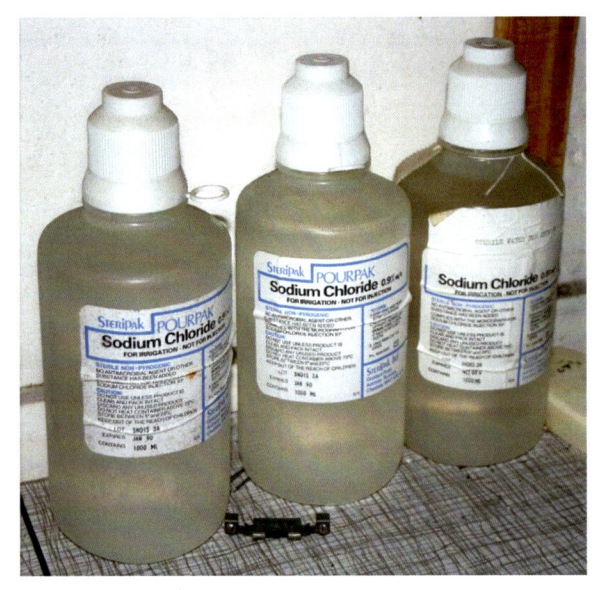

Left: Bottles of eyewash were provided in the latter days of service after several incidents where crew members had been exposed to the Formaldehyde-based chemical sanitary fluid used in the toilet.

Below: This letter from Maidstone Group Headquarters highlights the real dangers involved when mechanical failures occurred. At some posts it was common practise to leave the toilet door open so that observers at the bottom of the shaft could duck out of the way if something fell down the hatch.

0622 55674
26 February 1990

See Distribution

HEALTH AND SAFETY AT WORK
INCIDENTS INVOLVING MONITORING POST HATCHES

1. During 1989 the following two incidents were reported as occurring at Monitoring Posts:

   a. Incident No 1. The weld holding the locking bar to the underside of the hatch cover failed when personnel were securing the Post. The locking bar broke off and fell to the bottom of the shaft - fortunately the personnel were both outside.

   b. Incident No 2. As an Observer was leaving the Post the 'T' bracket holding the hatch cover sheared and the counter weight struck him on the lower back. The safety chain, slide bracket and pins were all intact.

2. As both incidents had the potential to cause death or serious injury, Post Chief Observers should be instructed to carry out an immediate close inspection of hatch covers and fittings and to report any defects to Group HQs for attention under reactive maintenance.

3. With these incidents in mind, the opportunity should be taken to remind all personnel of the dangers inherent in remaining at the bottom of a Post shaft when there is activity on either the ladder or at the hatch.

A S WALTON
Obs Lt
for Gp Comdt

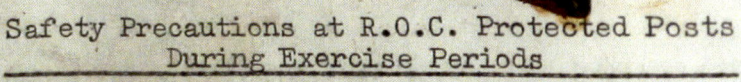

Safety Precautions at R.O.C. Protected Posts
During Exercise Periods

1. The ventilator shutter should remain open at all times.

2. When the post is occupied the hatch should be closed only when necessary for training purposes.

3. The use of naked lights is prohibited.

4. The storage or use of liquid fuels is prohibited.

5. Chemical fire extinguishers should not be used in the post. In case of fire sand and water are to be used.

6. Two persons should be present whenever work is being done in the post.

7. No heating is required in the post.

8. The battery and associated wiring is not to be touched.

Additional Precautions when Hatch is closed

9. Smoking is prohibited.

10. Cooking is prohibited.

11. Moving about should be kept to a minimum.

12. The post should on no account be closed down for more than eight hours consecutively.

ROC/1074/2/EQ
7th July, 1959

Above: The potential hazards of operating in a post were recognised early on. These original 1959 instructions regarding ventilation can still be seen in many posts today and detail when the post hatches should be closed along with various other safe working practises.

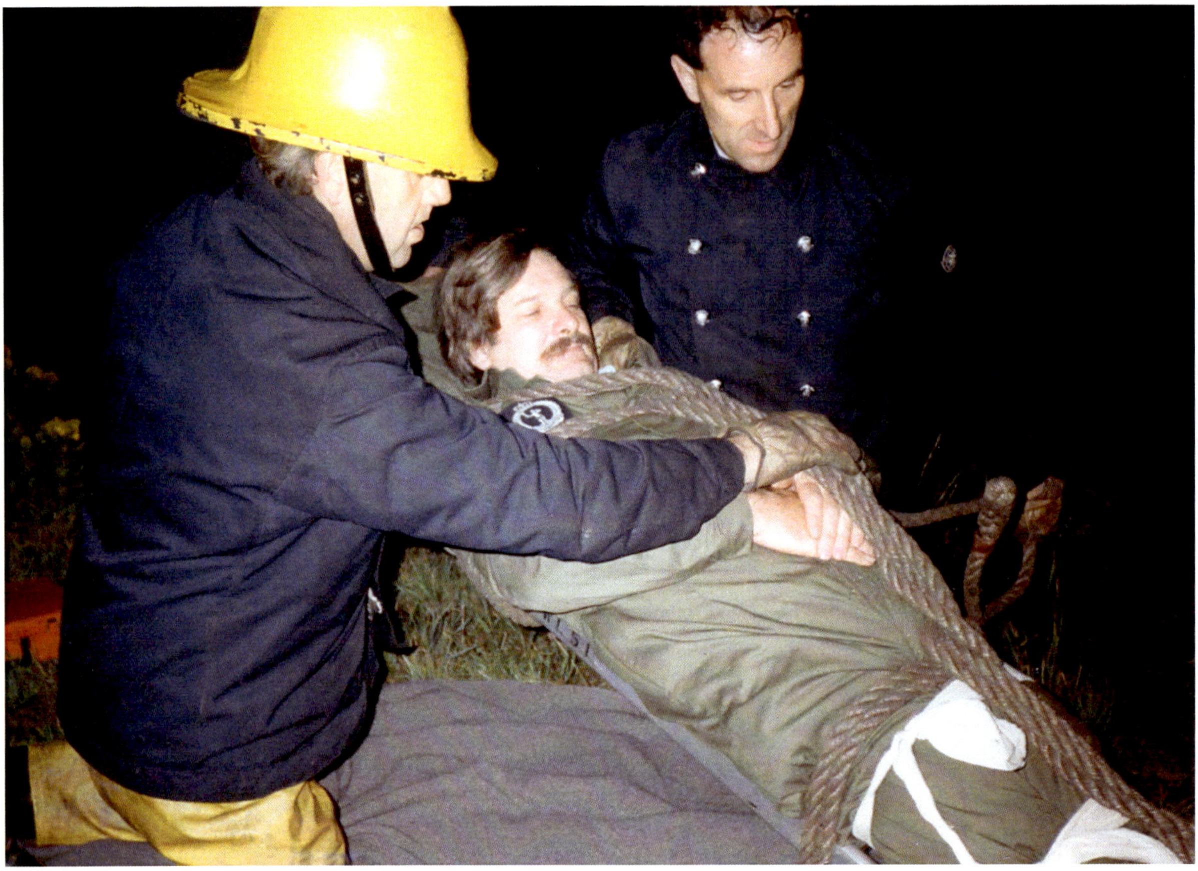

ABANDONED POSTS

Above: In order to recover injured crew members, the ROC worked in conjunction with local fire services to develop and practise methods of removing people safely from posts. This photograph, taken in the early 1980s, shows an exercise in Nottingham where the Derbyshire Fire Brigade practise rescuing an ROC member from the post at Whitwell.

Below right: When the posts first became operational they were issued with Bofors splints and also a smaller arm splint. While the splint instructions stated that the "splint is of such simple design that it can very well be used by those who have not received any training in First Aid or medical service", in reality it was a tricky and dangerous operation getting a badly injured crew member out of a post and the use of these splints by the crews was banned.

ABANDONED POSTS

Right: The danger of fire in such a small confined area with only a narrow exit meant that observers were prohibited from using naked lights and had to be careful when heating meals. Fire extinguishers could not be used as oxygen levels could be dangerously depleted, so water or a bucket filled with sand was the only realistic precaution. It was not until 1976 that asbestos fire blankets were issued. These in turn have now become a Health and Safety issue and it is very rare to find one still in its box in a post as these were one of the items that were listed to be removed at stand-down.

Homemade Equipment

Below: The post at Usk in Monmouthshire was bought several years ago for development purposes which never came to fruition. The post has slowly started to flood but still has a full set of British Telecom equipment in situ. The device sitting on the cupboard at the right of the photograph is a homemade maroon launcher.

Above: The homemade maroon trainer in the post at Usk. Many post crews built their own maroon trainers as the genuine training kits were usually held at group headquarters and were rotated around the posts. This meant that they were only available for short periods of time to individual post crews and this was not always convenient for crew training.

Above right: Another homemade maroon launcher can be seen in this photograph taken at Buckminster post in Leicestershire. The triangular three-tube arrangement of these homemade units are copies of the No.2 maroon that was in service in the 1980s. The post was flooded until ten years ago when it was pumped out – the tide mark can be seen on the furniture. Unfortunately water is again building up in the post.

Right: Another example of a piece of homemade training equipment can be seen in this photograph of a Bomb Power Indicator Trainer – a screw at the rear of the wooden backing could be turned to move the needle around the dial face.

Lighting and Power

Below: Power for the lights was provided by a battery pack that was kept near the door in the monitoring room. The battery box is a common find in abandoned posts. The original Alkaline 12 volt battery was supplied in this box along with the connecting strips for the individual cells.

Below: This photograph shows two of the later 'ALCAD' batteries that were in service at stand-down. Two batteries were provided when posts were equipped with radio; while non-radio posts only had one. Note the handle for the aerial mast pump at the bottom of the photograph.

Below left and right: Initially, lighting in posts was generally very poor, with only a 6 watt bulb available for illumination. If lights were left on for extended periods (for example, when observers were working on the surface), then the post battery could be drained unnecessarily. To prevent this, ninety-minute timers were introduced, starting in 1963. Observers still had to use torches to read instruments in some cases, so further improvements were made with the introduction of florescent lighting in selected posts from 1968 onwards.

ABANDONED POSTS

Right: Originally the batteries only needed to power a small filament bulb and when they needed recharging they were taken to the local garage. This was not particularly practical in a war situation, so Petrol Electric (PE) charging sets were provided from the late 1960s. Two similar designs were produced, one by A. C. Morrison of Southampton and the other by Engine Applications Ltd of Banbury. The version shown is the *Swan* unit produced by the latter company. The sets used a Villiers four-stroke petrol engine to drive a permanent magnet DC generator. It had a maximum output of 300 watts and provided 14 volt DC current to charge the battery.

Below: Manuals for the original PE sets plus the manual for the Yamaha 240 volt mains capable generator which started to replace the PE sets in the late 1980s.

Below: The PE sets were kept in the post in plastic bags and hauled out when they were needed. A four-and-a-half gallon Jerrycan was provided for collecting petrol but this was not to be stored in the post. Petrol was transferred from the Jerrycan into the smaller petrol container illustrated below, which was then used to fill the petrol tank of the PE set.

ABANDONED POSTS

Above right and left: Official procedure was to bury the petrol Jerrycan outside the post and uncover this as and when needed. In reality this was a tedious business and many post crews built more permanent storage areas in the grounds of the compound. Most were brick-lined holes with a simple cover, although some were more elaborate affairs – the metal example *(above right)* could be padlocked for extra security.

Below: The PE sets were usually set up near the post hatch, often on the hatch step or on a small concrete hard standing. The cables could then be fed down the shaft and connected to the battery. A few crews permanently wired the cables to the shaft and added a connection point near the top as illustrated at this post at Pattingham near Wolverhampton. Posts equipped with radio could plug into the two-pin socket located under the post outlet box on the ventilator.

Below: The master posts were re-wired with the introduction of the Burndept radios in the early 1980s. This included a new battery change-over box. In the 'off' position only the lighting would be available. If the 'A.Batt' position was selected then Battery 'A' would be available for charging, with Battery 'B' supplying power to the lighting and the radio. The 'B.Batt' position operated in the same way with Battery 'B' now available for charging.

 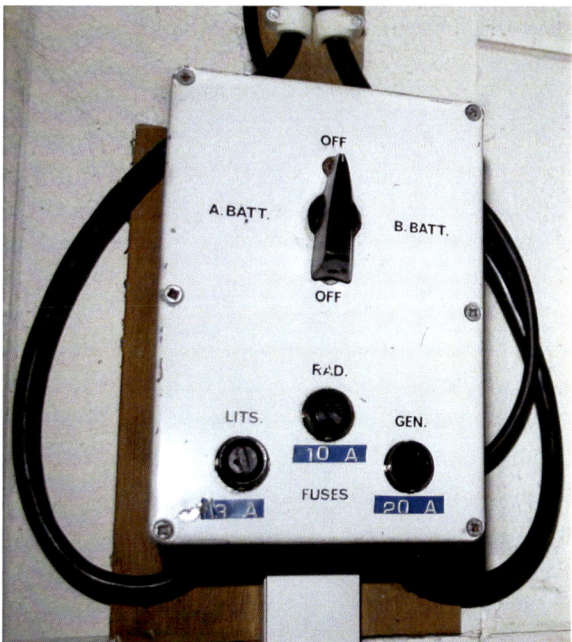

ABANDONED POSTS

Right: Group Officer Andrew Grant setting up a Yamaha EF1000 generator at Girvan Post, Ayrshire, in the late 1980s. Trials of such generators were conducted towards the end of the ROC's life as potential replacements for the old style Petrol Electric (PE) sets. Whilst being able to supply power at 240 AC it was found that the units were much heavier to lift up and down the post shaft when compared to the PE sets.

Local Modifications

Penrith Post, Cumbria

Below: The Penrith post in Cumbria was sold as part of a sale of surrounding farmland in 2008. This was one of the best preserved unrestored posts in the UK at the time but sadly, since the sale, several unique items have been removed.

Above and below: These photographs show the high standard of modifications that the crew at Penrith made to their post. As can be seen, they have fitted cupboards, tool boards, a carpet and even a roller-towel rail.

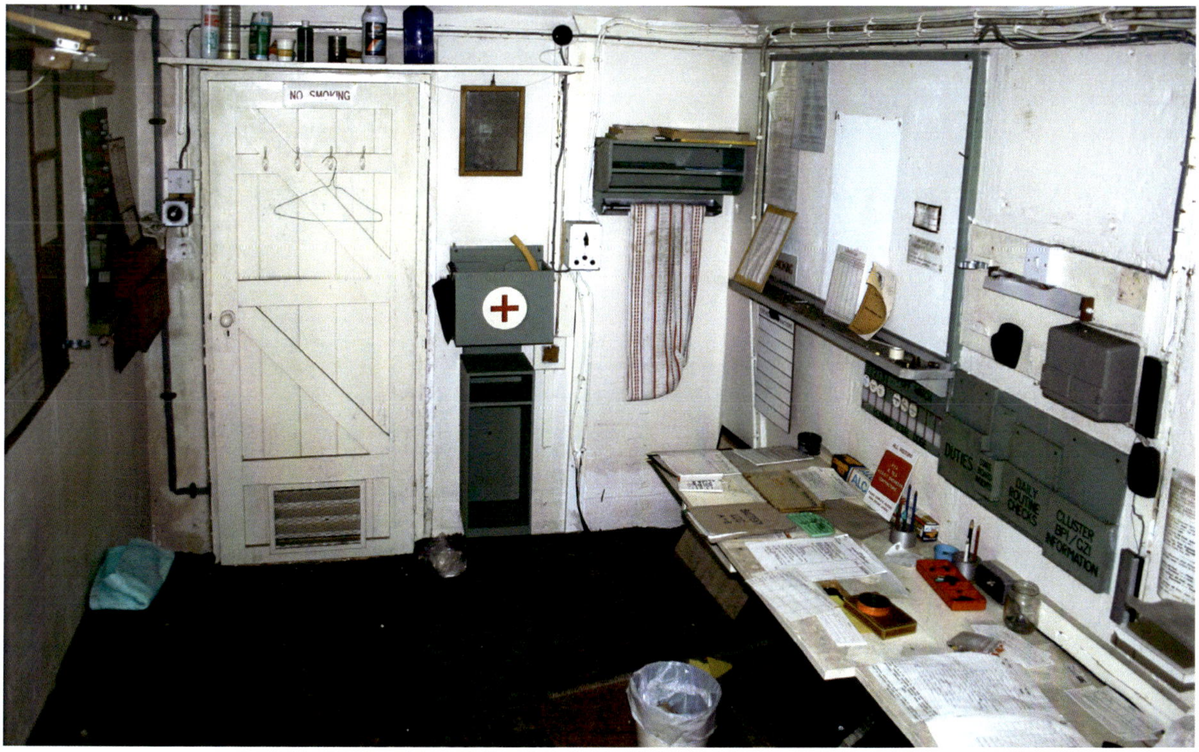

ABANDONED POSTS

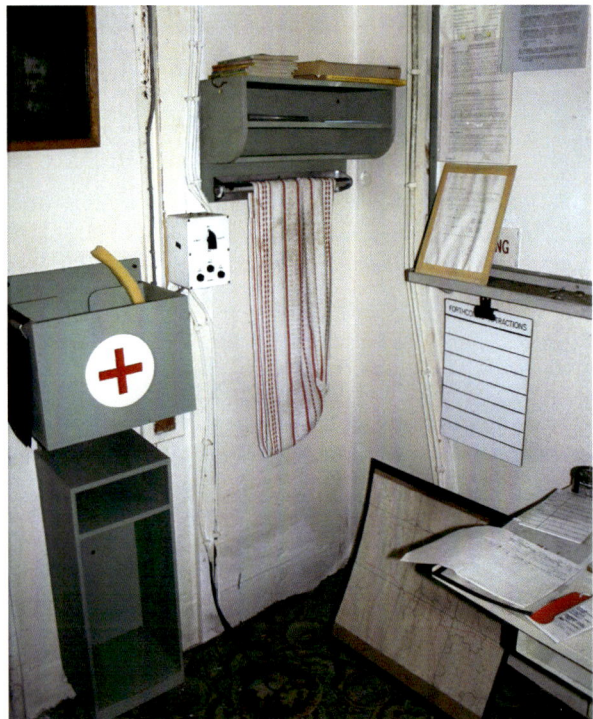

Above: Detail of the towel rail and First Aid box. A cluster map is propped up against the wall and, above, is a clipboard used for listing 'forthcoming attractions'.

Below: Even the toilet area has handmade tool racks.

Above: The tall white unit at the rear of the post is a purpose-built Jerrycan tipper. Water was stored in the post in Jerrycans and, to make it easier to dispense, the cans could be placed in the red painted metal cradles and be pivoted to pour water. This was not a standard piece of issued furniture and, although not found frequently, the same design has been found in posts all over the UK.

ABANDONED POSTS

Above: This map of Cumbria and the Borders shows the posts of the Carlisle Group. The bomb symbols are those used by the Group Control staff to plot explosions.

Below: Some enterprising crews took it upon themselves to plot the bigger picture by using information gleaned from other posts and then triangulating the data themselves.

POSTS	50	51	52		55	56	57	58
TIME								
PRESSURE								
BEARING	302	051						
ELEVATION	02	06						
TOUCHING/CLEAR								
SPOT SIZE								
DISTANCE								
GROUND ZERO								
POWER								
HEIGHT								

ABANDONED POSTS

Above: The working area of the post still contained post diaries, battery logs and other documentation when visited in 2008. Note the rack for the various ROC forms that has been constructed and hand painted by the crew.

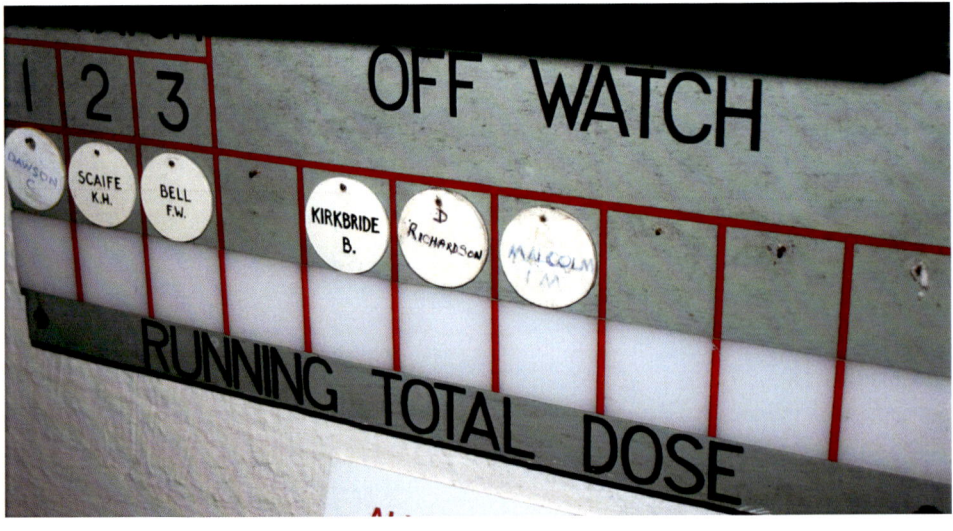

Right: Another useful addition is this board which allows the crew to understand, at a glance, the dose rates of individual members in a wartime situation. Note the wipe-clean plastic insert in the wooden board so that dose rates could be updated.

Corwen Post, Merionethshire

Above: Exterior view of Corwen post in Merionethshire, Mid Wales.

Below: Corwen is another example of a post where the crew have improved the interior by adding cupboards and storage space for paperwork. A homemade cupboard was built over the bed space. The plastic mugs are standard issue items. The copper earthing straps and cables indicate Corwen was equipped with radio.

Below: This photograph indicates that the sump and outflow pipe have also been earthed. All the tools in the post were painted a bright blue for some reason.

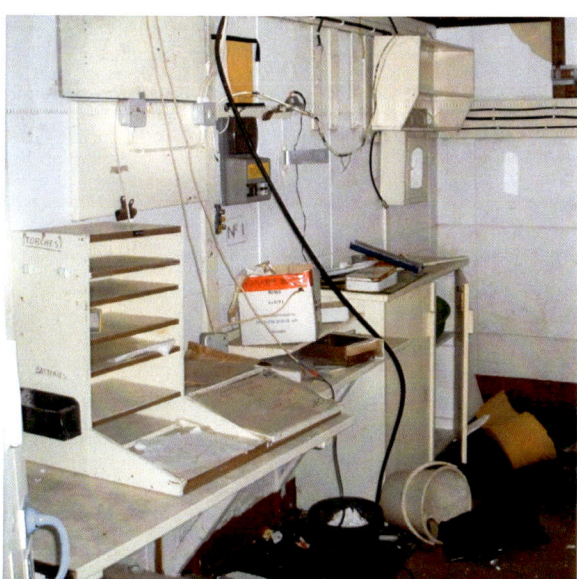

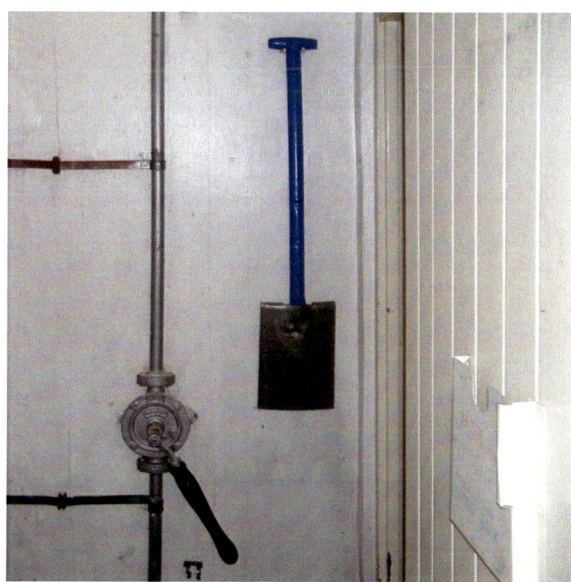

Thankerton Post, Ayrshire

Above: Thankerton post in Ayrshire is in good condition externally. Note that it has small holes for ventilation rather than louvres.

Below: The interior was modified to include a curtain that could be dropped down to cover the bed area. This would have allowed off-duty crew members some privacy while they tried to rest.

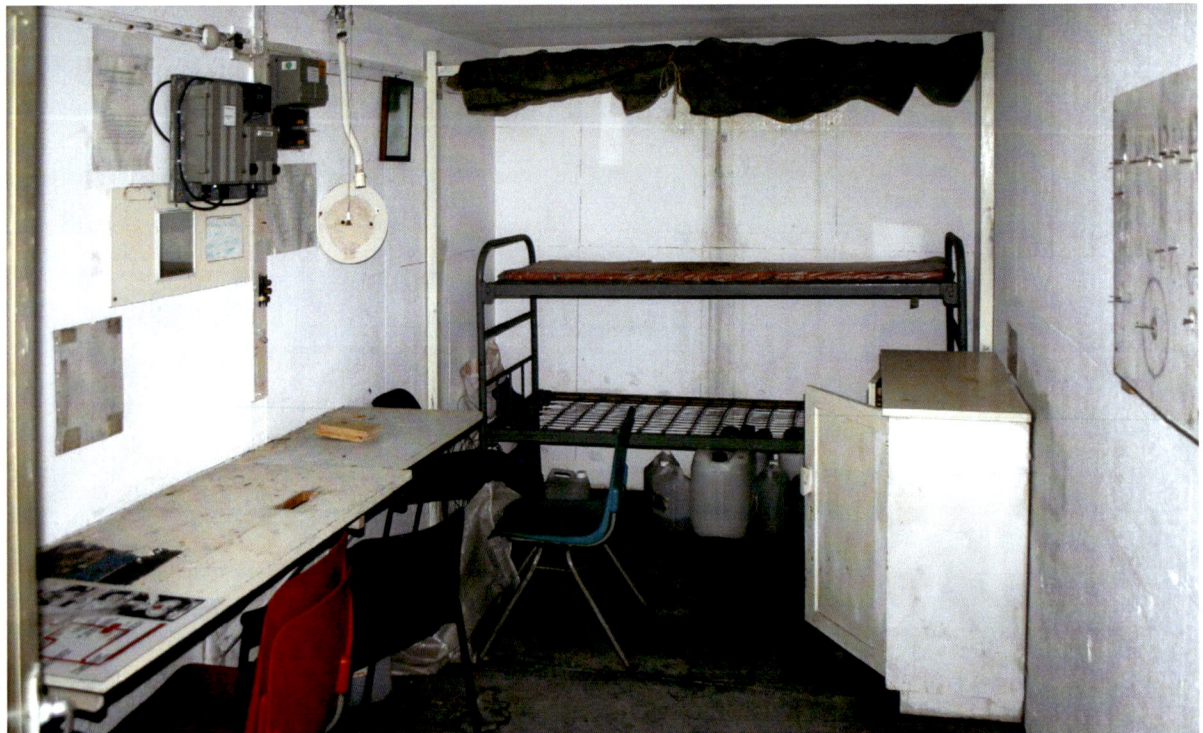

ABANDONED POSTS

Right: A large number of water containers are under the bed. Jerrycans were standard issue for this purpose in posts but were heavy when full and cumbersome to handle in the confines of the post. This crew have decided to use smaller, more manageable containers. This post is unusual in that the bunk beds remain. Most 1991 closures had these removed at stand-down. The posts had originally been equipped with a single bed as well, but these were removed following the reduction in crew size from four to three in the late 1960s.

Right: Various items stored in the toilet cubicle. The light green net on the toilet seat was the post net and along with the post rope was the standard-issue equipment for hauling things up and down the access shaft.

Below: Detail of the WB1400 carrier receiver.

Page 141

ABANDONED POSTS

Audlem Post, Cheshire

Above: Audlem post in Cheshire is in a small compound surrounded by stock-proof fencing. Note the concrete steps leading up to the entrance hatch. Most posts usually have a single step in this position but there are also many examples, similar to Audlem, where additional steps have been added in various positions around the hatch.

Right: Inside there is another example of a curtain having been erected to cover the bed space. The orange coloured mattresses remain sealed in plastic packaging, but the beds themselves have been removed. This was the result of a specific directive which instructed that the beds be removed and returned to stock when the posts closed.

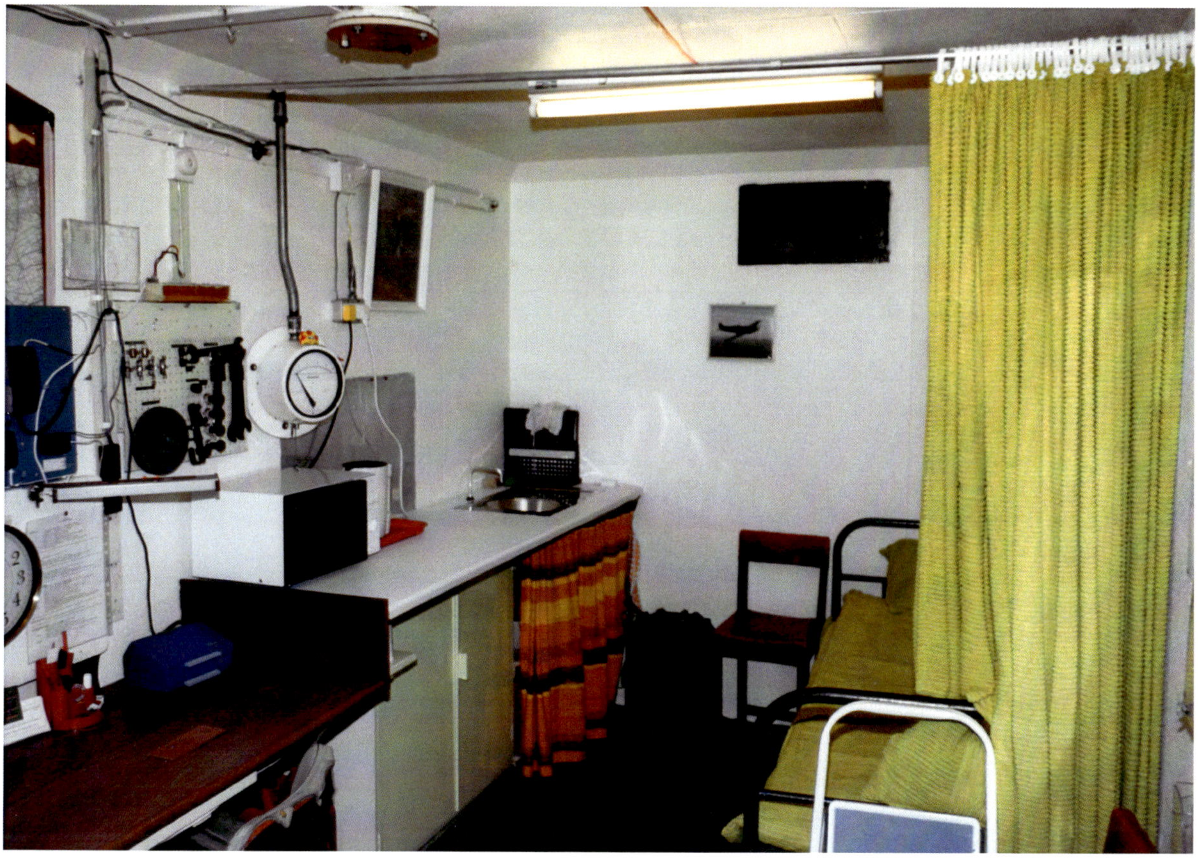

ABANDONED POSTS

Lytham Post, Lancashire

Above: This post at Lytham near Blackpool probably has the distinction of being one of the most comfortable in the Corps. The crew installed a curtain which split the post into a working and a living area, and they also added a sink at the far end of the monitoring room.

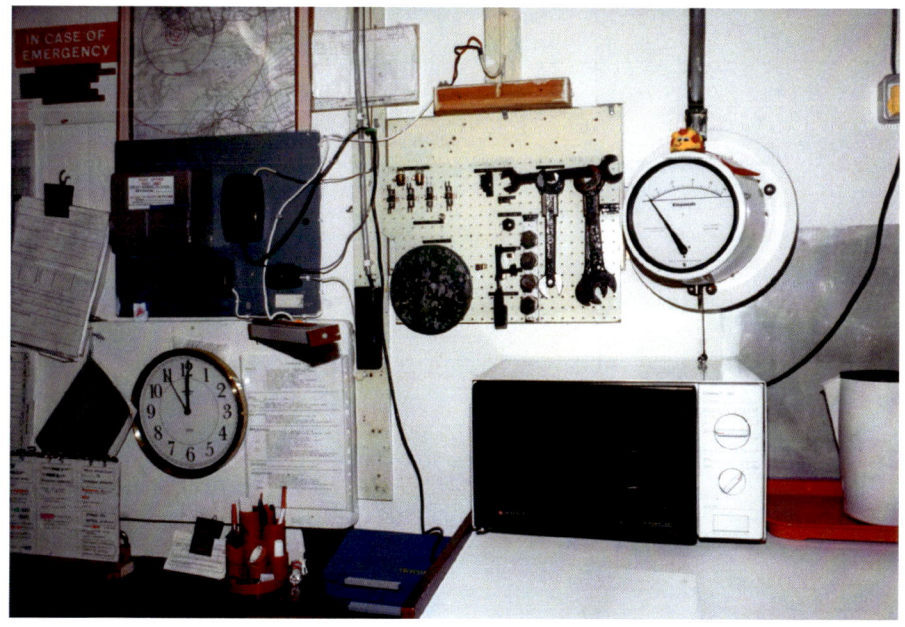

Left: The post was connected to mains power and had its own electricity meter. This allowed mains lighting and the use of a microwave oven and kettle. These photographs were taken in December 1990 – less than a year later the post was closed and was demolished soon after.

ABANDONED POSTS

Master Posts

In every cluster the master post had additional duties including 'deposition' (discontinued in 1968), control of cluster air changes, ROCMET weather reporting and radio operations. Master posts tended to receive new instruments first so that each cluster had a level of capability early in the rollout programme. A number of changes to the structure of the posts were made to allow radios to be used, with initial plans for these changes being drawn up in July 1964. Permanent masts were too vulnerable, so a pneumatic mast manufactured by the Clark Masts company was introduced. Compact enough to be stored in the post, these could be moved to the surface and extended pneumatically to full operational height. Connections for the aerial feed and mast air-line were provided at the surface, feeding down into the monitoring room.

Roadhead, Cumberland

Below: The post at Roadhead in Cumberland was equipped with radio. Copper earthing straps have been added to the front ventilator and anchor points have been positioned to stabilize the mast.

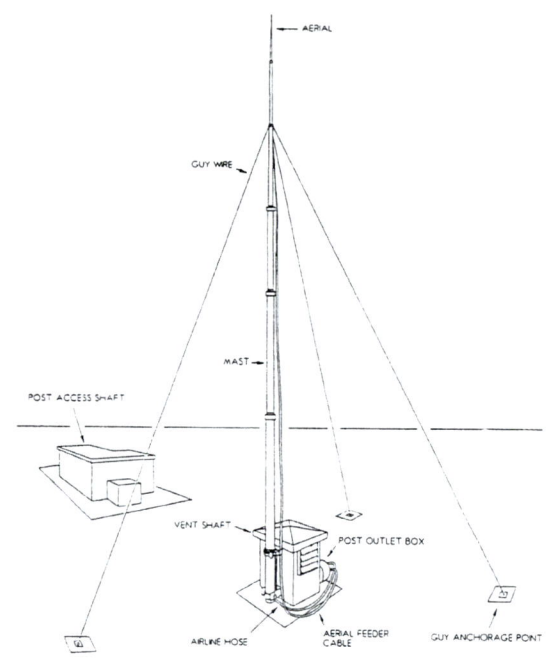

Above: When in operation, the mast was stabilized using guy ropes which were attached to three anchor points. These were usually situated in a triangular pattern around the turret ventilator and consisted of a metal hoop set in a small metal box with a flapped cover. The whole tie down point was set in concrete and usually buried so that only the flapped cover was visible.

ABANDONED POSTS

Above and below left: The connections at the surface were terminated within a round metal unit that protruded from the turret ventilator on the side opposite to the mast bracket. This was known as the 'post outlet box' and looked a little like a top hat. This circular metal cap could be wound on or off on a screw-thread using a special locking bar tool. This cover protected the connection points when the radio was not in use.

Right: A detail photograph of one of the mast anchor points. The flap lid has become detached.

ABANDONED POSTS

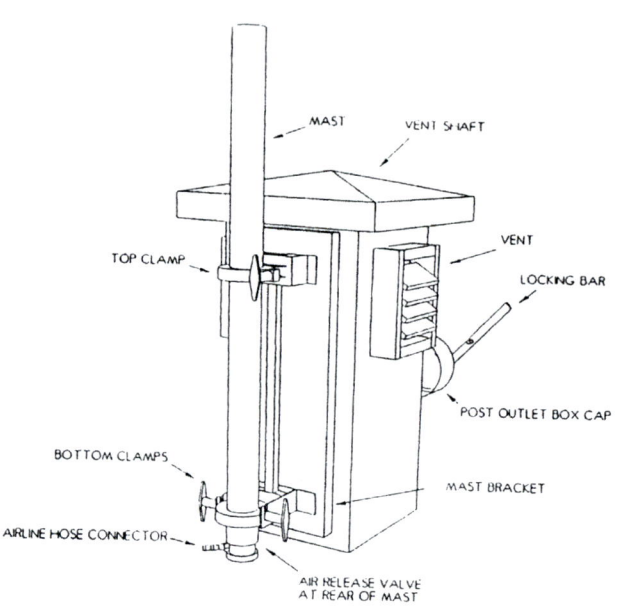

Above: The locking bar for the post outlet box. This is the more common type; there was also a version which was fabricated from a flat plate instead of a bar.

Right: A new metal mounting bracket was attached to the outside of the turret ventilator. The mast could then be clamped to this bracket. The aerial feed had to enter the post to be connected to the radio in the monitoring room. An air hose was also required so that the mast could be pumped up from inside the post. The easiest way to accomplish this was to feed the cable and hose down through the vent shaft to the room below.

Trumpet, Herefordshire

Right and below: These pictures of Trumpet post in Herefordshire show the back of the outlet box with the cables running down the vent shaft. The air-line is the large diameter pipe at the rear, while the aerial feed is the lowest of the three. Note the wooden formers used to build the post have been left lining the inside of the shaft.

The new cable and hose ran down the vent shaft and were guided past the shaft dog-leg and into the monitoring room via two mild steel tubes which were added at the bottom of the shaft. These exited through new holes created below the rear vent opening.

The master posts were re-wired with the introduction of the Burndept radios in the early 1980s. This included a new battery change-over box which allowed radio operation off one battery while the other could be charged. Other changes included the addition of earthing straps inside and outside the post, and the replacement of the large metal radio bracket inside the post with wooden battens which the new, much lighter, radio box could be bolted to. New fixings were also provided which allowed crews to store the mast and dipole in the entrance shaft rather than in the monitoring room.

Above: Inside the post a mounting plate for the Clark's hand-pump was bolted to the floor in the left-hand corner of the monitoring room. It required thirty-five strokes of the pump to erect the mast. Wooden battens were added to the wall to fix the new cabling and air hose.

Above: A view looking inside the 'top hat'. At some point after the original drawings were issued, a connection point for the generator was also added. This is the large two-pin socket. The aerial connection is directly above this. This arrangement meant master post crews no longer had to feed cables down the main entrance shaft when they wanted to recharge the batteries, instead they could plug into the connection point on the ventilator. Internally, this required the creation of a third hole below the vent exit. It is likely that this change took place during the early 1980s upgrades.

Fleetwood, Lancashire

Right: This series of photographs shows the crew of Fleetwood post in Lancashire conducting radio operations in October 1990. Here the crew attach the mast to the ventilator. The mast would be tethered with guy ropes prior to it being extended – these can be seen coiled-up on top of the ventilator. A Yamaha generator can be seen in the background.

Above: In this photograph C/Obs Harry Wilkinson has already fixed the aerial dipole to the top of the mast and is securing the feeder cable. From the early 1980s the mast was stored in the post using fixing brackets which attached it to the side of the entrance shaft ladder. The aerial dipole was stored by using brackets to attach it to the sump pipe running up the entrance shaft.

ABANDONED POSTS

Above: Detail of the dipole connection and the anchor points for the guy ropes.

Below: C/Obs Harry Wilkinson using the Burndept post radio at Fleetwood post.

Page 149

ABANDONED POSTS

Broughton-in-Furness, Cumbria

Above: This post, opened in 1965 as Post H4 of No.22 Group, Carlisle, is one of very few left still configured to the original 1964 master post design. Reallocated to No.21 Group, Preston as Post A2 following the 1968 cuts, it acted as master post to A1 Eskdale (the cluster only consisted of two posts) until 1982. The posts were reorganised again in 1982 with Eskdale reallocated to No.22 Group. Broughton remained in No.21 Group but was re-designated as 17 Post in a cluster with Barrow-in-Furness (16) and Flookburgh (15). The latter was modified to accept the new radio system and became the new master post, leaving Broughton-in-Furness with the original fittings of a first generation master post.

Right: This view shows that the post has not been modified with the addition of earthing straps or other later alterations. Water is getting into the post and the insulating tiles have become detached from the ceiling. The aerial mast and dipole were originally stored in the monitoring-room. The two metal 'U'-shaped brackets fixed to the right-hand wall are a local modification to store either or both of these. The separation between the table and the instrument shelf to the left of the cupboard is also in keeping with the 1964 drawings. The wooden item on the shelf is a homemade support for the PDRM82F, allowing the user to see the LCD screen clearly when sitting down.

ABANDONED POSTS

Right: This detail of the interior of the Broughton-in-Furness post shows the original metal radio bracket still in place. It also shows the batten arrangement and the two holes below the vent for the aerial and air hose. The wire at the top of the picture is the GPO line out for the carrier receiver and the Teletalk.

Longridge, Lancashire

Below left: The Longridge post in May 1983.

Below right: A photograph of the same spot taken twenty-eight years later. The hatch has been damaged and cannot be closed properly so water is starting to build up in the post – the sump is full and the carpet is soaking wet.

ABANDONED POSTS

Above: At the Longridge post in May 1983. *L to R* Lloyd Martin, Terry Tracey and Robert Plummer. The post is set up for radio operations.

Below: The interior of the post has been emptied but the routing of the air hose can be clearly seen running up from bottom left, along the top of the left wall and then to one of the holes under the vent. The three holes below the vent, the two vertical, green painted battens to the right of the BPI extension pipe, and the earthing straps are all evidence that the post was modified to accept the Burndept radio update in the 1980s.

ABANDONED POSTS

Reservoir Posts

Posts near major conurbations were generally more susceptible to vandalism and some were provided with improved compound fencing to deter break-in attempts. A neat solution to the issue was to place posts within areas which were already well protected. Frankley and Erdington posts in No.8, Coventry, Group were both built in existing protected reservoir compounds near large areas of housing in the Birmingham suburbs.

Frankley Reservoir

Below and right: Severn Trent Water manages the Frankley reservoir and agreed to open the post in 2008. Air quality meters were used prior to entry as the post had apparently not been opened since 1992.

ABANDONED POSTS

Right: There is a 'top hat' cover and a mast bracket on the turret ventilator indicating that Frankley was modified for radio installation. However, there are no earthing straps or any of the other internal modifications associated with radio operations. When the 'top hat' cover was removed using the standard tool, it was found that there were no connection sockets installed either. A decision must have been made to reassign the master post after work had started here. At closure, Frankley, Erdington and Shirley posts were in the same cluster, with Shirley equipped with radio and acting as the master post.

Below: The interior of the Frankley post was in excellent condition and included the post diary.

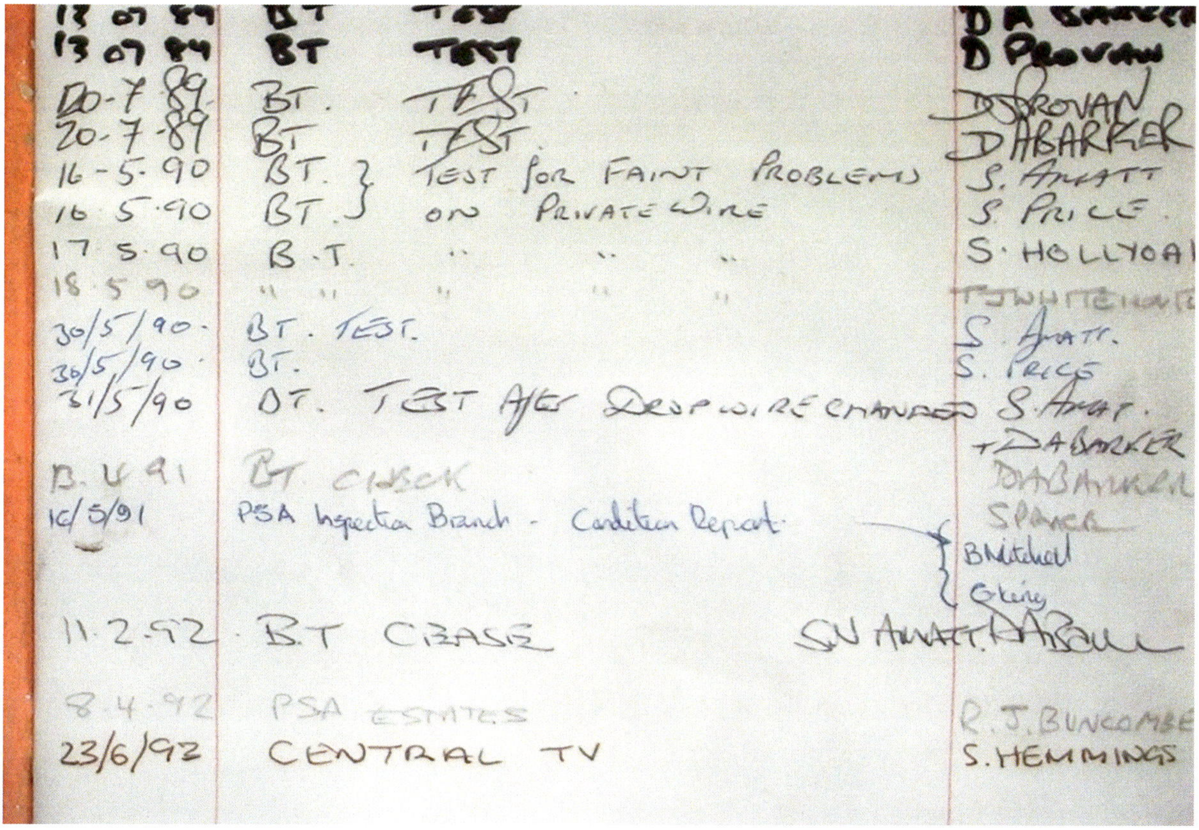
13 07 89 BT TEST D Provan
20-7-89 BT. TEST D Provan
20-7-89 BT TEST D A Barker
16-5-90 BT. } TEST for FAINT PROBLEMS S. Amatt
16 5 90 BT. } on PRIVATE WIRE S. Price
17 5 90 B.T. " " "
18 5 90 " " " " "
30/5/90 BT. TEST. S. Amatt.
30/5/90 BT. S. Price
31/5/90 BT. TEST After DROP WIRE CHANGED S. Amatt. + D A Barker
16/5/91 PSA Inspection Branch - Condition Report.
11.2.92 B.T CEASE
8.4.92 PSA ESTATES R.J. Buncombe
23/6/92 CENTRAL TV S. HEMMINGS

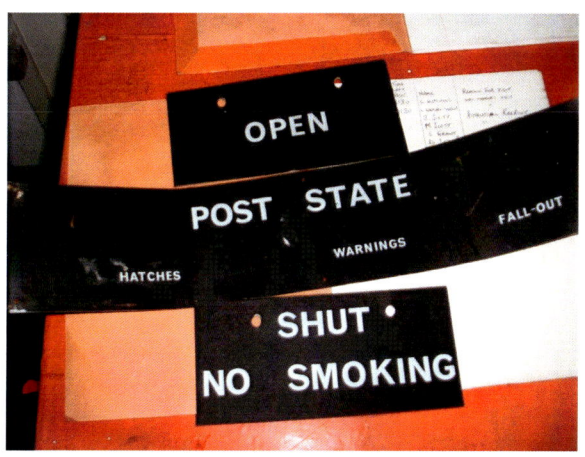

Above: The post diary which shows that on 23 June 1992, S. Hemmings of Central TV was the last official visitor to the site.

Right: In times of crisis there was always a fall-back plan - humour.

Below: These status boards are a unique local addition and are not usually seen in ROC posts.

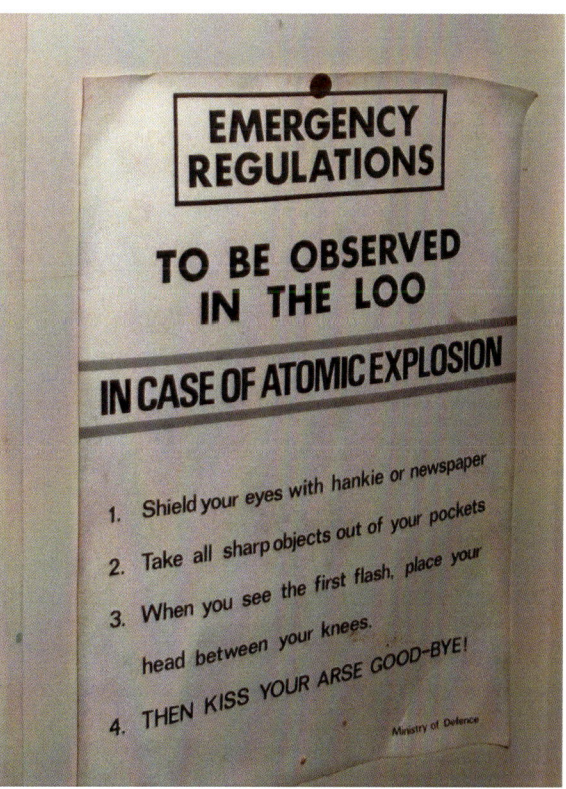

ABANDONED POSTS

Erdington Reservoir

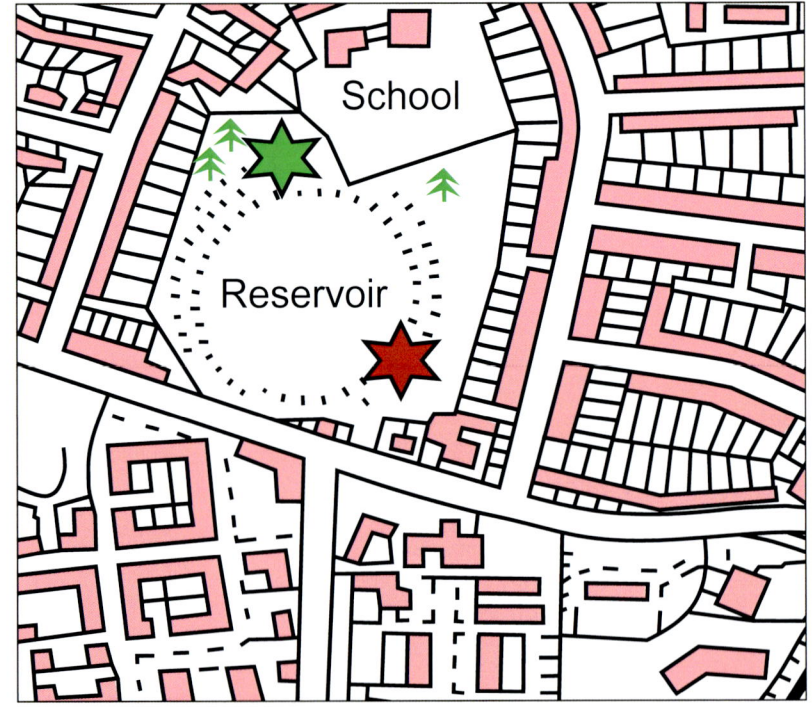

Above and right: During the visit to Frankley, the Severn Trent Water staff mentioned that there was a similar structure at the Erdington reservoir near central Birmingham. A previous Subterranea Britannica trip to Erdington had not found the post and it was presumed to have been demolished. The grid reference listed in the ROC's *Schedule of Posts* located it in the south-east corner of the reservoir, when it was actually in an inner compound at the north-west corner of the reservoir. The red star indicates the believed position (grid ref SP102917) and the green star, the actual.

ABANDONED POSTS

Above and below: The interior of Erdington has been decorated in a similar manner to Frankley post with some additional OXO posters for good measure.

Page 157

Above: Another OXO poster at Erdington, this one with aeronautical overtones.

Above: Besides the ROC, other organisations also had access to the posts for maintenance and testing. This sign on the monitoring room door was standard practice in some groups as a reminder to visitors of their obligation to record their visit.

Below: The site at Erdington was established in 1937 for aircraft reporting and this continued until the early 1960s when the underground post was built. This plotting table was found in the underground post and dates from those earlier aircraft tracking days.

Weather Reporting

A secondary role of the ROC was to provide a weather service. This would supplement the information coming in from the Meteorological Office and also from the eight Upper Air Stations. The Upper Air Stations were situated throughout the UK and gathered data by sending radiosonde equipment into the upper atmosphere using weather balloons. These are still operational today, although with some location changes since the Corps stood down.

This weather information was vital to the Corps and the UKWMO for fallout plotting and each sector control had three trained meteorologists on staff to make interpretations and predictions based on all the data available to them.

In the event that data from the Meteorological Office and the Upper Air Stations was no longer available, the UKWMO could still continue with fallout prediction as all ROC posts could report basic weather information using standard collection and reporting methods.

Bampton, Westmorland

Below: The underground monitoring post at Bampton in a seemingly idyllic setting.

Above: The Bampton post has started to flood. The sump grille has been removed and placed against the wall – a real hazard to the unwary visitor descending the ladder.

Below: One of the surviving artefacts is this homemade weather vane. All crews were trained to provide supplementary weather reports using the SUPMET scheme using codes to signify different weather observations, Cloudy, Thunderstorm etc, and also different visibility distances. Wind speed was determined using the Beaufort Scale and direction reported in 10 degree increments from true north. The circular card shown below was probably placed over the GZI mount and aligned to the cardinal points in line with the GZI orientation. The weather vane would then have been placed on top of the GZI handle.

Above: The crew of this post have modified the old aircraft plotting table by adding a weather vane and an angular scale. They have also added a distance scale, including local landmarks, to make visibility estimates more accurate.

Below: These weather forms were used for collecting and reporting weather information until they were replaced by the new METAR forms in the 1980s.

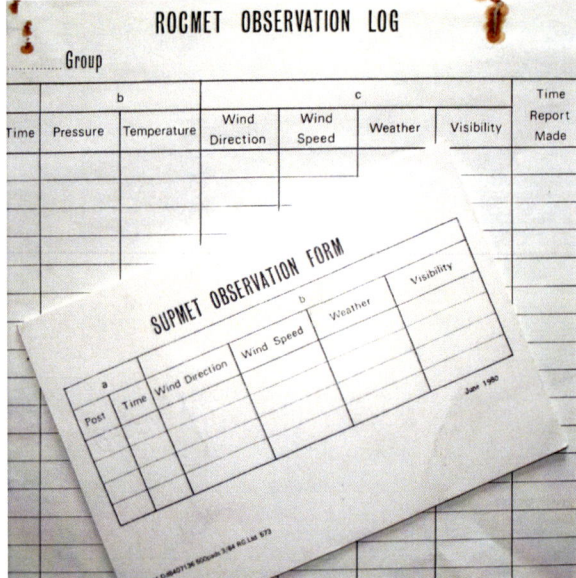

ABANDONED POSTS

Eighty-seven posts within the network were classed as ROCMET posts and these reported additional information including outside air temperature and atmospheric pressure. In practise, this meant that two or three posts in every group could report more detailed weather information. Reporting originally used the ROCMET system which later became known as METAR A.

Kirkbean, Scotland

Below: Kirkbean has several reminders of the weather reporting system that the ROC was using at stand-down. The cloud charts on the wall were commercially produced by the BP oil company and were provided to ROC posts in the 1980s. Originally the reporting of clouds was limited to three categories of coverage: 'No Cloud', 'Partly Cloudy' and 'Overcast'. The new METAR form required much more detail. Coverage was reported in terms of 'Oktas', (eighths of the sky covered). Cloud types and heights were also reported.

Above: This Short & Mason barometer was hung on the monitoring room wall above the working area and enabled the crew to report atmospheric pressure to the nearest millibar.

ABANDONED POSTS

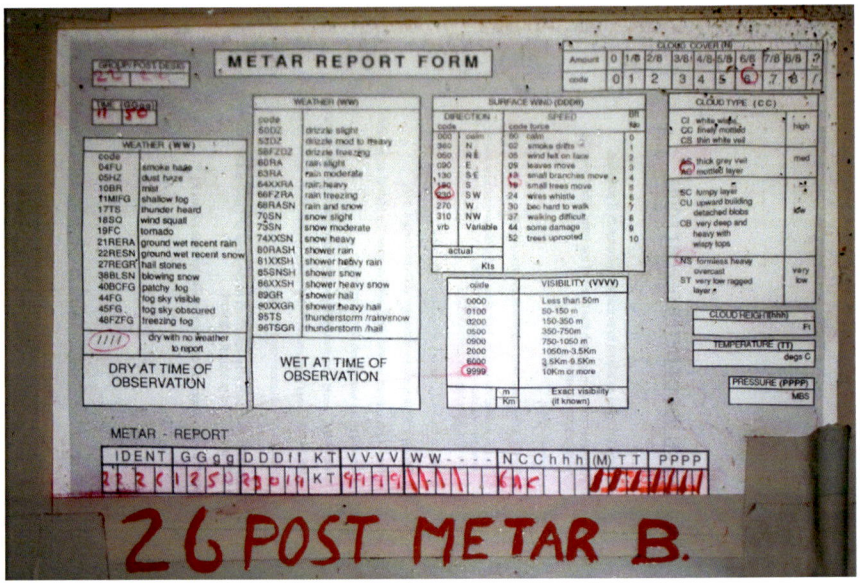

Right: The Kirkbean crew have stuck this METAR form onto a hardboard backing and covered it with a wipe-clean clear plastic covering. They have even added a rudimentary pen holder. METAR B replaced SUPMET as the process for all posts to report basic weather information.

Left: Three meteorological instruments were issued to these posts: the Short & Mason barometer *(previous page)*, the Whirling Frame Psychrometer *(below)* and a Munro anemometer. The Munro anemometer, seen here, was used to provide more accurate wind speed measurements than those possible using the Beaufort Scale.

Below: The Whirling Frame Psychrometer was used to measure the outside air temperature. The device would be spun at least ten times and the temperature reading was then taken from the lower thermometer.

New Uses for Abandoned ROC Posts

Following closure, many posts reverted to the original land owners with the MoD being obliged to demolish the post and return the land to its original condition. In reality the MoD came to agreements with many farmers and would pay them to allow the post to remain on their land, rather than spend more money on an expensive demolition process. The MoD also sold off a large number of the posts on the open market. As many of the sites were on high ground they were snapped up by companies as possible mast sites for the then nascent mobile telephone industry.

Some posts were purchased by private individuals and ex-ROC personnel with a view to preserving a piece of history, while others were purchased as investments for possible commercial or residential development. As the years go by the ownership of some posts can be difficult to determine, with some landowners not even being aware that the structures exist on their land. On many sites where there is no active management, posts have been adopted for a range of purposes, from being used by homeless people sleeping rough to acting as hiding places for the recent sport of 'geocaching', where participants use GPS systems to hide and seek containers called 'geocaches'.

Below: This extremely well protected site at Powick in Worcestershire has been developed as a communications site. The underground post can still be found in a well-protected inner compound to the right rear of the larger mast compound.

Below: J. H. Walter was the Lincolnshire-based firm that handled the sale of several post sites in the early 2000s. This post at Baumber was back on the market in 2011 and beat the guide price to raise £11,500 at auction. The post has been heavily modified inside with the addition of new internal cladding, improved security and a wood-burning stove with the FSM pipe acting as a chimney. Dent post in Yorkshire had a similar stove arrangement and featured in the Telegraph Magazine in January 2008 when the then owner was advertising the bunker as an overnight holiday destination.

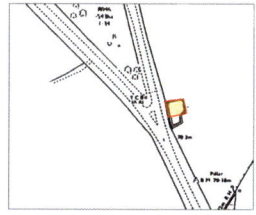

Opposite and right: Markfield post in Leicestershire has been extensively modified and now incorporates a very large commercial communications mast which protrudes from where the turret ventilator used to be. The hatch is secured with a large metal plate and when visited in 2011 was undergoing maintenance work as evidenced by the paint pots and brushes around the mast.

Above left and right: Mundford post is hidden away in Thetford Forest in Norfolk. The ROC crew built a second underground shelter while the post was still in service and this was used for storage. It still has a few bits and pieces left in it today.

Left: This post at Pleasley in Nottinghamshire now sits in the back garden of a farm house and has been converted into use as a wine cellar. Other posts have ended up as water tanks (for example Dulwich) and Fulford post is literally a cellar – the surface features were removed and a house built on the site. Entrance to the post is now through a trapdoor in the hallway.

Above: This post at Brampton now sits in the (rather extended) back garden of a private house and has been adorned with a range of weather measurement apparatus, including a Campbell-Stokes sunshine recorder which sits on top of the forward ventilator.

Below: Some posts in private ownership, like this one at Stottesdon in Shropshire, offer superb views of the countryside and many are used as retreats and weekend bolt-holes.

ABANDONED POSTS

Cley-next-the-Sea

Right: One of the earliest 're-uses' was of this post at Cley in Norfolk. The new use of this 1968 closure for bird watching was reported in the *ROC Journal* in 1985 – one of the few occasions when a picture of a post actually appeared in the magazine.

Below: Cley post is still used and owned by the Norfolk Ornithology Association today. The sloping ground has been cut away on one side and a door and window inserted to provide a bird hide.

UNDERGROUND POST WITH A VIEW

On the North Norfolk coast stands what must be one of the most unusual ROC Posts in the country.

The former 6/H1 (Cley Post) has been converted to a bird observation point and wardens post by the Norfolk Ornithologists Association.

The earth bank on one side of the post has been removed and a door and window cut into the side.

The post which is now known as "Walsey Hill, Migration Watch Point" is just off the A149 between the villages of Cley and Salthouse, map reference TG062441.

The site was first used by the Corps in 1953, the present underground post being built in 1958. The post was closed in the reorganisation in 1968 and purchased by the Norfolk Ornithologists Association in 1973.

The site is well worth a visit by Corps members who will find the warden very helpful.

Perhaps other members know of unusual posts in their area and I am sure that this would be of interest to readers of "The Journal".   Chief Observer T. H. Burlingham, 6/74

ABANDONED POSTS

Seismic Stations

The Strategic Arms Limitation Talks of the 1970s, (SALT 1 and SALT 2), gave rise to a need to police and verify underground nuclear testing. This fell to the Atomic Weapons Establishment at Aldermaston, who installed seismic equipment at certain ROC posts to monitor underground earth tremors. The posts with seismic equipment were at St. Breward, South Creake, Middlesmoor and Barham in England and Lampeter and Llanuwchllyn in Wales. Sharpitor post was also used for this purpose until 1983. Wroughton post has also recently been used as a seismic station, although by the British Geographical Survey rather than the Atomic Weapons Establishment.

By 1994 Barham had been abandoned but equipment was still functioning in South Creak post when visited in 1998. The six posts were included as potential monitoring stations for use with the Comprehensive Test Ban Treaty which came into being in 1996. However, by 2010 the equipment had been removed from both South Creake and Middlesmoor. The three remaining posts at Lampeter, St. Breward and Llanuwchllyn all underwent a modification programme during the late 2000s. All the posts have similar sensor equipment installed, although all three have different types of satellite communication dishes attached. It is presumed that these posts are still operating as seismic stations for the Atomic Weapons Establishment.

Below: Multiple BT boxes were added to route the signal from the seismic equipment out of the post and onwards to the AWE Blacknest Seismological Recording Centre. These photographs were taken at St. Breward post in Cornwall in the early 1980s while the post was still being operated by the ROC. The seismograph station was part of the UKNET and the Chief Observer had to send a monthly form back to the AWE which included readings from the equipment operating inside the post.

Below: The system used was the Seismometer SP Mk II. The main sensor was buried in a trench outside the post. Equipment inside the post included this cylindrical unit and voltmeter arrangement.

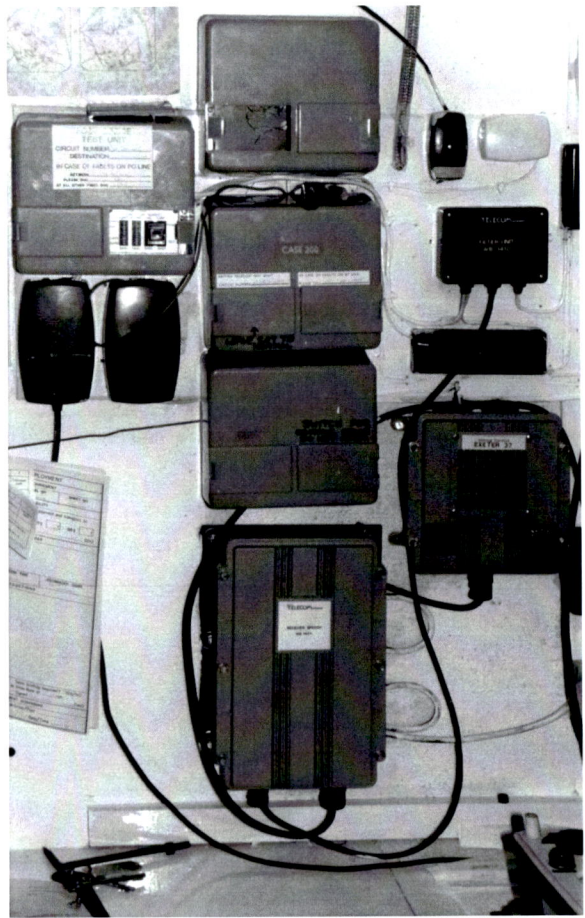

ABANDONED POSTS

Right: St. Breward post. When visited in 2006 the post had acquired two white metal boxes, some form of sensor and a large communications dish. Apparently the post is still operated by the Atomic Weapons Establishment. The new modifications suggest that data is now transmitted via the dish rather than over the GPO lines, which was the method used when the seismic equipment was originally installed.

Below left and right: Llanuwchllyn, Merionethshire. This post was one of six identified as being used as seismic stations. When visited in March 2008 the post was in the process of being modified and the mound next to the post had been dug up – presumably to modify or replace the seismic sensor. By March 2009 the modification programme had been completed and the post had acquired an external sensor and metal box the same as at St. Breward and Lampeter. A large communications dish had also been bolted to the side of the ventilator.

Chapter 8

RESTORED POSTS

Restoring ROC underground monitoring posts has increased in popularity in recent years. The internet has brought renewed interest in the subject and has attracted a younger generation, many of whom would have been too young to serve when the Corps closed down, and quite a few who had not even been born in 1991. However, immediately after stand-down there were only a few attempts made to preserve the posts. Ex-observers at Dersingham in Norfolk and Rushden Spencer in Staffordshire were some of the first to maintain and restore posts. They were followed by private individuals when posts were sold off in the mid-1990s; Knockholt in Kent being an example. Some were subsequently opened to the public on a limited basis, while others have been restored as private museums, such as at West Harptree in Somerset. Interest increased in the late 1990s as Cold War subjects became more popular with Subterranea Britannica members and the society conducted a nationwide survey of the remaining posts.

A further round of auctions was held in the early 2000s as posts originally bought by communications companies were sold off. Again, some were restored or changed hands and then restored; Machynlleth in Mid Wales being an example. Posts continue to come up for sale; several feature on online auction site, eBay, every year and appear to easily find new owners.

Many individuals and groups have restored posts in the last few years without having any ownership rights but by making agreements with landowners; posts at Kettering, Skipsea, Chopgate and Cuckfield being examples. Other posts are kept essentially unrestored but are re-equipped occasionally and opened to the public; for example Holbeach in Lincolnshire and Broadway in Worcestershire.

This chapter in no way attempts to cover all the posts that have been restored in the UK; the numbers have now grown to the point where English Heritage have little concern that this aspect of the Cold War infrastructure will be lost. The chapter does try to show the different types of challenges faced by post restorers and the results of that effort. All the post restorers featured are keen to point out that equipment and paperwork seen in the photographs are only on display during open days and that at all other times are removed from the posts. Many of the posts are open to the public on a limited basis and appropriate internet searches will soon determine the latest information.

Below: Dersingham, one of the first ROC posts to be restored.

Brandsby, Yorkshire

Right: The post in 2009 before John Jenkinson's restoration started. The post structure had been exposed when the farmer, whose field it is sited in, removed the earth mound to maximize his field area. The original protective brick tanking can be seen around the entrance shaft and ventilator.

This photograph shows that the concrete apron around the entrance shaft has been badly damaged in the past. The BPI blast pipe appears to be missing completely.

Left: The post painted and the damaged wooden louvers replaced. Note the GPO conduit in the right foreground, which has been badly bent.

Right: To quickly rebuild the mound, John hit on the idea of using bales of old tyres to fill the void and then to add an earth covering. Here a mini-digger is preparing the ground. Note that a replacement BPI pipe has been fabricated.

Left: Bales of tyres packed around the FSM pipe. The tyres quickly fill up the space which used to be a purely earthen mound.

Right: Another truckload of tyres being delivered to the site.

Left: The mini-digger was used to move earth onto the tyre-bales. Half the mound has already been covered. One of the team does some spade work to finish it off.

Right: The finished mound after a long day's work.

RESTORED POSTS

Right: The finished post in 2010. The mound has now grassed over and there is no way of knowing that it was created by using tyre-bales. John is also a military vehicle enthusiast and the Landrover is painted in the distinctive scheme of the British Army's Berlin Brigade, stationed in Berlin during the Cold War.

Left: John Jenkinson and Paul Brown in observer uniform outside the restored Brandsby post, which is approximately fifteen miles north of York. John bought the post in 2009 and since finishing the restoration has opened it to interested members of the public on several occasions. John's next project is to dismantle the *Orlit B* at Tollerton and transport it the eight miles back to Brandsby to re-erect it so that visitors can appreciate the ROC aircraft plotting role.

Chop Gate, Yorkshire

Right: Ex-ROC members, including David Hugill and Des Brown, have visited Chop Gate post since its restoration and have provided archive images of when it was in operation. This photograph shows members of the crew at the post in the 1980s.

RESTORED POSTS

Right: Fifteen-year-old Jack Hanlon got interested in the ROC after visiting and photographing a few of the local underground posts. He decided to approach the owner of Chop Gate ROC post to see if he could restore it. Chop Gate is owned by ex-Observer David Hugill. He and ex-Chief Observer Des Brown had kept the post secure after stand-down but had not restored it. Enthusiast Nat Ham volunteered to help Jack and, by August 2010 they were ready for their first open day. This photograph shows Jack *(seated)* and Nat *(standing)* in the restored monitoring room.

Below: The post as Jack and Nat found it. David Hugill and Des Brown had opened the post in 2004 to show a few people around but they did not have access to any of the old equipment. Jack approached the owners of Reeth, Croft and Middlesmoor posts who all subsequently donated items to help with the restoration.

Below: The operational area full of paperwork and equipment in the fully restored post. Fellow post restorer Ed Gamble kindly loans his GZI and BPI for Chop Gate open days. Now that the restoration has been completed, Jack and Nat hope to open the post to the public two or three times a year.

Page 173

RESTORED POSTS

Location 'Classified'

Above and below: The interior of the post fully equipped as it would have been at stand-down in 1991. The newspapers add a bit of 'set-dressing' to reflect events during the 1991 Gulf War.

This post was in extremely good condition when visited and was subsequently sympathetically restored with help from various members of an online enthusiasts forum.

The post sits in farmland and when the farm changed ownership the new owner found that he did not actually own the post or access rights to the field it was in. However, after a lot of effort he was finally able to purchase the post from the MoD. Although the farmer was happy for the restoration to go ahead, he did not want the location made public and does not encourage visitors.

Page 174

RESTORED POSTS

Above: The monitoring room. The gloomy lighting is representative of typical interior conditions in the posts.

Right: This *Eltex* toilet is still in its original packaging. The standard, government-issue, 'shiny' toilet paper has been replaced by this crew with something slightly softer.

Below: Some ROC humour.

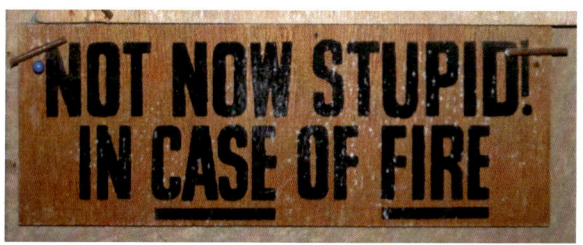

RESTORED POSTS

Surface to be painted	Surface Material	Primer (1)	Undercoat (2)	Finish (3)	Recoat Time	Colour (Finish)	Notes
External surfaces of access hatch and ventilator shaft	Concrete	Dulux Primer Sealer	Dulux Drab	Dulux Drab	hrs. 1. 16/24 2. 16 3. 8	Olive 58 B54-050	Brush
Access hatch cover	Steel	Dulux Metal Primer Chromate	Dulux Drab	Dulux Drab	1. 16/24 2. 16 3. 8	Olive 58 B54-050	Brush
Ventilator louvres	Wood	*Wood primer White lead	Dulux Drab	Dulux Drab	1. 16/24 2. 16 3. 8	Olive 58 B54-050	Brush *Handle with care – wash hands thoroughly after use.
Probe Pipe – External BPI Pipe – External	Steel Steel	Dulux Metal Primer Chromate	Dulux Drab	Dulux Drab	1. 16/24 2. 16 3. 8	Olive 58 B54-050	Brush
Interior – walls, ceiling, access shaft, closet	Concrete	None	Dulux Super Cover Acrylic Vinyl Emulsion	Same as u/c	1. – 2. 1–4 3. 1–4	White	Brush or roller
Floor & Sump interior	Concrete	None	None	∅ Dulux Floor Paint	1. – 2. – 3. 16	Buffalo B53-037	Apply 1st coat thinned 50% white spirit – sub. coats unthinned. Brush 1st coat – roller sub. coats. ∅ Gives off heavy vapour – open all ventilators and hatch cover.
Interior woodwork – doors, tables, cupboard and misc.	Wood	Wood Primer a. Leadless White, or b. Dulux Acrylic Primer/ u/c	Dulux White	+ Dulux Gloss	1a.16/24 1b. 4 2. 16 3. 8	White	If Dulux Acrylic Primer/undercoat is used, the u/c (col 2) can be omitted. Brush. + Dulux Super 3 may be used as an alternative
Interior metalwork – BPI pipe, probe pipe flange, ventilators	Steel	Dulux Metal Primer Chromate	Dulux White	+Dulux Gloss	1. 16/24 2. 16 3. 8	White	Brush
Ladder Sump Grid	Steel	Dulux Metal Primer Chromate	–	Dulux Aluminium Paint	1. 16/24 2. – 3. 16		Brush

General note on primers:
Use only on bare surfaces

Above, right and below: The observers on this post were extremely well organised and the post was very well maintained. The above paint-chart lists everything required to keep the post in good order and the check-charts for tools and instruments ensure that tasks are clear and well defined.

Time/Readings	Instrument checks/Actions
0800	R.S.M. No 2 (3) F.S.M. (2) B.P.I.(3) Time Check (2)
1200	Dosimeters GZ.I. Papers March 21st – Sept 21st
1600	F.S.M.
2400	F.S.M.
Even Hour	3 Previous Readings, Up Plus, Down Minus, Same Minus
0x1 rph	First Fallout
0x3 rph	Fire Maroons
350 rph	Prepare Probe for shielded readings
400 rph	Retract Probe to reading of 40
Falls to 400 rph	Extension of Probe
Below 0x3 B.P.I.	Log do not report

Above Ground Tools & Components. No 2 Observer		
No.	Item	
1	Cock Wrench	
1	BPI Baffle	
2	Double Ended Spanners	
1	Single Ended Spanner	
1	Plastic dome cover ring & studs	
1	Replacement Gasket	
1	Spade & Plastic Bags	
1	Siren, Minus Handle	
1	G. Z. I, Loaded	
Returned Tools & Components		
1	Cock Wrench	
1	B.P.I. Blast Pipe Cap	
2	Double Ended Spanners	
1	Single Ended Spanner	
1	Cover Plate from F.S.M. Probe	
4	Sets of Nuts & Bolts	
1	New or Old Gasket	
1	Spade	
Prepare Maroons Close Toilet Door Prepare B.P.I., F.S.M.		

RESTORED POSTS

Above and below: Two more photographs showing the post with the standard equipment in place.

Right: This shelf has been added by the crew to improve storage. The FSM probe hole in the ceiling could be difficult to reach, hence the homemade step. The ribbed metal frame on the shelf below is an arm splint. This would be used to secure an injured limb until the crew member could be evacuated.

RESTORED POSTS

Above: The team who set up the 'Classified' post for the photographs above give the salute: *L to R* Jamie Cross, Craig Smith and son, Jonathon, in ROC uniform jacket, and Mark Russell.

Cuckfield, Sussex

Right: Mark Russell approached the local Parish Council with the idea of restoring this post at Cuckfield so that members of the public could visit on open days and see how the ROC lived and worked underground during the Cold War. Mark was later joined by Ed Combes and between them they now provide tours of the site when the post is open. The post sits on private property and visits are by appointment only.

RESTORED POSTS

Above: The post part-way through the restoration process. It took Mark from late 2009 until April 2010 to complete the major part of the restoration – "eight long months of cold lonely days," according to Mark, who undertook the majority of the restoration single-handedly with only a small radio for company.

Right: The interior was in good condition when Mark took on the post although he still needed to source equipment and acquire some bunk beds. The First Aid cupboard is a non-standard piece of furniture that the observers added to the post.

Left: The finished interior. Mark has managed to source most of the equipment required – the post radio being a recent addition.

RESTORED POSTS

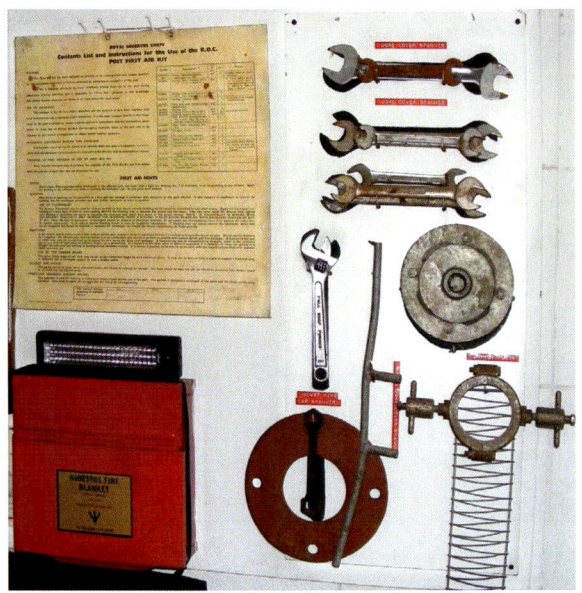

Above: Detail of the tool board in the monitoring room. The circular item at bottom right is a clamp for the radio mast. Mark supplements the lighting in the post by using battery-powered LED lamps – one of these can be seen on top of the fire-blanket box.

Below: Cuckfield has had a long association with the ROC as recorded by this plaque which is attached to the access shaft. The original post sign is now on display at the Newhaven Fort Museum and this also states: 'One of the first posts in Britain'. The late Derek Wood, author of *Attack Warning Red*, the definitive published history of the ROC, served at this post as an observer. Derek's widow has since visited the restored post when she signed copies of *Attack Warning Red* for Mark and Ed.

Above: Typical period items include the standard ROC teapot, 'Glitto' scouring powder and a variety of tinned and dried foodstuffs. The stacks of cylindrical tins on the bottom left are 'Tommy cookers', used to heat food.

Below: Storage space in the posts was limited. The chemical toilet closet invariably became an additional storage area. The foul-weather jacket on the hanger was recovered from an abandoned post in a very poor condition and had to be washed multiple times to make it presentable. There was usually only one toilet in a post and they were rarely used.

Herriard, Hampshire

Right: Andrew Ramek was interested in the Cold War and found out more about the ROC after a visit to the 'Secret Bunker' tourist attraction at Hack Green in Cheshire.

Left: On his next visit to Hack Green, in March 2008, Andrew took along this model of an ROC post, which set off a chain of events leading to him taking out a lease on Herriard post less than two months later.

Right: Herriard was opened in March 1959 and closed in 1991. The diagonal slot in the wall of the hatch entrance may be a cable access point. The original posts were designed to be built with two 3-inch-square holes in the access shaft wall at the surface, one for the sump pipe and one for cable access. Changes to the design in 1959 moved the cable access point and stated that the hole in the shaft wall should be grouted closed.

RESTORED POSTS

Above: Andy cleared the site on his first visit and found that there were many problems with the post. The concrete on the turret vent was damaged to such an extent that only the exposed reinforcing bars held the structure together. The blanking plates for the probe and the blast pipe were also missing and the hatch mechanism had fallen off.

Left: The interior was in reasonable condition but the rotary sump pump had been removed and some of the furniture needed repair.

Opposite: The entrance shaft and hatch partially through the restoration process.

Above: This photograph was taken while Andy was re-wiring the post. The box in the foreground contained the original post battery while the crate in the background is for the siren, which has since been removed. The three bolts sticking out of the floor were used to bolt down the hand-pump for erecting the radio mast, indicating that Herriard was a radio post.

Right: This detail, taken during the restoration of the interior, shows the sump grille and a new sump pump in place.

RESTORED POSTS

Above left and right: These photographs, taken during the restoration, show the turret ventilator with fresh cement and the hatch mechanism repaired and repainted.

Below and opposite: The interior and exterior of the post after the restoration was completed. The amount of work done can be clearly seen when compared with the previous photographs of the post in its original condition.

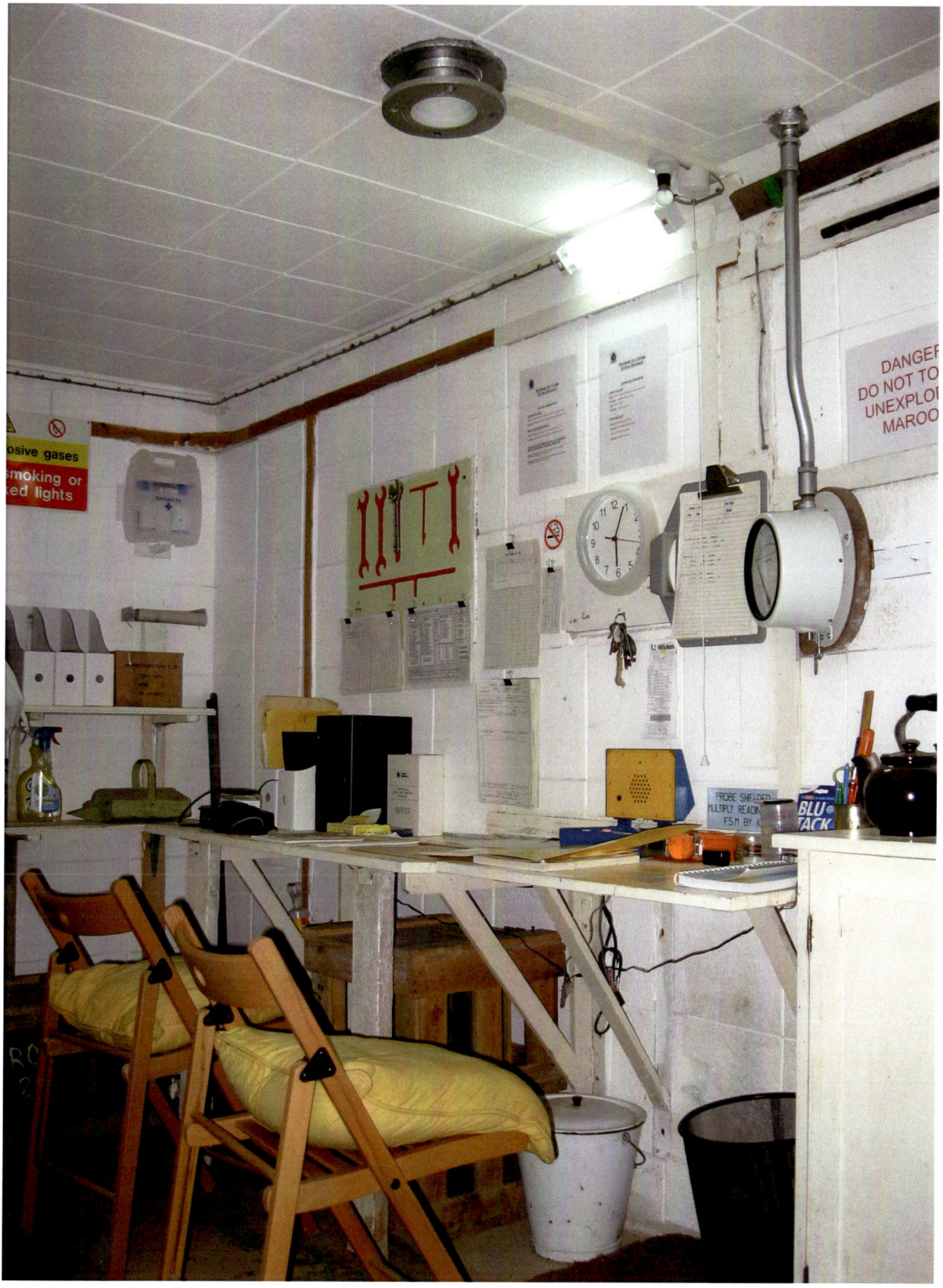

RESTORED POSTS

Above: Kettering post has been restored and painted in a very light green colour scheme which is reminiscent of the 'anti-flash' white schemes of the 1960s. Note the unusual exposed conduit, modified to take the telephone line underground, in the right foreground. The steps were added in the 1980s to aid one of the crew members who suffered from polio.

Kettering

Penshurst Subterranea Britannica member John Smiles bought this post in Kent in 2002 when a large number of posts were sold off by the Crown Castle communications company. These had been bought as potential satellite phone mast sites and were subsequently sold off when the company decided they were no longer required.

Below left and right: John's first task at Penshurst was to clear up the site and paint the exterior.

RESTORED POSTS

Above: Penshurst post was flooded to chest height due to a leak that was eventually traced to the telecoms access pipe.

Below: John pumped the post dry in July 2003. This was relatively easy compared to another of his projects which was to help pump out the huge former RAF *ROTOR* radar bunker at Wartling in Sussex.

Right: Penshurst after it was pumped out. John left the post for about a year so that it would dry out and then returned in the spring of 2004 to clean, paint and refurbish the original fittings. The post had a raised wooden floor which was rotten and had to be stripped out. John also rewired the post and rebuilt the desks.

RESTORED POSTS

Above and right: The post after the restoration work was finished. John now holds occasional open days when people can venture inside. The post is empty and locked at all other times.

Above: A non-standard holder for the FSM. The item on the left is the Fixed Survey Meter probe head.

Below: The battery change-over switch. This is the rarer 'Scottish Office' type which had an internal battery test unit. When the 'test' button was pressed a red, yellow or green LED would light up, depending on the state of charge of the battery.

Below: The exterior of the post fully restored.

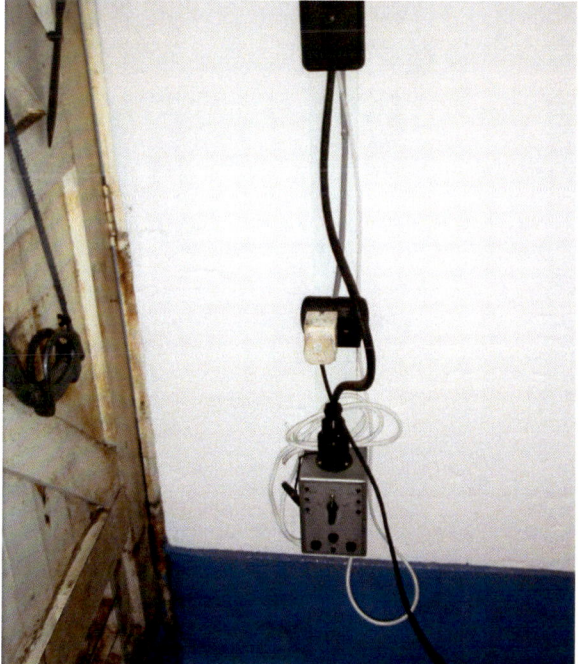

RESTORED POSTS

Portadown, Northern Ireland

Alistair McCann has had a long standing interest in military aviation and Northern Irish heritage and has been a long-time member of the Ulster Aviation Society.

Alistair's interest in the ROC started when he found some of his late grandfather's papers. His grandfather had served in the Corps during the war monitoring aircraft from the various road and rail bridges on the Firth of Forth while at veterinary college at Edinburgh, and later served briefly with the Corps in Northern Ireland.

Alistair visited all the remaining posts in Northern Ireland during 2006 and 2007 but did not decide to restore a post until 2009, when he took on Ballynahinch post in County Down.

After completing Ballynahinch, Alistair decided to restore Portadown post in County Armagh. This had good access and was in very good condition already. Minor repairs, cleaning, painting and a re-wire were quickly completed and the post was opened on 25 June 2010. The first open day soon followed and was a great success with over seventy visitors including the local media and BBC News, who conducted a live broadcast from inside the post.

Below: Ballynahinch was Alistair's first post restoration project. Alistair completed this project, but the post was in a remote location and difficult to get to from the road. Portadown post was much more accessible so he decided to shift his attention to restoring this site.

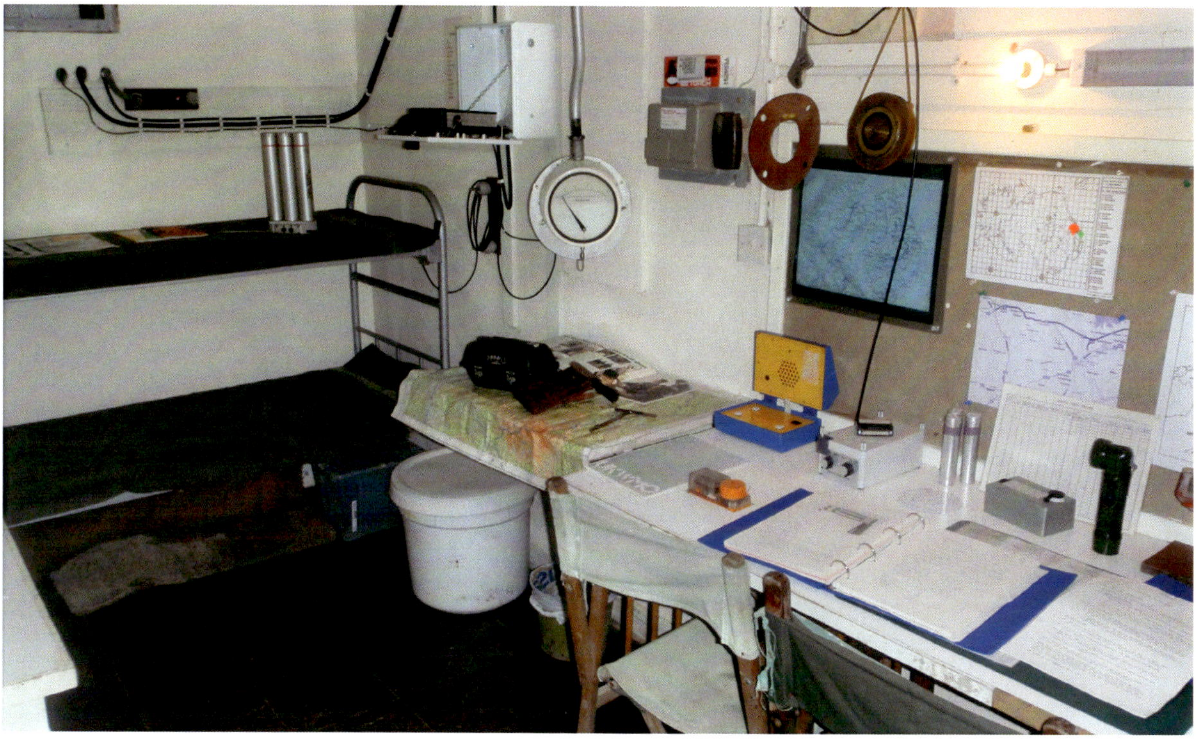

RESTORED POSTS

Above and below: The furniture is on the right-hand side of the room when entering it, meaning that the post was built incorrectly to the original plans and is one of many 'mirror' posts. The radio and external mast bracket indicate that Portadown was a master post. The weather instruments on the equipment shelf would have been used for enhanced weather reporting as part of the ROCMET system, although Portadown was never a ROCMET post while in service.

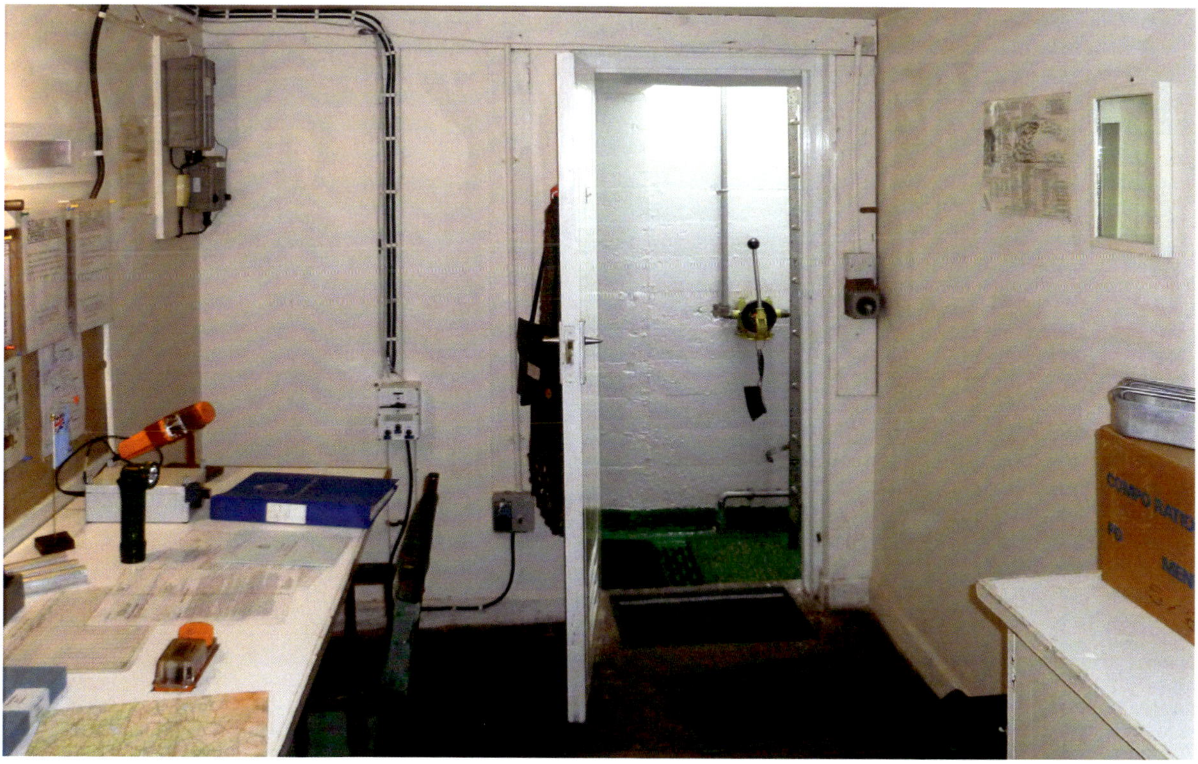

RESTORED POSTS

Left: The restored exterior of Portadown post. The post was opened in 1960 and closed in 1968. It was subsequently reopened in the 1980s when the post at Lurgan was closed for security reasons.

Below: One of several open days held at the post. Alistair McCann is to the left of the photograph in ROC uniform.

The Royal Observer Corps in Northern Ireland

Above: No.31 Group on parade at Banbridge in the 1980s. The ROC was not established in Northern Ireland until relatively late into the history of the Corps, with the first man being officially enrolled into what became No.31 Group on 1 April 1954.

Right: There was no Second World War ROC post infrastructure or sites to use and develop when the ROC formed in Northern Ireland. The *Orlit* post building programme on the UK mainland was almost complete by mid-1954 and these structures were not used in Northern Ireland. Instead the Northern Ireland aircraft posts were built from brick to a similar general design to the mainland prefabricated *Orlits*. This photograph shows a crew on an aircraft plotting exercise, probably at Armagh post.

RESTORED POSTS

Above: Both surface and elevated structures were built. This post at Hillsborough has a similar overall layout to a mainland *Orlit B* but the position of the doorway and other details show that it is a structure unique to the Corps in Northern Ireland.

Right: Many of the Northern Ireland underground posts were built during the early part of the programme, starting in 1957. There was a high degree of change in the post establishment because, during the Troubles, posts were closed, and earlier closures reopened, as security threats materialised. A unique feature of the Northern Ireland underground posts was that the posts equipped with radio had a separate mast mount rather than having the mast attached to the turret ventilator. No.31 Group never operated the original *Countryman* system and was not equipped with radio until the 1980s Burndept system was introduced.

RESTORED POSTS

Right: In 1966 No.31 Group was operating fifty-eight posts in fifteen clusters. This reduced to thirty-three after the 1968 cuts. By 1972 the security situation in Northern Ireland had deteriorated to such an extent that posts were rarely used and training was confined to cluster meetings and attendance at the Group Headquarters. By 1976, four of the thirty-three posts had been sealed, four were classed as 'Cat B – difficult to visit' and five were classed as 'Cat C – dangerous to visit'.

```
                          SECURITY - NORTHERN IRELAND
"SECURITY

1. In recent months the external difficulties facing the Corps in Northern
Ireland have increased and it has been decided to issue firm instructions for
the safety and guidance of all members. These instructions are of a temporary
nature and will be relaxed as soon as possible.

2. With one single exception noted below uniform is not to be worn on any
occasion whatsoever. The single exception is that it may be worn by officers
inside the protected Headquarters building at Lisburn. However uniform is not to
be carried frequently between home and Group Headquarters but arrangements made,
when desirable, to store the uniform at the Headquarters so that it can be put on
for duty.

3. Post and Crew meetings are to continue normally, Head Observers of Posts are
to consider their local knowledge and experience when arranging them and are to
consult HQ No 31 Group in cases of doubt.

4. Cluster Meetings are to continue normally, Group Officers are always to
consult HQ No 31 Group on timings and dates before making arrangements.

5. Any other meetings proposed are to be referred to HQ No 31 Group before
the arrangements are made.

6. Routine inspection visits to Posts are to be made at random from time to
time but Head Observers and Group Officers are always to consider their local
knowledge and refer to HQ No 31 Group before any such visits are made.

7. In arranging any meetings no members are to be placed at undue risk.
All members to take normal precautions by not discussing meetings, publicly,
by holding them in closed quarters and by checking entry.

8. It is with regret that I face the ceasing of the wearing of uniform but I
feel that it would be unfair to members in Northern Ireland who have shown and
are showing their support for the Crown, and to the Security Forces, to continue
to wear uniform. It is hoped that these measures can be relaxed soon and that
meetings can be attended again in the manner consistent with the traditions
of the Royal Observer Corps.

                                           Signed    K TERRY
                                                     Observer Captain
                                                     Western Sector Commandant
                                                     ROYAL OBSERVER CORPS
```

Left: In 1978 the then Group Commandant, Obs Cdr Jack Barnes, convinced ROC Headquarters that a limited reopening of some posts was feasible and most were soon open again. This photograph shows the crew of Portadown post in the mid-1980s.

Right: In later years there were still security issues and several posts were abandoned due to attacks by armed groups in the 1980s. Vulnerable posts were armoured with steel plating to protect entrance and ventilator shafts. This post at Downpatrick still has the steel protective plating in place.

RESTORED POSTS

Rushton Spencer, Staffordshire

It could be argued that the crew of Rushton Spencer never stood down at all. They decided to approach the local farmer with a view to occupying the post after the official stand-down and this was agreed. The owners had a relative who was a wartime observer, and felt that keeping the post open would be a good way to retain their link with the Corps. The crew and other ex-observers then turned the post into a museum and were in the fortunate position of being able to acquire a wide range of equipment as the rest of the Corps stood down.

Above: Members of the Rushton Spencer ROC Post Museum carrying out maintenance on the post in May 2011. *L to R*
L/Obs Alan Heron (19/21 Grp),
Obs Dave Taylor (16 Grp),
Obs Martin Chester (16 Grp),
C/Obs Dave Arnold (16 Grp),
Obs Nick Garside (21 Grp).

Right: The post is very exposed on high ground and regular maintenance is necessary to keep it in good condition. In this picture the team have been using an angle-grinder to remove the old paint prior to repainting the exterior of the post.

RESTORED POSTS

Right: This *Orlit A* was recovered from Cheslyn Hay post site and erected at Rushton Spencer in 1999. The site also features a flag pole and a large beacon.

Right: The interior of the post has been modified by adding a shelf onto the top of the cupboard and moving the beds around. The ROC crest that can be seen on the wall behind the GZI, and the tote board behind the FSM dome on the cupboard, were both acquired from the Shewsbury Group Headquarters building when it was closed. The post is lit with an 18 watt filament bulb in this photograph – three times the power of the original bulb.

Right: This photograph was taken with the fluorescent light turned on. This was the only lighting available operationally in the later years of service and shows the typically gloomy interior. Prior to this, the lighting was even poorer, with only a 6 watt filament bulb in place during the early years. The crew have wired the post so that either the filament bulb or the fluorescent light can be used. Illuminating the interior more brightly would have been possible but would have increased battery discharge and hence reduced the time between recharging.

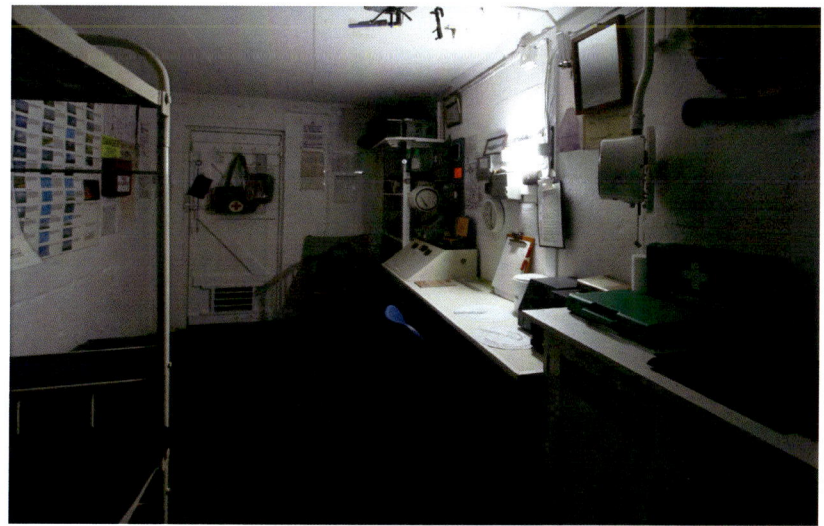

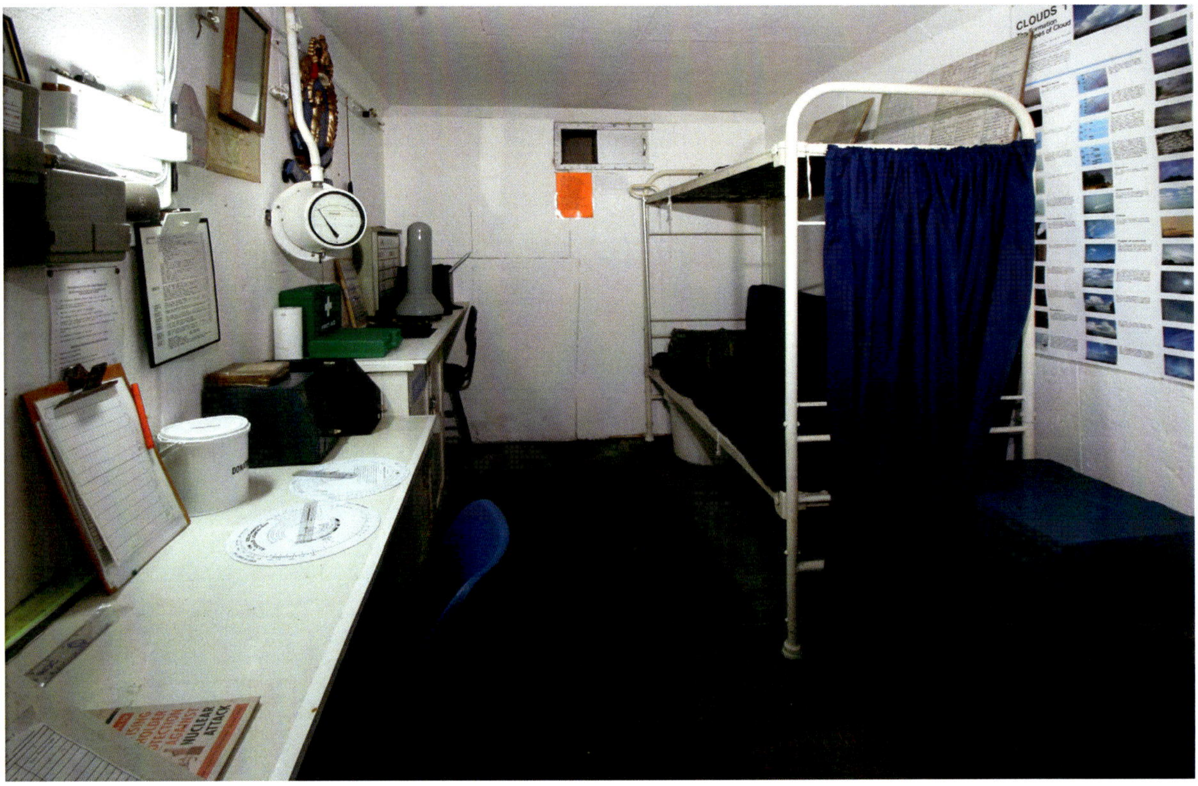

Above: The circular dial devices on the table are triangulation calculators which would have been used at Group Headquarters to calculate the position and power of the bomb burst based on information provided by the posts. The large white container under the bed was used to store the GZI and was actually originally part of a home brewing kit. The ROC purchased a job lot and then issued them as standard equipment.

Below: The former Chief Observer of the post made these units as training aids that could be removed from the post. On the left is a model of the later Maroon No.2 and on the right a extremely good facsimile of an AD3460 Teletalk.

Below: The original storage crate for the Maroon 3-Burst No.1. Live maroons would not be kept in the post; this is and example of the very rare training version.

RESTORED POSTS

Right: The PE set in its original delivery container – this included cabling (not shown) and a socket tool. These sets were usually removed from their containers and stored in a heavy duty plastic bags in the toilet cubicles.

Below left and right: The team also salvaged all the original signs from the Group Headquarters and these now adorn the toilet cubicle and monitoring room doors.

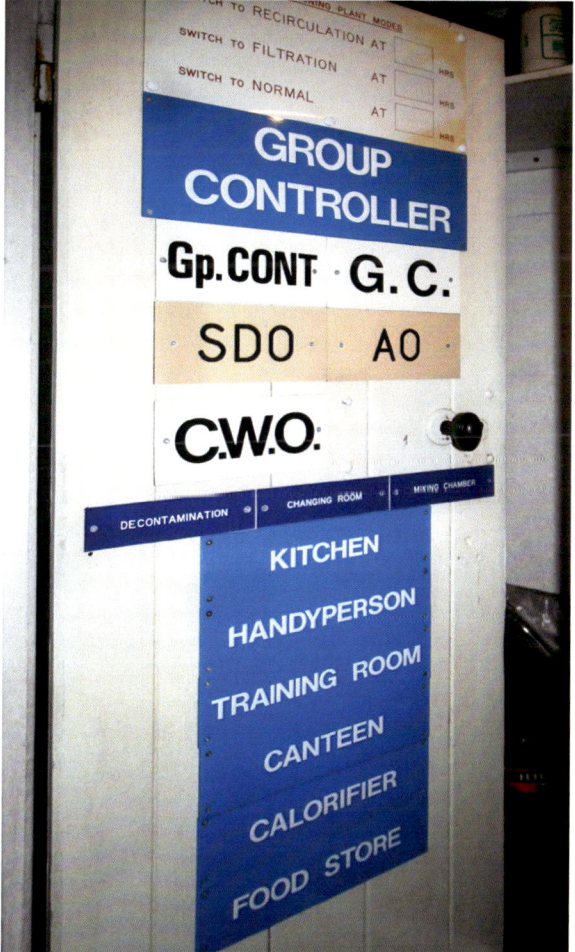

RESTORED POSTS

Skelmorlie, Ayrshire

Right: Frank Alexander joined the ROC in 1983 and started in the Corps as an observer and then became Leading Observer at Skelmorlie post. He then moved on to become Chief Observer at Gourock post. Frank stayed with the Corps after the posts were stood down and finished his service as an Obs Lt in the Nuclear Reporting Cell (NRC) at Greenock Naval Base. The picture of the Queen is a print of a portrait which was commissioned by the ROC in 1988 to mark the fiftieth anniversary (in 1991) of the 'Royal' title. The Queen herself (then Princess Elizabeth) visited the ROC post situated in Brunswick Tower at Windsor Castle during June 1944 and witnessed the work of the Observers as V-1 flying bombs flew across the night sky.

Below: Frank uses small speakers, positioned inside the Teletalk and radio, which are connected to tape cassette players so that he can play original recordings of transmissions to give a feel for the sounds of the post when it was in operation. The No.25 Group Headquarters sign was saved but the headquarters itself was demolished in 2001.

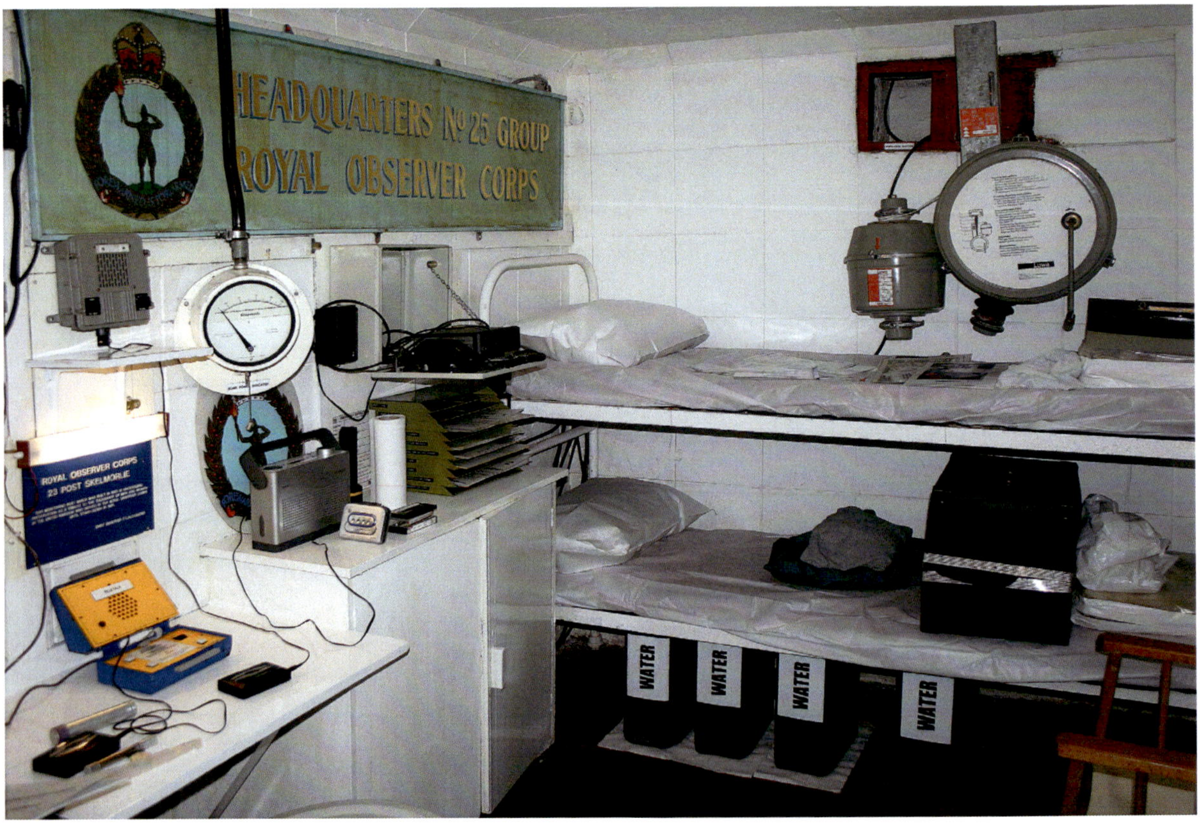

RESTORED POSTS

Left: Frank started the restoration of Skelmorlie post in 2003. The post is opened to the public several times a year and is used as an educational resource. Frank, with support from No.25 Group ROCA (Royal Observer Corps Association), applied successfully for a Lottery grant to buy a trailer so that he could store and transport equipment to and from the post for open days. Frank is now working towards opening an ROC museum in his home town of Largs.

Right: This map of the No.25 Group posts shows the other posts in the Skelmorlie cluster. These were Gourock, Kilchattan Bay and Tighnabruaich. Tighnabruaich was prone to flooding and was removed from the ROC schedule of posts in 1990 and effectively abandoned. Frank has restored Kilchattan Bay post as well as Skelmorlie and was hoping to restore the complete cluster. Unfortunately, Gourock post is situated in a public park and repeated vandalism meant that this was not a viable option. Frank has also conducted radio broadcast trials from Skelmorlie and was allocated a specific frequency and callsign to enable this.

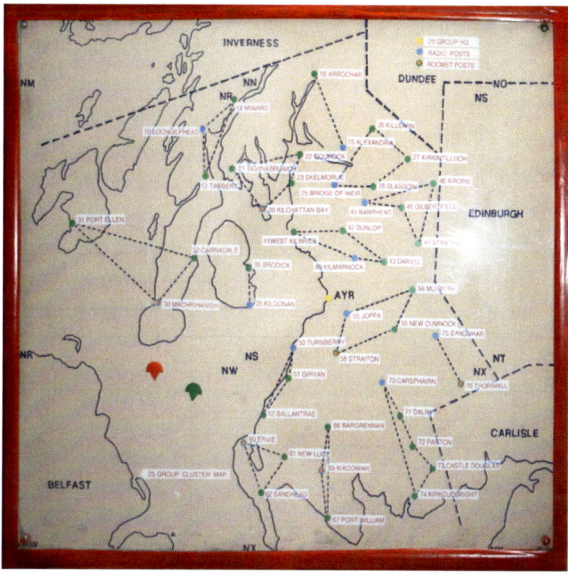

Right: Frank has acquired a Carrier Control Point and has wired this up to the WB1400 carrier receiver that was standard equipment in the post. The unit is fully operational and Frank can now give the 'attack warning red' message over the CCP phones which is then broadcast through the WB1401 speaker unit.

RESTORED POSTS

Stoke Golding, Leicestershire

An above-ground aircraft post was constructed at Stoke Golding in 1937 and was designated G2 as part of No.5 Group. The post overlooked RAF Nuneaton and worked in conjunction with the RAF station during the war. The post was stood down in 1945 but reactivated in 1947 and became part of No. 8 Group in 1953. The underground post was built in 1960, although the aircraft reporting role continued at the site until 1962.

Left: The crew using the aircraft post at Stoke Golding in the early-to-mid 1960s.
L to R L/Obs Mick Wood, W/Obs Kathleen Cooke, Obs/Officer Ron Smith and Obs Mark Swain. The crew are using RAF-issue fixed focus binoculars and are using the 'finger plotting' method to track and report aircraft.

Right: The crew prepares the underground post for operations. Ron Smith (in peaked cap) was the Observer Group Officer responsible for Stoke Golding and several other posts in the area. Martin Cooke is holding the GZI. Martin served on the post until stand-down.

Right: The crew conducting operations in the 1960s. Note the observer on the top bunk wearing the GZI satchel. The steel helmet was used by the crew to stop them hurting their heads on the hatch counterweight.

At the time, Stoke Golding crew were also operating the new post at nearby Bedworth, which had yet to be allocated a crew. Sometimes they would physically stay at Stoke Golding but also act as the Bedworth crew, reporting two different sets of results to Group HQ during exercises. In this case W/Obs Kathleen Cooke is using two FMST units to report two different sets of fallout readings.

Left: W/Obs Bev Chippendale, L/Obs John Hirst and Obs Bernard Owen conducting a training exercise in the 1970s. The post is more cluttered when compared to the earlier photograph.

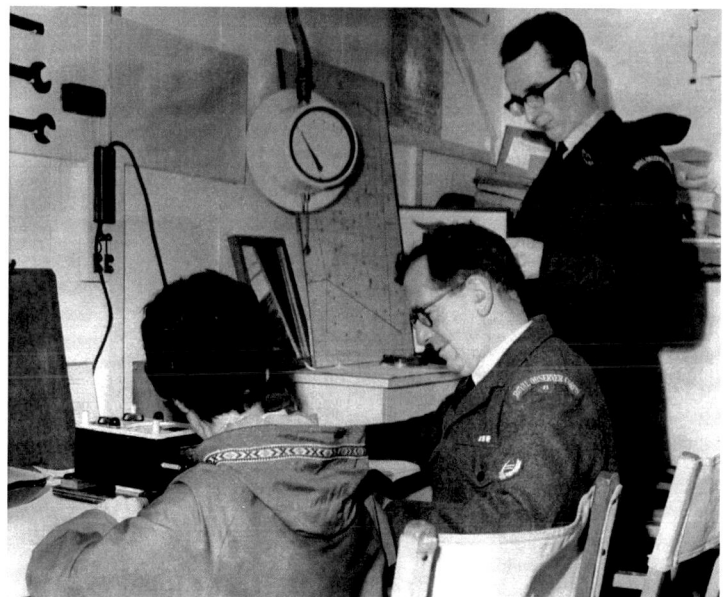

Right: L/Obs John Hirst and Obs Bernard Owen attaching the FSM plastic cover onto the probe pipe sometime in the early-to-mid 1970s. The aircraft post can be seen in the background still in good condition. It remained on site until 1983 when it was finally demolished, although the base and some brickwork can still be seen on the site today.

RESTORED POSTS

Right: This photograph shows Obs Brian Headley and Obs Gerry Collinson on an overnight NATO exercise in the mid-to-late 1970s. By this time the post had been modified to accept the first generation of radios.

Below: Obs David Heppingstall, C/Obs Martin Cooke and Obs John Campton conducting the last exercise at the post on 20 April 1991. The 1980s upgrades can be seen behind the crew – the post radio is a modern Burndept unit and earthing strips and an air tube for the pump-up mast have been added.

RESTORED POSTS

Left: By 1999 the post was open and the interior fire-damaged, although there were some interesting items remaining which were removed and donated to the ROC museum at the Norfolk and Suffolk Aviation Museum before the hatch was welded shut to stop further damage.

Above right: By 2005 the post was heavily overgrown and the exterior badly damaged. The concrete vent shaft had been broken through and the FSM probe pipe broken off.

Below: In 2008 the post and surrounding land was sold to local resident Terry Bottrill. Once Terry had cleared the site he started a restoration project. The hatch ventilator was refabricated and a new concrete apron built around the hatch. High levels of hatch security were added and the FSM probe pipe repaired.

RESTORED POSTS

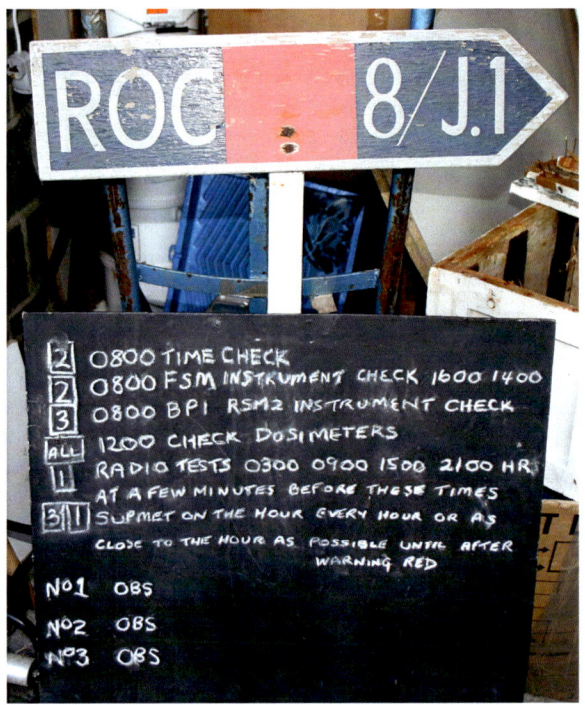

Right: Ray Allard, the ROC curator at the Norfolk and Suffolk Aviation Museum, kindly agreed to return the items, including the blackboard and sign, shown in the photograph, removed from the post in 1999.

The photograph shows the blackboard and sign in Terry's garage after their return. '8/J1' refers to the ROC designation of Stoke Golding as No.8, Coventry, Group, Post Juliet 1. This meant that Stoke Golding was No.1 post in the 'Juliet' cluster, the No.1 usually signifying the master post. Posts were designated alpha-numerically until paper-tape data-processing was introduced in 1967. The alpha-numeric system was retained for administration but a new purely numeric designation was required for the data-processing system to work.

Further renumbering occurred after the closures of 1968, and the alpha-numeric system was finally dropped in 1982 following the communications upgrades. The final numeric-only system identified master posts by using a '0' or '5' for the second digit, with Stoke Golding being No.55 post at stand-down.

Below: The finished interior. Period carpet tiles have been added and fire-damaged polystyrene wall and ceiling tiles have been repaired or replaced. Terry has also added the new fold-down table visible on the right of the photograph and also various wooden battens to allow mounting points for signs and notices.

Above: Terry has completed the restoration and holds several open days a year. During restoration Terry was able to contact the former Chief Observer, Martin Cooke, who served on the post for thirty years, virtually the entire time that the post was in service. Martin's wife, Kathleen, served for twenty-seven years and even Martin's son spent seven years in the Corps – a combined family total of sixty-four years. Martin now helps run open days with Terry and has been a huge help in restoring the post, providing information and equipment through contacts with his former colleagues in the Corps.

Right: Terry Bottrill and Martin Cooke at the post in February 2011. Terry's next project is to rebuild the aircraft post.

RESTORED POSTS

Upton Magna, Shropshire

Right: The post at Upton Magna in Shropshire is in good condition but is essentially empty with no remaining paperwork or artefacts. Occasionally it is equipped to show how the posts would have looked. This external photograph shows a *Secomak* siren in the foreground with a homemade maroon launcher and GZI beyond.

Below: Most restored posts are set up with equipment as at the 1991 stand-down, but in this case it has been set up to represent a post in the early 1980s just before the new equipment programmes took effect. The radio headphones would have been plugged into a jack socket under the table and not directly into the radio as in this mock-up.

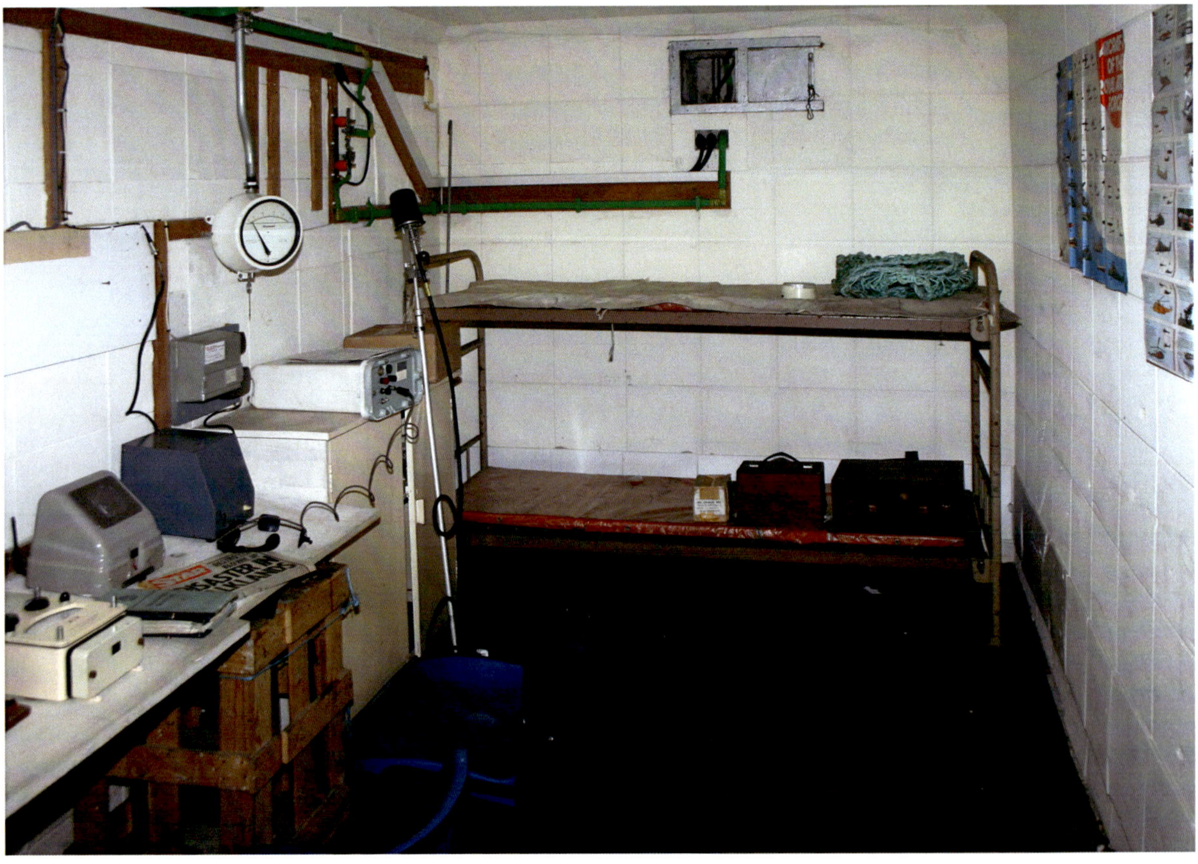

RESTORED POSTS

Above: Further detail of the earlier generation equipment. The radio would have been wall-mounted and the headphones are actually of a type used by Post Plotters at headquarters rather than the correct post headphones.

Below: Detail of the Teletalk and WB400 carrier receiver. Both the FSM and FSM Trainer unit can be seen to the rear along with one of the training manuals that would have been in use during that time period.

Above: Detail of the radio and BPI. The later Burndept radio would have been secured to the two vertical wooden battens to the right of the BPI.

RESTORED POSTS

Veryan, Cornwall

The Truro branch of the Royal Observer Corps Association (ROCA) decided to acquire and preserve an underground post in the mid-1990s, and contacted the National Trust, who own Nare Head on the Roseland Peninsular, with a view to restoring Veryan post. A lease was signed in September of 1995 with the branch paying a peppercorn rent but on condition they took out public liability insurance to enable the public to visit.

The post was bare when the Association took it on but the team managed to acquire most of the equipment from up and down the country during the following year and opened for their first visitors on 20 October 1996. Since then the post has had a large number of visitors – by 2006 (the tenth anniversary of opening) over 1,220 had visited the post.

Right: Veryan post is situated at Nare Head and is just off the Coastal Footpath which can be seen in the foreground. This has resulted in a large number of walkers being introduced to the ROC over the years. These included many Americans in the late 1990s as an American walking tour company regularly took its customers to the post as part of its itinerary.

Left: Carlton TV filming on a rainy day in July 2003. The filming was for the TV series *West Country Top Secret*. Due to the efforts of Truro branch members, Veryan has featured more frequently in the media than any other restored post. The post has featured several times in local newspapers and it has been filmed several times for videos and DVDs. It has also featured in regional TV and radio news programmes and nationally on Radio 4.

RESTORED POSTS

Above: ROCA Truro branch member Lawrence Holmes explains the BPI to visitors at an open day. In some years the post has been opened to visitors on as many as seventeen occasions with several hundred people visiting.

Below: ITV Presenter Kathy Wilshere, cameraman Matt Mulcrone and Veryan post members Dave McCree and Alan January during filming for *The Westcountry Tonight* in February 2010.

Below: Cameraman Matt Mulcrone sets up a shot for the recording outside the post. The filming was part of a feature about the 'Historic West' which was broadcast on the regional news programme.

Chapter 9

THE ROYAL OBSERVER CORPS LEGACY

September 2011 saw the twentieth anniversary of the stand-down of the majority of the ROC and the closure of the monitoring post network. Since then the physical infrastructure has suffered. For example, of the thirty-five posts operational in No.8 Group at stand-down, twelve have been demolished, three are capped with concrete, two are flooded and at least one has been burnt out. The condition of the remainder ranges from badly vandalised to one post which has been completely restored.

The majority of the iconic semi-sunken group headquarters have survived in various guises with only a few being totally demolished. Several, including those at Dundee, Oxford, Yeovil, Coventry and Lincoln have had surface structures removed or have been extensively modified internally. The survival of one of these structures both internally and externally has now been assured as English Heritage have acquired and restored the Group Headquarters at York to the condition it was in at stand-down.

Both of the Anti-Aircraft Operations Rooms modified for the Corps still survive, as does the former RAF Sector Operations bunker at Preston. This is in good condition and, although

Below: The fire-damaged operations room at the Exeter Group Headquarters at Poltimore Park – note the messages written on the tote boards. The site has been used as a paintball venue and the interior is in poor condition, although some of the ROC internal fittings still remain.

not open to the public, does contain material explaining its former usage as well as a mock-up of an underground post. Its sister site at Inverness was not so fortunate and has long since been demolished.

Time has not been so kind to the headquarters built as surface structures and only four of the original thirteen now survive. Of these, Shrewsbury has been heavily modified internally and externally, Wrexham is in good external condition and Exeter has been badly vandalised and fire-damaged. Oban was in military hands for many years and was in good condition a decade ago. It was sold into private ownership in 2009 and it is unclear what its future holds.

The history of the Corps is featured in many displays within aviation and military museums up and down the country. Good examples can be found at the Norfolk and Suffolk Aviation Museum, Newark Air Museum, and at Newhaven Fort in Sussex. The ROC exhibits at Aeroventure in South Yorkshire and at the Ulster Aviation Society's museum at Long Kesh in Northern Ireland are more recent and welcome additions.

There are also several Cold War museums in the UK with at least four secret-bunker style attractions. These are at Kelvedon Hatch in Essex, Holmpton in Yorkshire, Anstruther in Scotland and Hack Green in Cheshire. All are in large, former RAF *ROTOR* period bunkers and are of much interest in their own right. All have some ROC material, with Hack Green having the most comprehensive range of ROC equipment on display. National museums such as the RAF

Below: The ROC exhibition at Long Kesh in Northern Ireland. This is one of the Ulster Aviation Society's displays at the former RAF airfield which later became the Maze prison.

THE ROC LEGACY

Museum at Hendon and the Imperial War Museum have some material on display but little on the ROC's nuclear role. The National Cold War Museum at RAF Cosford has some items of post equipment on display but the overall ROC representation is disappointingly small considering the contribution the Corps made to the United Kingdom during the Cold War period.

The people and the spirit of the ROC are still well represented today by the Royal Observer Corps Association (ROCA). This was formed in 1986 while the Corps was still active and now acts as an umbrella organisation with the old Groups running meetings, producing newsletters and arranging trips. There are also events organised on a national level, including parades and memorial services.

Right: The illuminated 'Display A' and 'Display B' boards which would have been used in the group operations room to track fallout plumes. These are part of the ROC exhibition at the Anstruther Secret Bunker museum near St. Andrews in Fife.

Bottom right: Group Officer Neville Cullingford was one of the driving forces behind the establishment of the Royal Observer Corps Museum, which came into existence when the Corps was still active, and for many years resided at the site of the Winchester Group Headquarters. Following the closure of the site and its subsequent demolition, Neville and other members of the team have placed the exhibits in storage. They now use them to mount temporary exhibitions nationwide. The museum is now a registered charity with Neville acting as the Honorary Curator. Here, Neville and Tony Maasz (Chairman of the Trustees and the last Group Commandant of No.14 Group), are in the museum storage facility 'somewhere in England'.

Above: The Royal Observer Corps Association celebrated its twenty-fifth anniversary at the National Memorial Arboretum at Alrewas in Staffordshire on 14 May 2011. A service was held in the Millennium Chapel and later a tree was dedicated to the Seaborne Observers at the Royal Observer Corps Association grove. Here ROCA members parade their standards following the dedication.

Below : The ROCA grove consists of twenty-five trees planted by members of the Association in memory of those who served in the Corps from 1925 to 1995. The plaque contains a short history of the Royal Observer Corps.

BIBLIOGRAPHY

Buckton, H., 1993, *Forewarned is Forearmed*, Ashford, Buchan & Enright, ISBN 1852532920

Catford, N., 2010, *Cold War Bunkers*, Folly Books, ISBN 978 0956440525

Clarke, B., 2005, *Four Minute Warning – Britain's Cold War*, Tempus, ISBN 9780752433943

Cocroft, W. D. and Thomas, R. J. C., 2003, *Cold War: Building for Nuclear Confrontation 1946-1989*, English Heritage, ISBN 9781873592816

Gething, J., 1993, *Sky Guardians: Britain's Air Defence 1918-1993*, Arms and Armour, ISBN 9780853689461

Gunston, B., 1983, *Modern Soviet Airforce*, Salamander Books, ISBN 0668054969

Hamilton, T., 1994, *Identification: Friend or Foe*, HMSO, ISBN 9780112904960

Isaacs, J. and Downing, T., 1998, *Cold War*, Bantam, ISBN 9780593043097

Wood, D., 1992, *Attack Warning Red*, Carmichael & Sweet Ltd, ISBN 0951728318

Newsletters

Mitchell, C. and Holmes, L., 2010, *St. Breward – The Seismic Post*, 10 Group ROCA Newsletter No.61

Rodley, K., 1997, *Unusual Aspects of Building Royal Observer Corps Posts*, 10 Group ROCA Newsletter No.22

Swain, R., 1992, *Fiery Fred*, Wingspan, July and August 1992

The Royal Observer Corps Journal – Various editions 1980-1991

Internet Resources

http://www.subbrit.org.uk

http://www.derelictplaces.co.uk

http://www.28dayslater.co.uk

http://www.rocremembered.com

http://www.ringbell.co.uk/ukwmo/index.htm

http://www.rocassoc.org